LIVING IN THE FUTURE

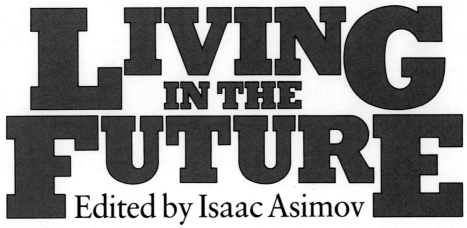

LIVING IN THE FUTURE

Edited by Isaac Asimov

Devised by Peter Nicholls

Beaufort Books
Publishers
New York

This book was devised and produced by
Multimedia Publications (UK) Limited

Editor: Michael March
Design: Roger Walker
Illustration: Lynn Williams
Picture Research: Juliet Brightmore, Sheila Corr
Production: Arnon Orbach, Judy Rasmussen

Library of Congress Cataloging in Publication Data
Main entry under title:
Living in the future.
    Bibliography: p.
    Includes index.
    1. Twenty-first century—Forecasts—Addresses,
essays, lectures. I. Asimov, Isaac, 1920-
CB161.L496 1984   303.4′909′05   84-9179
ISBN 0-8253-0225-0

Published in the United States by Beaufort Books Publishers, New York.

First American edition 1985

Films by D.S. Colour Ltd, London
Typeset by Rowland Phototypesetting (London) Limited
Printed in Spain by Mateu Cromo Artes Graficas, Pinto, Madrid

10 9 8 7 6 5 4 3 2 1

Frontispiece: Modern architecture. The Moshe Zur Zefa housing system
in Jerusalem.

Contents

Introduction

FUTURISM

ISAAC ASIMOV

We are all concerned about the future, every one of us. Probably every human being who has ever lived has felt such concern. The tendency is to worry about our personal future – about how we're going to meet our expenses, if our health will hold up, if our children will make happy marriages or, more trivially but often more intensively, if our favourite team will win tomorrow.

It is impossible for human beings to experience so universal a concern without a few trying to capitalize on it. Even in prehistoric times, there must have been those who claimed to be able to foretell the personal future by the behaviour of birds in flight, or by the random fall of sticks, or by any of a thousand other pieces of trivia.

Even today, in this age we like to think of as hi-tec, there are people who claim to be able to tell you what will happen to you by studying the configuration of the planets, or by gazing into a glass object, or by scrutinizing the lines in your palm, or by observing the fall of tea-leaves, and so on.

Such practices have almost always proved successful with almost all people for a variety of reasons. First, people *want* to believe because it increases their sense of security to consider the future as knowable and therefore controllable. Second, people tend to remember those predictions that seem to come true, and to forget those (possibly a far greater number) that do not. Third, fortune tellers carefully make their predictions vague: 'You will make a long journey' or 'Beware of a dark woman' or 'Financial problems will require care.' The eager believer is sure to interpret almost anything that happens as the fulfilment of such vagueness. Astrology fits the bill perfectly.

Yet astrology and all other forms of fortune telling are mere charlatanry. No one has ever shown that they successfully predict the future. Nor have the principles on which they are based ever been explained in a way that shows them to be founded on any physical evidence, or to be anything more than bare assertions.

There is authentic foretelling of a limited kind, to be sure. A meteorologist can predict that it will rain the day after tomorrow, and a doctor can tell you that you have six months to live (or that you will

A polarized light photograph multiplied 40 times of pyridoxal (a derivative of Vitamin B6).

recover), and such things are legitimate. Predictions of this type are based on rational scientific principles that can be explained and understood by everyone, and which experience shows to be correct.

Divine revelation

Another way of looking at the future is to ignore the personal aspects and to try to see what will happen to humanity/the earth/the universe as a whole.

To us of the Western tradition, the most familiar of such attempts prior to the modern scientific era are to be found in the Bible. Various biblical prophets who lived between the eighth and fifth centuries BC attempted to explain what God's plan for the future would be like.

Some, thinking of God's goodness and mercy, concentrated on the ideal future waiting for those who obeyed God. Thus, the prophet Isaiah said:

And it shall come to pass in the last days, that the mountain of the Lord's house shall be established in the top of the mountains, and shall be exalted above the hills; and all nations shall flow into it... And he shall judge among the nations, and shall rebuke many people: and they shall beat their swords into plowshares, and their spears into pruninghooks: nation shall not lift up sword against nation, neither shall they learn war any more.

Other prophets, thinking of God's anger, concentrated on his punishment of sinners once history has run its course. Thus, Joel speaks of 'the day of the Lord' (or, as we more commonly know it, Judgement Day) in the following terms: 'Let all the inhabitants of the land tremble: for the day of the Lord cometh, for it is nigh at hand; a day of darkness and of gloominess, a day of clouds and of thick darkness...'

The most famous of all the biblical foretellings of the future of humanity is to be found in The Revelation, alternatively known as The Apocalypse (from the Greek word meaning 'uncover'). There, in gruesome detail, the end of the world is described as a series of disasters, featuring a universal war between the forces of good and evil, and the physical collapse of the earth and sky. Only a small body of human beings is saved from the universal disaster, and then, on the ruins, a new heaven and earth are built.

Only one non-Christian mythology, that of the Scandinavians, goes into similar detail about the end of the world. In the Icelandic tale of *Ragnarök* (the twilight of the Gods) the world again comes to a grinding end, destroyed by a universal war between the forces of good and evil; and, again, on the ruins a new heaven and earth are built. (Since the earliest versions of *Ragnarök* date back to a time when Christianity was already establishing itself among the Scandinavian nations, the Norse tale may have been strongly influenced by The Revelation.)

The prophecies of the Bible are not based on anything that we would today recognize as scientific evidence or objective reasoning. Those who accept them as valid portrayals of the future believe that they are inspired by an omniscient God and are therefore a far greater indication of truth than any amount of evidence or reasoning.

As the centuries have passed, and the universe has come to be better understood, more and more people have grown dubious about the reliability of divine revelation. The old prophecies have lost their force among the more educated and sophisticated portions of society. Nevertheless there are people who remain firmly convinced, even now, of the literal truth of the apocalyptic passages of the Bible.

The prophets who were responsible for these portrayals of the end of the world gave the impression that it was imminent. The early Christians seemed to have believed it would come in their lifetime. It did not, but succeeding generations, or at least some of them, kept their expectations and hopes alive, and tried to live in a way that would ensure them a place among the survivors. Enthusiasts would read The Revelation carefully and try to extract from its obscure symbolism some indication as to *when* the end would come.

In 1818 William Miller, a devoutly religious farmer decided, from his study of the Bible, that Judgement Day would come in 1843. Gradually he attracted disciples, known as Millerites.

Overnight in 1833 there came a shower of meteorites, perhaps the most spectacular in history. The meteor trails were as thick as snowflakes – it seemed as if every star in the sky was falling, as predicted by a verse in The Revelation. That seemed awfully convincing to many, even though, on the next night, all the familiar stars were still in their rightful places in the sky. In 1843 a great comet appeared; that too was taken as a sign of the forthcoming end.

By then, Miller had calculated that the end would come some time between 21 March 1843 and 21 March 1844. The year passed without anything happening, and a new date was set: 22 October 1844. That too passed without incident. Miller died in 1849, a puzzled and disappointed man, but some of his followers continued to keep faith, feeling that only the specific date was in error.

The Seventh Day Adventists and Jehovah's Witnesses are offshoots of the Millerite movement and they continue, to this day, to believe in and to preach the nearness of the end, though they are careful not to mention exact dates.

Of course, the end may indeed come soon. At any time. An intense and ferocious nuclear war would put a virtual end to humanity, perhaps even to life in general upon the earth.

Towards futurism

Neither personal fortune telling nor apocalyptic forecasts represent what we today call 'futurism'. What then is futurism?

All through history changes have taken place in the nature of human society; in some cases very profound changes. If these changes can be foreseen and their consequences weighed, that would be futurism.

It is unreasonable to suppose, however, that all changes can be foreseen, even dimly. A conqueror may arise, a great leader of men and armies, one who may overthrow nations and establish an empire, as Cyrus of Persia or Alexander of Macedon did. Or a plague may strike, and cripple or fatally weaken great nations. Such a plague struck Athens in the time of Pericles, and Rome in the time of Marcus Aurelius; there was also the Black Death in fourteenth-century Europe and the worldwide epidemic of Spanish Influenza in 1918.

Such things can't be predicted, depending as they do upon the chance mixing of genes that contribute to the talents of a particular human being or to the infectiousness of a particular microorganism.

But then changes like these are not truly important. Conquerors, plagues and natural disasters make themselves deeply felt in the history books, but they are not permanent; they go away. And once they are gone, the survivors pick up the pieces and life goes on as before.

There are some events, however, that produce permanent changes with consequences that are never undone. In almost all cases, such changes are technological in nature.

Consider the development of agriculture. It took many thousands of years for agriculture to be worked out, to catch on, and to spread outward. The process was not nearly as dramatic as the thundering advance of a conquering band of nomad horsemen. Once agriculture was established, however, think how different the lives of a group of farmers would have been from those of a group of hunters, how widespread and complex the consequences of farming life with its multiplying numbers of sedentary people requiring a relatively stable food supply. From an invention like farming there was no retreat. Society was bound to continue to expand those consequences into the indefinite future.

One can name other slow and undramatic changes, rooted in technology, that have changed the world more deeply and permanently than Julius Caesar or Genghiz Khan ever did. What about the invention of pottery, or metallurgy, or herding or iron smelting, or the compass needle, the invention of printing or papermaking, or the construction of a practical steam engine?

Human beings alive today have, in their lifetimes, seen crucial technological novelties coming ever more rapidly thanks to the advance of science, novelties the consequences of which are deep and permanent. They have seen the aeroplane and its greater offspring, the jet aircraft, turn us into a world of long-distance travellers. Television has permanently altered entertainment, news gathering and politics. Nuclear weapons have added a horrible new dimension to international disputes. Lasers may give us nuclear fusion as an energy source. Rockets have taken us to the moon and have taken our cameras as far as Saturn. Computers, microcomputers and robots are changing everything they touch.

Even those important changes in history that are deep and permanent and that are, apparently, unrelated to technology may not be so unrelated after all.

The spread of Christianity was a change of the first magnitude, but would it have taken place if the Roman roads had not knitted the Mediterranean world together, making it possible for the Roman armies to keep the peace and Christian missionaries to travel freely?

The Crusades permanently altered European history, but would they have taken place if the horse collar, and the mould-board plough had not increased agricultural production and multiplied the populations of France and Germany to the point where landless members of the freely-breeding noble families became a menace to society and were shipped off to the Holy Land to fight the enemies of Christ?

The Protestant Reformation was another huge change, but would Martin Luther have succeeded where earlier rebels against the Church had failed if he had not had at his command the new invention of printing which spread his ideas far and wide across western Europe?

The technological dimension

The importance of technology was not recognized until relatively recently. Histories written before the modern era deal extensively with war and intrigue, but seldom ever mention technology. The reason is that until recent times technological advance was slow compared with human lifetimes. Innovations were few and spread quite slowly. It was easy to overlook technological change because few individuals notice any progress at all in their often short lifetimes.

Technological change, however, is a cumulative phenomenon. That is, technological advance produces conditions that favour further technological advance. Each new idea, properly applied, produces consequences that demand and give rise to additional new ideas. The result is that throughout history the rate of technological advance has, more or less, steadily increased.

Even during periods that seem to be retrogressive, technological advance continues. The Middle Ages were once pictured as a time when western Europe retreated from the high cultures of Greece and Rome, to advance again only when the Reformation broke the grip of the Church's dead hand. Not so! The Middle Ages were a time of intellectual ferment and lively advance. It was then that the magnetic compass came into use, and the mechanical clock, and gunpowder, and spectacles, and the printing press, and the windmill – to say nothing of the horseshoe, horse collar, and mould-board ploughing I mentioned earlier. Most of these advances were made first in China, so western Europe may have borrowed them rather than truly invented them; nevertheless Europeans applied them in such imaginative ways that by 1700 they were masters of the world, including China.

There inevitably came a time when the rate of technological advance became fast enough to be seen by people in the course of their own lifetimes; when the fact of change could no longer be denied; when it could be seen with the living, naked eye, rather than through the long glass of history. When did that happen?

To me it seems quite obvious that it happened with the coming of the Industrial Revolution.

The beginning of the Industrial Revolution is usually pinned to James Watt's development, in 1769, of a practical steam engine. It took a generation for people to realize what had happened, but by 1800 at the latest, it was clear to most of James Watt's compatriots capable of looking beyond their noses that Britain would never be the same again. And, as the decades passed, the same realization came to those other nations to which the Industrial Revolution spread.

Science and the future – fact and fiction

With the acceptance of rapid technological change, a new curiosity arose among human beings, possibly the first *new* curiosity in recorded history.

What would the future be like?

Not one's own – personal future – that was as obscure as ever, and remained in the hands of fortune tellers and astrologers – and not apocalyptic futures either – those remained in the realm of religious mysticism. But the future of society. What would the future of society be like, given continued technological advance?

Here at least one can speculate honestly, for each existing advance suggests others that seem, to a rational mind, to be attainable. What is more, each existing advance suggests consequences that may make themselves felt with considerable force in the near future.

To go back to the Industrial Revolution, once a steam engine was hooked to a paddle wheel of a ship, so that that ship could move without sails against wind and current, it was not so difficult to imagine a steam engine attached to a land vehicle, which could then move without horses.

Or, once the steam locomotive was shown to be practical, it was easy to envisage a nation criss-crossed by railroad tracks, with its population mobile beyond precedent. What would society be like if travel were made swift and easy?

And if balloons could be constructed to carry men a few miles downwind, why not construct larger balloons, with gondolas equipped with steam engines hooked to propellors so that they could manoeuvre against the wind and carry human beings across the ocean?

A demand usually creates a supply. As people grew curious about the consequences of continuing technological advances, writers began to write fiction describing such advances and their consequences. Early nineteenth-century writers such as Mary Shelley, Edgar Allen Poe, and Nathaniel Hawthorne produced the earliest science fiction, although the term was not officially coined until 1929. And it was with Jules Verne that the genre came into full bloom.

In 1863 Jules Verne (then 35 years old, and a failure at everything he had tried) wrote *Five Weeks in a Balloon*. It sold magnificently and the astonished Verne decided to write other 'extraordinary voyages' (as his publisher called them). He described trips that circumnavigated the earth in record time, that made their way to the centre of earth, to the bottom of the sea, to the moon, to deep space by way of a comet, and so on. He was the first writer to devote himself almost entirely to science fiction, and the first to make a living out of it. In fact, he grew rich and famous as a result.

What is more, he was a deliberate futurist. He attempted to make his scientific descriptions accurate (at least according to the knowledge of the time) and to allow for reasonable and rational advances in technology. Sometimes he made errors of fact (he was, after all, a journalist rather than a scientist) and sometimes his conceptions were entirely wrong. One can't reach the centre of the earth by threading one's way through caves and natural passages, since these cannot exist deeper than a couple of miles below the surface. Nor can one fire a vessel carrying human beings into space out of a giant cannon; the acceleration would kill the crew immediately.

Nevertheless, Verne's novels gave a sense of the future that was valid. As time went on, some of his concepts gained the nuts and bolts of reality.

H.G. Wells, who began to write science fiction in the 1890s, proved to be even more popular than Jules Verne. He was not quite content to venture carefully into the realm of technological advance, but let his forceful imagination roam freely. He wrote of time travel, anti-gravity, and invading Martians, none of which is ever likely to gain reality.

On the other hand, as early as 1902, almost as soon as scientists discovered that a vast new source of energy existed in the atomic nucleus, Wells wrote of what he called atomic bombs. In general, his pre-World War I predictions of what wars of the future would be like were considerably closer to the mark than anything that army officers and government officials were expecting. (If more people had taken Wells seriously, the major wars of this century might have been avoided by horrified policy makers.')

Science fiction continued to be the major source of futurism into the middle of this century. Science fiction writers wrote (not always clearly, not always correctly) of interplanetary travel, of robots and computers, of nuclear bombs, of over-population, of television, and so on. By and large, however, their scenarios tended to be ignored by 'practical' people as 'just science fiction'.

But time was passing and technological advance continued to accelerate. Things that were 'just science fiction' began to turn into fact with surprising speed. The turning point came in 1945 with the dropping of the atomic bomb on Hiroshima. Suddenly, science fiction writers were vindicated, and from then on the better ones among them were accorded a certain respect.

Yet science fiction is not a perfect vehicle for futurism. Predicting the future is not the science fiction writer's job; it is, at best, the by-product of his attempt to write a successful piece of fiction. If the plot requires it, he will make use of a device he may well know will not and cannot exist in any reasonable future. Faster-than-light travel, for instance, is an absolute necessity in many science fiction tales, and is adopted without qualm even by those writers who know very well how unlikely it is that the speed of light will ever be exceeded.

After World War II, however, the pace of technological change and the surprising successes of some science fiction writers at foreseeing the nature of that change, led to the development of professional 'futurism'. People began to weigh the direction and consequences of further technological change, not in order to write a dramatic and successful piece of fiction, but in order to guide business or government in making decisons.

After all, although a decision may be made today (let us say, to build a large nuclear power plant), it may take years to put it into effect. In that time, unexpected developments may prove to have made the project unnecessary, or obsolete, or dangerous.

Even more subtly, if certain social security measures are taken by a government now, how will they affect the economy 50 years down the road when the average age of the population will have increased markedly? Or, if large numbers of robots are placed on assembly lines now, what measures will need to be taken to ease the economic dislocations that will inevitably follow, and how do we predict what those dislocations will be?

Futurism is no longer at the service of mere curiosity. No longer does it serve the simple wish to be entertained and astonished. It has become an indispensable adjunct to business and government. The more accurate futurists can learn to be, the better the possibility of a rational economy and a good government.

This book is written by futurists, who are looking into the near future and trying to see what our lives will be like then. In so doing, they may actually change the future. For if people don't like what the future may hold if things continue as they are, they can take measures *now* that will change that future, and then create one they would find more attractive.

And that might be good thing!

'Hand with reflecting globe', M.C. Escher (1935).

Chapter One
ANALYSING THE FUTURE

After so many failed utopias and cancelled Armageddons, are the prophets of doom or salvation at last becoming a dying breed? Bruce Page looks behind the 'authoritarian and panicky' predictions at the assumptions and methods of those who made them, and traces the damage done by mechanistic accounts of the natural and social world, by 'iron laws' and 'objective necessities'. Intellectually, these linear, deterministic views of human progress have been overturned by quantum physics and the 'uncertainty principle'. Practically, they are challenged by the ever-increasing number of people who can participate in defining that progress. 'We are inclined to see *a* future', Page argues, 'and to forget that there are many futures, with more of them becoming possible all the time.'

Analysing the future

BRUCE PAGE

The future, we must all admit, is a very curious place. Nobody who goes there comes back alive – though all of us have contrived, somehow or another, to travel to the present from the past.

And we seem to be getting better at occasional journeys into the past. This isn't another attack on Ronald Reagan: the remarkable fact is that we know far more today about the fourth century BC and the Primal Bang than did people who were temporally rather closer to them. And this kind of knowledge, the result of imaginative expeditions, grows more profuse, and more convincing all the time.

Not so with the future, or anyway not just now. Until fairly recently people seemed to think they could see quite a way into the future, and intellectually respectable characters like Karl Marx and H. G. Wells – not to mention more recent, computer-based futurologists like the Club of Rome – could be found running their stands without embarrassment alongsde the racecourse touts, the newspaper astrologers and the ladies with crystal globes.

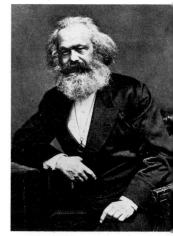

Futurologists who made their predictions without the benefit of computers: Karl Marx *(above)* and H.G. Wells, author of *War of the Worlds*.

Although futurology remains profitable, it has lost much of this intellectual standing. Too many large bets have come unstuck. Too many disasters have arrived unforeseen, and rather too many prophets of doom have gone through the humiliation of being rung up by the newspapers and asked what they plan to have for lunch on the day after the day they predicted so firmly as the last in the history of the world.

This is a rather curious situation. The past, or so we're told, is dead and gone – is beyond our influence. Yet we see further and further into it. The future, at least in theory, is something we should be able to have some influence on. Yet it becomes all the time more puzzling.

There are some kinds of predictions that can still be made with assurance, as when Jerry Pournelle says in the American computer-systems magazine *Byte* that – because of the continuing fall in the cost of semiconductor memory – in a few years' time anyone almost anywhere in the world will be able to know within a few seconds the answer to any question which is calculable. But, as Pournelle acknowledges, it's remarkably difficult to imagine what sort of a world that will be. Indeed, it's difficult to see people agreeing on what is and isn't calculable.

In particular, things have been very tough for Marx, who could be said to have mounted the first scientific expedition into the future. A well-funded academic industry, expecially active in the United States, is devoted to posthumous barracking of Marx: though you do wonder, as with those armchair explorers who patronize Columbus for getting Hispaniola mixed up with Cathay, whether the critics themselves could mount any voyage more testing than a cab-ride to the airport.

Giving the future a bad name

There was once a comfortable assumption that along with increasing mastery of the physical world would come – indeed did come – an increasing ability to anticipate and determine the future course of the world.

This belief, in fact, was something rather worse than comfortable: typically, it was philistine to the point of arrogance. Those who held it generally saw the future as one in which their own values and attitudes (unarguably superior to all others) would achieve universal pre-eminence. It is often associated with the Victorians, but it survived well beyond their period, and I remember encountering it in well-preserved form during the years when the Americans believed themselves to be organizing a mission of civilization in Vietnam.

I attended at Harvard an occasion called the Godkin Lecture, intended by its founder to celebrate the notion of intellectual liberty. It was given, in 1968, by MacGeorge Bundy, one of the 'action intellectuals', as Theodore White used to call them, who were then engaged in Washington government, and therefore in polishing up the Vietnamese[1]. These gentry – Dr Henry Kissinger represents the type with a minimum of intellectual adornment – certainly did have a great air of Victorianism about them. Bundy commenced by looking around the hall, which contained a large number of people looking almost exactly like himself (I cannot claim to have been conspicuously different). Well, he said, clearly there was no need to waste any time with definitions of liberty; an audience of this kind wouldn't have any doubt about such matters. The problem, he said, was how this clear vision was to be imposed upon the rest of the world.

Such a remark could only be made by a man who felt confident that along with physical power arrived the gift of prophecy. To the Bundyesque mind, matters presented themselves in a simple fashion. We (the leaders of America) are powerful fellows, so powerful that we can decide what the future will be. Therefore, in order to see into the future, we need only look into ourselves and decide what we think would be convenient.

One of the ways in which the 1980s are an improvement over the 1960s is that many ordinary Americans have become sceptical of this analysis. Their leaders may continue to believe it, but putting it into practice has become a good deal more difficult.

To MacGeorge Bundy, or to temporally Victorian apologists for the simple notion of bourgeois progress, like Samuel Smiles, the idea of a controllable future might seem attractive. The same attraction has not been felt by more complex intellects. To Max Weber, the greatest and subtlest of twentieth-century sociologists, the very notion seemed tragic: combined with the relentless organizing power of modern industry, it must lead to 'the disenchantment of the world', that is, to a world in which nothing remained to be left to chance, a world without surprise. (He did not think it would make much difference, incidentally, whether those who organized the future happened to call themselves socialists or capitalists.)

During the 1950s and 1960s derivative versions of Weber's nightmare certainly carried some conviction. Especially the critics of advertising and consumerism made out a case that great business bureaucracies, equipped with massive devices of persuasion, would be able to decide what popular tastes suited their own economic interest, and then bring those tastes efficiently into being.

It could perfectly well be said that these neatly packaged tracts, such as Vance Packard's *The Hidden Persuaders* and *The Waste Makers*, were themselves symptoms of the disease against which they claimed to be

prophylaxis. ('The mirror on the whorehouse ceiling', said Mary MacCarthy, in a phrase which today would probably get her burned at the feminist stake.) But the anxiety which they exploited was reasonable in itself. If Kellogg's, IBM and Watneys could predict and control the future just like that, the resulting world would indeed be one of disenchantment.

People today are, not foolishly, worried about the prospect of the human race blowing itself to bits. Thirty years ago there were some grounds for fearing that it might bore itself to death.

However, things have not turned out quite that way. Certainly the large corporations have too much power. But when it comes to making the future they don't seem to have as much as they would like. It is quite clear that Kellogg's did not want people to start eating health foods and muesli; IBM did not want to have to make a personal computer; and without doubt Watneys and other British brewers wanted the British customer to go on dirinking the almost comically bad beer which they found it convenient to manufacture. These organizations did not stint in their

Large corporations are often slow to respond to the requirements of consumers. The British computer company ICL started producing compact personal computers in addition to these mainframe computers only under duress.

efforts to create the futures which they considered appropriate.

But the cereal makers have found that making their own new products – if rather mediocre ones – was the only way to protect their markets. IBM found that there was no solution except to enter the personal computer market themselves – they have been immensely successful, but at the price of buying in products from outsiders in a way that IBM once would have scorned to do. (The perfect anecdote of the micro revolution concerns ICL, Britain's home-grown attempt to produce an IBM, complete with dedicated priesthood. 'This company will go into personal computers over my dead body', said the last-boss-but-one of ICL. 'It did', noted one of the trade papers a year or so after his demise.)

And the condition of the British beer merchants, though not deserving of the slightest pity, is in descriptive aspects pathetic. Having been forced by consumer pressure to improve somewhat the quality of their flat beers – and thus reduce their own margin of comfort – they had the crafty notion of inventing a British market for lager beer, on which they proposed to restore the situation.

They did not envisage a future in which this would simply create a British market for the far more expert and serious lager brewers of foreign counties like Australia and Germany – for whose products the irresponsible consumer would display an immediate affinity.

Battles continue on this territory, and it often does seem as though God fights on the side with the largest advertising agencies. But even within the consumer civilization there remain areas of unpredictable wilderness, and if anything they appear to be spreading, rather than shrinking.

Does the world owe anyone a future?

Underlying these visions of the future, whether vulgar or tragic, is a belief that the effect of knowledge is to decrease uncertainty. Comforting as this may be to the genuinely stupid, it is likely to disturb anyone with some claim to intelligence – indeed, it can lead to desperate and neurotic conclusions.

Friedrich Hayek, in *The Constitution of Liberty*, is forced to think that ignorance is the only real justification for freedom. And, as with a good many of Hayek's tortured thoughts, there is a certain plausibility in it.

One of these days, he suggests, we may know just what will happen next, and just what would be the best thing to happen. In that case, according to his massive logic, there would be no case for liberty – no case for allowing folk to conduct their own doomed inquiries. Only in the cases where we can't decide what's best do we allow all the messy experiments to go on.

If one supposes the growth of knowledge actually does decrease the area of the unknown, then one would have indeed to share Hayek's fears. However, the professor's great value to twentieth-century thought has been the reliability with which he has been found, on all relevant occasions, staring learnedly in quite the wrong direction. To adapt Lenin's crack about Zinoviev, if Hayek fears something then it is safe to assume our danger comes from some other quarter altogether.

Today, people are not inclined to fear that the future may be too well-mapped. On the contrary, they worry about the possibility that, precisely because of our accumulated knowledge and physical mastery, there may not be any kind of future whatever. The human race will reach a nuclear dead-end, after a bare million years or so of existence.

Anxiety about the future is nothing new. But the threat of wholesale nuclear destruction — more appalling by far than the devastation of Hiroshima *(left)* — has created a global insecurity.

This Senegalese family has more immediate problems — how to find enough food to survive in the drought-ravaged Sahel.

The feelings of insecurity which arise from this are generally considered to be unprecedented, and to date roughly from 1945, when the bombs incinerated Hiroshima and Nagasaki. Spokespersons of purity suggest that sexual excesses, drug abuse and other defects alleged to exist today in unusual luxuriance arise from lack of confidence in the general survival of civilization. My own guess is that insecurity is rather the older and more natural condition — that the hundred years up to 1945 were in truth the aberration, and that human societies have more often than not felt themselves to be hanging on by their fingernails.

Pre-Hellenic inhabitants of Attica, medieval peasants — and, surely, most of the people of present-day sub-Saharan Africa — would find the idea of any kind of assured future, whether individual or collective, distinctly bizarre. The Scythians, the Black Death, or cyclical drought must always have looked at least like an even-money bet in the race against fertility.

We know that many civilizations which seemed to themselves self-sufficient worlds have died of causes like these, or of causes which have yet to be explained. Could any of their dead visit their future, which is our present, they would be amused to find that the progress once taken to justify our arrogant conviction of collective immortality has now reduced us to a state of daily fear which is often more abject than their own. Doubtless, as heirs of the nineteenth century, we consider ourselves entitled to security, and react rather like first-class train passengers turned out to fend for themselves on a wet and barren moorland.

'The point, however, is to change it'

Really determined efforts to investigate the earthly future are, for the same sort of reasons, a fairly recent development.

Before you can get over-confident, you first have to acquire some kind of confidence. And until the societies of the West got the first reasonably firm grip on the physical circumstances of the present – something which only began with the Renaissance, and didn't seriously change most people's daily life until much later – the efforts of the best available intellects were concerned with rather more practical questions.

To medieval theologians it seemed futile to suppose that anything much could be done to change human existence, whether for better or worse. Living in a nastier climate than Plato, and no longer having slaves to bear the daily burden, their physical situation was probably more disadvantaged. Anyway, they did not suppose that anything could be done about it in time to improve things for themselves and their contemporaries – in which they were perfectly correct.

Meanwhile, everybody had to die, which clearly meant a change of state, and it might be worth figuring out the likely results. You couldn't hope to change the world, but by careful analysis you might find some way to get out of it alive.

Marx compressed the wholly-changed attitude of his own times into his famous remark that the old philosophers had merely interpreted the world – 'the point, however, is to change it'. Victorian engineers and railways magnates who would cheerfully have flogged Marx for his views on property ownership would as cheerfully have congratulated him on that particular expression.

The great event which separated the ebullient capitalists and revolutionaries of Victorian Europe from the medieval theologians was the seventeenth-century scientific revolution which was led by Newton. So dazzlingly successful was Newton in creating a science of terrestrial and celestial prediction that his immediate successors could not see the auto-destruct mechanisms which were built into it. When Bishop Berkeley identified them in *The Principles of Human Knowledge*, he was taken for just another of those clever Irish teases. Today, however, Berkeley's theological argument against regarding the Newtonian laws as anything more than a limited model looks like very prescient futurology.

It was easy enough for people to jump to the conclusion that prediction might imply control, because it was such a novel and impressive phenomenon. Columbus, after all, had been able totally to ignore the best contemporary maps, in the confidence that they were not all that superior to his own eccentric guesswork. The charts were actually much less inaccurate than Columbus. But when for the right reason – of which he was ignorant – he got to a most interesting wrong result, they still couldn't tell him anything useful about the situation he was in.

Geniuses of his time didn't need any theory of human error to maintain their intellectual humility factor. Sheer, visible muddle was always right alongside them in their grandest achievements.

By the early nineteenth century, things looked somewhat different. A clipper captain could set out from England or New England, using one of Matthew Maury's wonderful Antarctic courses, and take his ship – an artefact as unlike the *Santa Maria* as a Boeing 747 is unlike a biplane bomber – down through the Roaring Forties almost to the ice-cap before bearing north for Melbourne. And then, after 12 weeks without sight of land, he could time his arrival at Port Phillip Heads to the most advantageous movement of the local tides. This was a feat of prediction and control difficult for earlier minds to conceive, let alone perform.

Woodcut, 1493, of the *Santa Maria*, in which Columbus travelled to the New World. He arrived there by accident, largely because he distrusted unreliable existing maps.

This was precision. This was the result of deciphering Nature's legal system, and using it to serve her with writs of mandamus on behalf of humanity. Karl Marx was certainly not alone in supposing it equally possible – given the rate at which things were progressing – to find 'iron laws' governing the development of human society, which would enable properly trained helmsmen to perform equivalent feats of political and social navigation.

The mathematician and astronomer Laplace conceived of a universe in which the inexorability of cause and effect would make the future perfectly predictable.

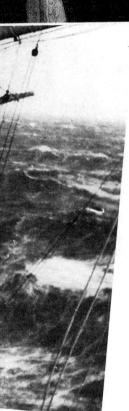

Clipper in heavy seas. By the nineteenth century, ships had accurate maps to guide their voyages. Sometimes they did not sight land for three months.

But the actual fact is that any specific advance in analysis or prediction is apt to make human society in general less predictable – or more 'anarchic', as it may appear to people who are in quite good shape the way things are.

To continue, for a moment, with nautical examples: ancient and medieval sailing ships could sail to windward scarcely, if at all. To predict the duration of any voyage they had to make against a prevailing wind direction was virtually impossible. High-technology sailing ships changed all that, because they could reliably make good a windward course. But each ship thus acquired what mathematicians would call another 'degree of freedom', making their collective and individual movements considerably harder to predict.

You can see the something similar happening in contemporary politics. Whereas voters once had to make their decisions in ignorance of other people's plans and intentions, they can now get a great deal of very accurate knowledge through opinion-polls.

This can have highly de-stabilizing results for any traditional party which relies on the argument that votes for minor parties are inevitably wasted. People may add up all the potential tactical votes, and decide that some piece of tactical behaviour is worth a try because others who share the same knowledge are likely to reach roughly similar conclusions.

Tactical voting has always been known to some extent among electorates in America, Australia and Europe, long-trained in the use of multi-faceted voting systems: in modern conditions it becomes more and more prevalent, and with the aid of new and more reliable information, even the British electorate is able to get some surprising results out of the antique machinery it has to use. Constituencies once as reliable as the rotten boroughs thus become marginals, likely at any moment to make monkeys out of serious people like candidates and headline-writers. Pundits refer to this sadly as 'the new volatility of the electorate': a term suggesting decline from some stern past into a gesticulating Latin present where no decencies remain secure.

Politicians of the established order who think opinion-polls should be prohibited in the run-up to an election 'are doubtless authoritarian. They are not, however, stupid. They have an intuitive grasp of the reality, and know that the one certain result of increasing human knowledge is to multiply uncertainties about the future.

In this they are correct, and a great genius of the Enlightenment like Laplace quite wrong. Laplace, the French mathematician and astronomer whose *Celestial Mechanics* rounded out and codified the work of Newton, thought that a perfect knowledge of the location and movement of any particle of the universe might in principle be acquired, thus making it possible to predict the same particle's path. Knowledge, he firmly proposed, would indeed drive out uncertainty:

We must envisage the present state of the universe as the effect of its previous state, and as the cause of that which will follow. An intelligence that could know, at a given instant, all the forces governing the natural world, and the respective positions of the entities which compose it, if in addition it was great enough to analyse all this information, would be able to embrace in a single formula the movements of the largest bodies in the universe and those of the lightest atom:

nothing would be uncertain for it, *and the future, like the past, would be directly present to its observation.*

'Everywhere uniform and immobile'

What happened to this great edifice of certainty which Newton and Laplace built – and which the founders of social science supposed themselves to be emulating? It collapsed because it was built upon an error no less preposterous than Columbus made when he halved the very accurate contemporary estimate of global circumference.

In accounting for the behaviour of bodies in space and time, Newton of course had to allow for *relative* motion. But instead of asking what a relative motion was relative *to*, he preferred to try to solve the problem with incantations. The universe, Newton said, contained absolute time, which 'in itself and without relation to anything external flows at a uniform rate', and also relative time, which 'is measured by movement'. Measured in relation to what? He didn't say.

He also declared the existence of absolute space, 'everywhere uniform and immobile', as quite distinct from relative space 'defined by our senses by its position relatively to bodies'. Acute contemporary critics like Berkeley and the German philosopher Leibniz asked him to provide a clear distinction between the two bands of time. Newton, characteristically, made no public answer, beyond causing a clerical protégé to assert that all these definitions existed satisfactorily in the mind of God ('. . . space and duration are not *hors de Dieu*, but are caused by and are immediate and necessary consequences of His existence').

It is quite impossible to know whether Newton actually believed this: indeed, it is hard to know very much at all about Newton's real beliefs, because he was a closet Unitarian in a time when questioning Christian orthodoxy was still an unhealthy practice, and he was genuinely interested in speculations about the Bible and about alchemical transmutation which today seem simply bizarre.

Berkeley complained that Newton's system – the practical brilliance of which he didn't deny – was based on theology, not science, and on hopelessly mixed-up theology at that. Today Berkeley receives a respect from professional philosophers which he didn't get in his own lifetime.

Newton was an experimental and theoretical physicist of gigantic – perhaps unparalleled – magnitude, capable not only of exploiting every technique of contemporary mathematics, but also of evolving a completely new one, the calculus. In the same way, the decisive attribute of Christopher Columbus was not his particular hypothesis about the circumference of the earth, but the brilliance of his seamanship and his relentless courage. In each case, genius needed some kind of framework or starting-point, and whatever came to hand was pressed into service.

Newton himself regarded his own work as an incomplete sketch of the universe, ending *Principia Mathematica* with a statement that he would have 'liked to say something of the highly subtle spirit which pervades crass bodies' and of the myriad possible connections between celestial mechanics and human existence.

Above: Isaac Newton (1642-1727). Despite Newton's mystical inclinations, his *Principia Mathematica* became the foundation stone of a strictly mechanistic world view.

PHILOSOPHIÆ
NATURALIS
PRINCIPIA
MATHEMATICA.

Autore *J S. NEWTON,* Trin. Coll. Cantab. Soc. Mathefeos Profeffore *Lucafiano,* & Societatis Regalis Sodali.

IMPRIMATUR·
S. P E P Y S, *Reg. Soc.* P R Æ S E S.
Julii 5. 1686.

L O N D I N I,
Juffu *Societatis Regiæ* ac Typis *Jofephi Streater.* Proftat apud plures Bibliopolas. *Anno* MDCLXXXVII.

But these matters cannot be expounded in a few words; nor is there a sufficiency of experiments by which the laws of this spirit's action would have to be accurately determined and demonstrated.

However, in spite of Newton's modesty, the historical fact is that within 150 years the mathematical structure which he had erected upon a foundation of inconsistent Christian mysticism was being taken as the chief justification for explaining the world as a strictly mechanical system whose every working – past and present – would soon be disclosed to human eyes. Laplace, as noted earlier, was Newton's greatest follower, and there is a famous story of the conversation he had with Napoleon after the Emperor had been leafing through part of his work. There didn't seem to be any mention of God, said Napoleon.

'I had no need of that hypothesis', said Laplace.

Today, we may not have 'need of that hypothesis' – this essay, anyway, isn't an attempt to reconstruct medieval notions of the supernatural. But we should ask whether Berkeley wasn't perhaps right to predict that dreadful harm would be done to human life and human morals if the success of Newton's science were to become a justification for considering its mechanics consistent and self-sufficient.

Within a mechanical system, there is no obvious place for morality, compassion, courage – or, one might say, unpredictability. Human nature being what it is, remarkably few people with a mechanical, materialist view of the world ever behave exactly as their theories suggest they ought to do. But the case does not appear to be unknown. The distinguishing point about Hitler, said Simone Weil – the pre-war French philosopher, not the present-day politician – was that he actually behaved as 'a man of pure force'.

Hitler, according to her diagnosis, believed crudely and simply that human societies and human individuals were machines, just as he thought the solar system was a machine. If that was his real intellectual and emotional position, it explains a lot of things. And no member of the demi-intelligentisia like Hitler would have believed such a thing before the triumph of 'mechanical' Newtonianism.

Einstein (inadvertently) causes the end of causality

Whether or not Berkeley was right, from the strict viewpoint of scientific prediction, it just didn't matter until quite late in the nineteenth century.

Newton's system appeared scientifically quite immaculate just so long as people remained largely ignorant about the nature of light and electromagnetic radiation generally. And that remained the case until the 1860s. Then, James Clerk Maxwell changed the world again, with a set of equations that tied up all the forms of electromagnetic radiation as wave motions travelling at the speed of light – and not at any other speed.

In the most literal and direct sense, Maxwell's equations brought into being the electrical and electronic systems on which our cities depend for their daily existence. But they were, in themselves, a Newtonian impossibility. Within the absolute space-time of Newtonian physics, any relative velocity could, in theory, be achieved. It's said that the resulting contradiction became visible to Einstein while he was still a child: that under Newton's 'laws' it would be possible for a vehicle to accelerate until it was travelling as fast as light or faster. For this to happen, you had to imagine that light could either 'disappear' (for the same sort of reason that the rise and fall of a wave 'disappears' for a boat which exactly keeps pace with the wave), or that there might be ways for electromagnetic radiation to travel at non-Maxwellian speeds.

Neither alternative would do. Though immensely high velocities can be achieved, the control required can only be exerted because – as Einstein showed – the Maxwell equations, with their constant velocity for the

Below, right: The Scottish physicist James Clerk Maxwell (1831-1879). Maxwell's equations challenged the absolute space-time of Newtonian physics and paved the way for electronic systems. A page from his manuscript is shown above.

given in ( )

To show that no other values are admissible let us suppose
that the values $F + F'$ $G + G'$ $H + H'$ fulfil the equations
then since F, G, H have been shown to fulfil the equations
we must have by the first equation

$$\frac{d}{dx}\left(\frac{dF'}{dx} + \frac{dG'}{dy} + \frac{dH'}{dz}\right) - \left(\frac{d^2F'}{dx^2} + \frac{d^2F'}{dy^2} + \frac{d^2F'}{dz^2}\right) = 0$$

or $$\frac{d}{dy}\left(\frac{dG'}{dx} - \frac{dF'}{dy}\right) = \frac{d}{dz}\left(\frac{dF'}{dz} - \frac{dH'}{dx}\right)$$

with two other equations of the same kind. Hence we find

$$\frac{dH'}{dy} - \frac{dG'}{dz} = \frac{dV}{dx}$$

$$\frac{dF'}{dz} - \frac{dH'}{dx} = \frac{dV}{dy}$$

$$\frac{dG'}{dx} - \frac{dF'}{dy} = \frac{dV}{dz}$$

where V is some function of x, y and z
Differentiating these expressions with respect to x y z respectively,
we find $$0 = \frac{d^2V}{dx^2} + \frac{d^2V}{dy^2} + \frac{d^2V}{dz^2}$$
the only finite and continuous solution of which is $V = 0$

Hence we must have $$F' = \frac{dW}{dx} \qquad G' = \frac{dW}{dy} \qquad H' = \frac{dW}{dz}$$

speed of light, aren't attacked by the kind of infinite acceleration that Newton allowed to be possible. The only coherent universe, he showed, was one in which movement was always relative, and no velocity could be greater than that of light.

Einstein had apparently constructed a system of a kind that Berkeley might have approved. It was scientifically consistent, and quite neutral in terms of religion and metaphysics. It did not assert or deny the existence of God – nor did it press God into service, along Newton's lines, as universal cosmological janitor to appear with a bucket whenever a leak developed.

But within 20 years, this sytem also 'auto-destructed'. At least, it led, with apparent inevitability, to conclusions which its creator Einstein regarded as horrible and repulsive, even though they were argued brilliantly by people he admired and respected. Einstein gave twentieth-century physicists a new way of looking at the world – a whole new degree of freedom – and found that he could not predict or control the use they made of it.

What they did, in fact, was create quantum theory, of which the most famous appendage is Werner Heisenberg's 'uncertainty principle'. At a practical level of operational physics, quantum mechanics co-exists with the modern formulations of Einstein's relativity theory. They are used for quite different purposes, just as a book is used for one purpose and a television set for another.

But in quantum mechanics there are no strict chains of cause and effect: probabilities can be estimated, but no exact predictions made. Even sceptics, after a little reflection, find it hard to doubt the essence of Heisenberg's statement, which is that we can't possibly know the position and the momentum of a particle with equal accuracy. The energy applied to measure its position is bound to change its momentum, and vice-versa.

Einstein, though he probably had no more commitment to orthodox religion than did Newton, at this point fell back, rather like Newton, on a statement which was basically one of religious faith. Whatever the results of mathematical logic and experimental fact, he did not wish to believe in a world where cause and effect were only linked by probabilities.

'God does not play dice with the world', he said, in a famous statement which seemed to him decisive.

Apparently it didn't strike him that lots of people would find heavenly gambling games a rather convincing explanation for what they saw around them. To judge by the twentieth-century experience, somebody – or something – appears to be playing dice with the world.

Nor did it occur to him – in this context at least – that to Weber's mind, maybe less powerful than his own, but equipped with a more sophisticated knowledge of the human predicament, the idea of a world without chance, a world of predictable mechanism, was intensely painful.

To reach the future, jumping is compulsory

The mathematician and engineer Rudy Kalman has argued – as indeed have others – that much flawed social science, of which bad futurology is an outgrowth, begins in an attempt to borrow the prestige of the 'natural' sciences. Yet all too often, the social scientists have worked with a mistaken or outdated model of the system they suppose themselves to be emulating.

Marx demonstrates in *Capital* a sound understanding of the 'hot' science of his immediate day, which was organic chemistry. But he was, in all sorts of ways, an exception. By the turn of the twentieth century Marx's conceptions about natural science were very seriously out of date, and as Kalman says, the attempts of a lesser figure like Freud to compare the 'charges' on the libido to the charges on an electric battery are at best embarrassingly naive, and at worst look like quackery or mumbo-jumbo designed to conceal the absence of thought. By the 1960s the efforts of the Club of Rome to use simple, linear computer-models to predict the future were becoming somewhat mischievous: fortunately, their pretensions were exposed by the passage of time and the scorn of mathematicians.

It isn't unfair to say that the social scientists discovered the mechanics of natural science just at the moment that the natural scientists were abandoning the model in use as obsolete. The timing of the matter is almost eerily coincident: during the same years 1890–1920, when the foundations of modern physics were being laid, Alfred Marshall was

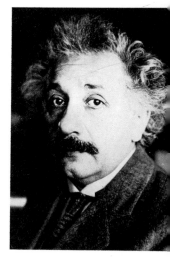

Albert Einstein (1879-1955) is said to have spotted the contradiction in Newton's theories while he was still a child.

Moment of totality. Eclipse of the sun, 29 May 1919, as photographed from off the coast of West Africa by Sir Arthur Eddington's expeditionary team. Eddington's photographs confirmed Einstein's theory of general relativity by showing that light from the stars was deflected by the sun's gravitational field.

consolidating his influence as the supreme exponent of 'scientific' economics, constructing an apparatus of rubbish which it is still rather less than fashionable to rate at its true value. (Professor Joan Robinson did once say, by way of a joke, that 'the more I read Marshall, the more I admire his intellect, and the less I admire his character', which is about as close as the British intellectual elite get to admitting that one of their international champions was actually a crook.)

It would be hard to over-estimate Marshall's influence. While less notorious than Marx's, it has been more extensive, chiefly because of its much greater political acceptability to the taxi-riding classes. Western academic economics, and its applied branches in government, finance and corporate operations – monetarist and 'Keynesian' alike – derive essentially from Marshall, and share Marshall's Newtonian mechanics. And because of the justified pre-eminence of economics among social sciences, the same influence diffuses itself through apparently independent disciplines like sociology and psychology. They studied to imitate economics, as economics studied to imitate physics.

Where Marx said 'the point, however, is to change it', Alfred Marshall also had his quintessential statement. On his own evidence, his world-view came down to a Latin tag: '*Natura non fecit saltum.*' Nature does not proceed by jumps.

The Newtonian idea that the world's machinery works smoothly and continuously (with a nice relationship of cause and effect) is an illusion, made possible by the crudity of our ordinary vision. Individual particles alter their energy-states only in quantum 'jumps'. We can make all sorts of statements about their likely aggregate movements, and these will work perfectly well so long as circumstances don't change very much: that is, so long as conditions of heat and pressure continue to resemble those that have applied in our tiny corner of the universe for the last few billion years. However, this doesn't enable us to say what any particular particle will do under the conditions found in the heart of a new-born star.

To blame Adam Smith, Karl Marx or David Ricardo for trying to import Newtonian science into the study of society would be unreasonable. It was the 'leading-edge' intellectual technology of their time. It was in many respects still difficult stuff, and nobody had shown that there was anything scientifically dubious about it.

We should be harder on Marshall and his successors – many of whom still infest the academic system. They had only to read the newspapers to discover that something wholly explosive was going on in the natural sciences. Relativity and quantum mechanics have today – fair enough, too – become a matter of textbook acceptance. But that, curiously, may have caused them to be less understood outside professional scientific circles. In the 1920s, they were front-page news, and – as the period's literature shows – a subject of everyday conversation.

Historians, poets, soldiers – ordinary people of every kind – could have told the economists, had they been ready to listen, that Marshall was talking through his mortar-board. Everybody knows, if their heads have not been stuffed with nonsense, that human beings are fairly predictable in the aggregate, and sometimes very unpredictable individually. Furthermore, they know that the unpredictable behaviour of an individual may cause all sorts of unexpected events in the larger community.

To be sure, social affairs generally do jog along quite smoothly and continuously, in a Newtonian kind of way. But then then there is a jump, and the February Revolution of 1917 has turned into the October Revolution, bringing the Bolsheviks to power; or the Americans have recovered from Pearl Harbour and won the Battle of Midway; or Clive Sinclair has invented a computer which is so much cheaper than anyone else's that it almost amounts to a different product.

Many of these events take place in battle, or in other kinds of conflict when indeed the conditions of heat and pressure are far removed from those of ordinary life. And as every soldier's recollections tell us, it is nearly impossible to predict behaviour in the one state from observations made in the other.

You can look at the Jewish girls and boys of the Warsaw Ghetto Uprising, and know as a historian that courage of that sort appears and reappears through the ages, and that there is generally more of it around than Hitler and his like allow for – indeed, Hitler was amazed to have such a thing occur in 1943 on long-conquered territory[2]. Still you cannot predict, individually, *why* Leon Rodal, *why* Regina Fuden:

… the 40 ZOB fighters led by Regina Fuden … crawled through the sewers all through the night and the following day and emerged through the manhole at the intersection of Ogrodowa and Zelazna Streets during the night of 29 April.

Human beings may behave more or less predictably in the aggregate, but extraordinary circumstances create unforeseen acts of courage, such as the resistance of these women, pictured here after being taken captive, at the time of the Warsaw Ghetto uprising in 1943.

Regina Fuden insisted on going back and guiding those groups which had remained in the ghetto ... she was last seen badly wounded in the knee after a clash with the Germans ...

Dammit, as Orwell said, the revolutionaries *do* remain silent under torture, the battleships *do* go down with flags flying and guns still firing – often enough to get the human race into unexpected trouble, and quite often to get us unexpectedly out of it.

Let us rephrase Marshall, so that we have a more reasonable, even useful statement. We can say: 'Nature does not make jumps – so long as there is not much going on. When things start happening, look out for all sorts of jumps.'

As a matter of fact, the economics deriving from Marshall works rather well so long as it confines itself to fairly limited states of human society – the ones within which people decide where to get their dry-cleaning done, whether to buy GM or Ford, and whether to go to Yugoslavia or Cornwall for their windsurfing. And it will do very well for making aggregate predictions within which these activities can be coordinated neatly without loss of individual freedom. It is probably easier to compute the seasonal forward-currency requirements of the travel business than it is to predict which car company will increase its market share next year, but these two endeavours are of a similar order.

If you set out to do something altogether more ambitious, like reshape the moral attitude of society by fiddling about with the money supply – which is the recorded ambition of Mrs Margaret Thatcher – you may well have a rather interesting time. But there is not the slightest chance that your economists (or futorologists) will be able to forecast the outturn. (Keynes, who was in a quite different moral and intellectual class from Marshall and most other economists, got things exactly right when he compared his own trade to dentistry. Modern dentistry is one of the great achievements of civilization, but we do not expect a dentist to cure our moral problems as an intrinsic part of any operations on our teeth. As citizens dentists have a right, even a duty, to seek nuclear disarmament or a balanced national budget: they must be careful, though, about suggesting that dentistry can be a specific means to either of those ends.)

There is further complication of the 'Newtonian inheritance' (I hope it is clear that I'm not blaming Newton for it) which contributes to the present low state of social science and futurology. There is a combined reading of Marx and Marshall – together, of course, with many intellectual fellow-travellers trundling along their way – which suggests that individuals don't make any difference to the movement of history. Thus, we aren't necessarily liberated by the knowledge that individuals are unpredictable. Indeed a great number of 'educated' people think they are educated precisely because they don't share the vulgar notion that individual action changes the course of events.

Though it would shock the average Tory governor or Republican school-board member, the version of history and social science that our schools actually churn out is heavily watered Marx-and-Marshall. Just as in the case of the relationship between the Church of England and Christian evangelism, the dilution applied is so great that the dose is little more than homeopathic. And for this reason those few people who have noticed what is going on assume little harm is done.

However, they miss a point: homeopathic medicine is only harmless as long as you don't need medicine. If you actually need a beneficial drug such as penicillin – because, shall we say, you are suffering from some massive infection – and you take instead a harmlessly small dose of some obsolete poison, you will very likely die. If you need the guidance of real history, pseudo-history can be lethal.

Guiltily though they read and enjoy stories in which individuals turn events, the educated folk of our time think they are supposed to think that collective movements, not individuals, decide the course of history. This is true only in the sense that human individuals never exist except within a collective, which is trivially obvious.

The course of the world is not decided by individuals *or* collectivities, but by complex interactions between the two states, neither of which has any meaning without the other. Homeopathic Marxism has always been in a tangle about this, which derives from a tangle Marx was in. In his case, however, it derives from his attempts to solve an immediate problem with conceptual tools which not even his formidable skills could make adequate to the job.

He was rightly concerned to criticize the social effects of the Industrial Revolution. Not only were they horrible, but to a great extent the attenuation of those horrors resulted from his criticism. Yet he immensely admired many of the achievements of the early industrial entrepreneurs, and it was not easy, in a Newtonian world of strict causality, to see how admirable actions led to evil results.

How much was intended, how much accidental? Marx solved the problem by suggesting that individual moral behaviour didn't affect the progress of society. A capitalist might be an excellent fellow individually – take his friend Engels, for example. It was only from an 'objective' position of class analysis that good and bad effects arose.

Marx meant no harm by this. Subsequently, though, it has been used to justify thousands, even millions of murders which were made physically possible by the progress of mechanical science.

And it is when we look at the fears and passions of contemporary society, in which the most prevalent vision of the future is a nuclear Armageddon, that we may think Bishop Berkeley was, after all, something more than a trader in Irish paradox. Berkeley's warning, without undue distortion, can be boiled down roughly like this. He thought that to accept Newton's brilliant improvisation as a consistent account of the world was dangerous, because it was likely to produce a civilization equipped with relatively great mechanical power, and a simplified, mechanistic view of human nature inadequate to the task of moderating that power.

Futurology as a participant sport

Visions of the future generally alternate – lurch might be a better word – between fatuous Utopianism and wild-eyed despair.

Just at the moment, despair is a bit more prevalent. We are supposed to be within a very short distance of blowing ourselves up, running out of resources, poisoning the entire atmosphere, and/or surrendering to every kind of political and moral perversion. Utopian visions, however, are also freely available. We are about to enter a period of limitless abundance and perfect amity based on the international exchange of information between microprocessor systems.

Both types of visionary are likely, on close examination, to disclose authoritarian tendencies. In order for Utopia to be realized, it will be necessary for all of us to submit to certain dictates of reason – purely scientific ones – which their author is qualified to set out. Indeed, it usually turns out that he or she is ready to administer them in person.

Equally, if doom is to be averted, the only way is for everyone to adopt, without further argument, the specific political arrangements proposed by those who are issuing the warning. Even if, as I do, you support the general aims of the Campaign for Nuclear Disarmament, the authoritarian quality of much CND rhetoric is difficult to miss. The opposition is often allowed to be deluded, and sometimes malicious. But no other possibility – such as that the other side might be partly in the right – is willingly contemplated.

At this point the primitive streak of Samuel Johnson which resides in every sane human being tempts us to say, 'The future, Sir, is likely to be principally remarkable for its close resemblance to the past.' A dash of Johnson makes a useful antidote to the more extreme brands of arm-waving, and we know that every future is bound to contain a great deal of past (we carry it about with us, like snails). But all the same it isn't a complete answer: the bit that resembles the past isn't the distinctive bit of the future.

What I am arguing here is that these authoritarian and panicky views of the future – and you need never scratch far beneath the surface of a Utopia to find panic – derive from over-simplified, mechanistic views about the effects of new knowledge, and that these remain deeply embedded in our culture. The inheritance of the last three centuries makes us prone to see the future in linear, mechanical terms. We are inclined to see *a* future, and to forget that there are many futures, with more of them becoming possible all the time.

In this context, we should be clear that it is not just *one* future out of many that terminates with a nuclear blank. Of the myriads, there must be many which contain the utter extinction of humanity. To hope that we can somehow 'return' to a situation in which this ceases to be true is both naive and dangerous. We shall never again be sure of human survival. And as I argued earlier, it was only a recent arrogance of ours which enabled us to think we could.

At one level, it seems difficult and paradoxical to say that each time we make an increase in predictive capacity we make the future less predictable. At a plain, practical level it is not really so hard.

Because we understand and control the physical world much better than we used to do, we can reasonably expect that nearly all children born into a modern industrial democracy will grow up to become individuals with several degrees of freedom attaching to them. This now happens for millions of people, where once it happened only for thousands or hundreds. And it is legitimate to hope that it may begin to happen for many more millions – though this will require much work, much intelligence, and a good many lucky rolls of the dice.

The politics of Europe have become highly unpredictable as more and more of its inhabitants have become actors and improvisors, rather than extras or items of human scenery. And not all of this unpredictability has been on the perverse and lethal side. It may be true that in 1910 no sane person could have imagined a future which included the Final Solution. However, twenty or thirty years ago very few sensible people were able to imagine a future, our present, in which – touch wood – there is no West European city where the secret policeman has free-range rights, and no state of Western Europe in which basic liberties are wholly denied. Totalitarianism may remain firmly installed in Eastern Europe, but the bullet in the back of the neck is a rarity now, and that once would have been a difficult thing to predict.

We should not close our ears to the voices of warning, because if they are wrong to suggest a return to Arcadia is possible, they are no doubt right in saying that this is a time of unusual danger. Our period is one of acute, maybe lethal disproportion between the understanding of social sciences and physical sciences. However, on the argument presented here, this is a disability which can be ameliorated. Like the great European witch-craze, it arose from intellectual errors which can in principle be overcome (provided the time available isn't too short).

'A curious place'

A real science of the future – a valid futorology – is possible, in spite of the fact that the future grows more complicated with every passing moment. Physics, after all, did not come to a stop because the physicists had to admit that there were large areas of uncertainty whose existence they had not suspected. To the contrary, they got on with doing the physics they could do with a much clearer mind, and were able to enter a period of immense and even alarming creativity.

The first requirement is to accept some limitations, and develop a sense of proper categories. Economists, after far too many years devoted to the frantic boast and foolish word, are at last settling down to the hard, technical work of trying to analyse the movements of particular exchange rates at specific times, and are making rather fewer attempts to deduce whole systems of political morality from, for instance, the ratio between public spending and gross domestic produce.

A useful science of the future will be based on history – and not because of the exploded claim that history enables us to predict the future. The real business of history, drawing on every other scientific discipline which it can, is to describe the present, and the path by which we arrived at it, with sufficient accuracy to estimate some probabilities about the future. The less inaccurate those probabilities, the greater is our freedom of action.

The best description of the process is given by R. G. Collingwood, who was both a historian and a philosopher, in his *Autobiography*. Collingwood was first abused, and then largely ignored in his native country, England: firstly because he was an academic who displayed a healthy loathing for academic discussion. Those who make their living from it have never attempted to forgive him. On top of that, he made a complicated but valid argument for saying that all social sciences are branches of history, which completed the alienation of any academics left over from his first exercise in un-tact. Slowly, and in large part because of work done in the United States, his reputation is being dug out from under the vast pile of dead cats within which his Oxford colleagues interred it. A historian (a social scientist), says Collingwood, is obviously not a fortune-teller as the religious Marxists used to suppose. The best parallel is that of an expert woodsman who accompanies a traveller into unexplored territory.

'Nothing here but grass and trees', says the traveller with confidence.

'Are you sure of that?' says the woodsman. 'Don't you think that might be a tiger over there in the bushes?'

The traveller is very likely to respond with alarm, saying: 'Yes, it is a tiger – give me a gun.' At this point, says Collingwood, the historian must be careful to resist the contemporary fashion which claims that intellectual guides are no good if they only indicate where the tigers might be, and don't offer to lend a hand with shooting them. (That is what the 'action intellectuals' of 1960s' Washington offered to do.) The guide's only proper response is to say:

If you think that is a tiger, and the only thing you think about tigers is that they ought to be shot, then go to a gunsmith. That is where you will get a proper gun (though do not expect him to sell you a gun which can see tigers as well as shoot them). But are you certain it's a tiger? What if it is your own children playing Indians?

The historian, the expert, the scientist can only furnish certain kinds of help to the time-traveller. (And, of course, just as all motorists are pedestrians, all guides themselves are travellers, whatever their individual qualifications.) Moral decisions cannot be shifted away from the individuals to whom the movement of time presents them. Nor is there ever a technical answer to a moral or political problem. Much of the disaster the Americans caused in Vietnam resulted from the delusion that somehow or somewhere could be found a gun – a piece of military technology – with the capacity to see tigers as well as shoot them.

Nor is there, in any situation, certainty. Assess the probabilities however we may, action contains a major component of blindness. One possible course of action is to refuse to shoot anything that looks even slightly like a child. The difficulty about this is that when the tigers hear it they start dressing up as children, and one kind of future which is not the slightest bit difficult to foresee the nature of is one in which the tigers get their own way with everyone and everything.

I believe that we shall get better and better at predicting things. The chief reason for this is the spread of cheap computing power – which means the much wider distribution of the capacity to ask, and re-ask, the 'what if' questions which are the basis of all attempts to look beyond the present.

Certainly it is true that more and more people own machines on which models of the future can be built, and run and tested. Perhaps within this development we can see a way to circumvent the problems of space and resources within a world of rising physical aspirations. Much of the waste, inefficiency and conflict of our world is due to the poverty of our information systems and process-control systems: we bump into each other, ignore each other's cries for help, apply the wrong resources to things, simply because much of the time we don't know what's going on.

Clearly enough, the tenor of my argument, following Collingwood, is to say that futures are made by the actions of human beings, from which it follows that the more people involved in making them, the more possible futures there are. I do not mean to be racist, sexist or Eurocentric in saying that the world of the present – the contingent, dangerous world which seems capable of blowing up in our faces – has been largely the creation of the male half of a middle-sized culture based until recently on just one corner of the Eurasian land mass. The significance of the remark is simply that if so much excitement, danger, and change has been generated from so small a base, then it seems likely that a great deal more will happen as the rest of the human talent-pool comes on stream, as seems to be happening. (Again, touch wood.)

I have suggested here that the Newtonian scientists who gave us the physical basis of the modern world also infected some of us with the dangerous heresy that knowledge decreases the area of what's unknown – whereas the truth is that knowledge increases it. In conclusion, we should remind ourselves that Newton himself perceived very accurately how things stood, expressing his view in justly famous and deeply moving words:

I do not know what I may appear to the world; but to myself I seem to have been only like a boy playing on the seashore, and diverting myself in now and then finding a smoother pebble or a prettier shell than ordinary, whilst the great ocean of truth lay all undiscovered before me.

Some two centuries later, after new shells had at last been found to outshine Newton's, J. B. S. Haldane put a similar thought into rather different words, and produced a motto which ought to be displayed between programs on the computer screen of every serious futurologist. On the evidence of modern physics, he said, the universe 'is a much more curious place than we suppose. Indeed, it is probably a more curious place than we *can* suppose.'

References

1   White was the author of various editions of *The Making of the President:* a nonpareil exponent of devotional journalism. The bijou cited gives some idea why I.F. Stone said 'a man with a prose style like that need never lunch alone'.
2   The Ghetto Revolt should not be confused with the Warsaw Uprising of 1944. Though both were heroic, the earlier and almost wholly Jewish revolt was launched when there seemed hardly a flaw in the Nazi hegemony over Central Europe. It was the first open challenge on occupied territory. See Reuben Ainsztein, *The Warsaw Ghetto Revolt*, Holocaust Library, New York 1970.

Chapter Two

KEEPING PEOPLE ALIVE AND FED

In recent years we have almost eliminated what were once the most virulent diseases, from smallpox to tuberculosis. Yet at least five million Third World children still die each year for want of the most basic medicines. And in the West, new illnesses are replacing the old, illnesses linked to environment, diet and lifestyle. Norman Myers looks at the ways the developed and developing countries must learn from each other in the necessary transition from curative to preventive medicine. He examines, too, the new problems created by the increasing proportion of old people in Western societies, and reconsiders the factors affecting the, still critical, problem of population growth.

But does the world even have the capacity to feed its present population. Magnus Pyke outlines recent agricultural innovations and argues that the real issue is no longer one of nutritional resources but of organization, planning and political choice. How can we make better use of available land? How willing are we to reduce the amount of meat we consume? And will we come to accept the substitutes now being developed, from soya to algae?

Western food aid to African and other Third World nations can be a stopgap measure only.

Population and health

Norman Myers

People in the developed world now live better than their forebears one century ago would have dreamed. On average they survive much longer, and their health is greatly improved all round. But this applies to a distinct minority of humankind. At least three billion people in the developing world do not fare any better than did our great-grandparents, while half a billion at the bottom of the pile enjoy – or rather endure – lives that are nasty, brutish, and short, as was the norm in the Western world several centuries ago.

By the year 2000, our present global community of 4.7 billion will have increased to well over 6 billion. By 2100, when population growth is projected to level out at zero growth, there could well be more than 10 billion of us. How many of these will join the developed-world elite who are favoured with a long life and a healthy one? Will the future be a simple extension of the past, with some winners and many losers? Or will there be basic improvements in the patterns of health world-wide? The most likely

Population in billions

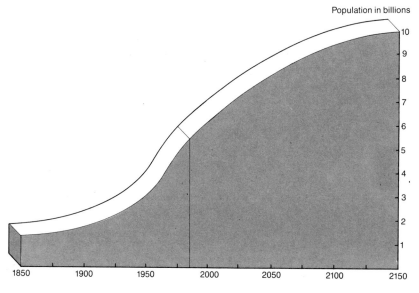

Graph of world population growth 1850-2150 (projection).

answer is that there will be a mixture of both. Certainly we can look forward to some splendid advances in modern medicine, and we can also anticipate some massive road-blocks on our path towards the United Nations' goal of Health for All.

First of all, just what do we mean by 'health'? According to the World Health Organization, 'Health is a state of complete physical, mental and social well-being, and not merely the absence of disease or infirmity.' To our discredit, we have not undertaken much detailed analysis of this concept, so we must obtain our picture of health (so to speak) from what we know about diseases and deaths – a far from complete picture in terms of health overall, especially with respect to mental and emotional health, and psychic welfare in general. Fortunately we possess plenty of data on major causes of death, as on life expectancy and related factors, all of which are helpful: after all, a society's ways of death reflect its ways of life.

Moreover, we are beginning to recognize that health is not only a fundamental human right, it is an extremely valuable resource. Only healthy people can realize their full potential, just as only healthy societies can make progress in the proper sense of the term. In 1977 the Thirtieth World Health Assembly resolved that 'The main social target of governments and WHO in the coming decades should be the attainment by all citizens of the world by the year 2000 of a level of health that will permit them to lead a socially and economically productive life.' To this end, WHO tries to persuade governments to shift their emphasis from curative to preventive medicine, and to promote general good health all round. An individual can be deemed healthy only if he/she is well fed, decently housed and adequately educated, enjoys pure water, proper sanitation and a clean environment – and is able to secure work, live at peace, and play a significant part in the community.

Life expectancy

Many of us now live longer – but only a little. Despite our best efforts, we seem unable to push longevity much beyond the biblical three-score-years-and-ten, and there is evidence to suggest that we shall not manage to extend it much beyond about 85 years or so – whatever the 'perpetual youth' cults in California may desire.

The global average for life expectancy at birth is now about 62 years. It ranges from well over 70 years for one billion people in the developed world, to only 45 or so for one billion people in the most impoverished parts of the Third World, notably the Indian sub-continent and black Africa. (In any case, longevity is a recent phenomenon: in Great Britain and the United States at the end of the last century, when these two nations were still in their developing phase, the average was no better than 50.) Fortunately there has been some progress in the Third World, from an average for low-income countries of 41 in 1960 to 51 in 1980, and for middle-income countries from 50 to 60 – due not so much to improvements in health care, as advances in environmental hygiene, especially in terms of water supplies, sanitation, housing, spraying against malaria, and, above all, nutrition.

Malnutrition

It is nutrition, or rather the lack of it, that holds up progress in the Third World. One child in five in Latin America suffers from malnutrition, and one in three in Africa and India. As a result, it is a direct or associated cause in almost three-fifths of all Third World deaths, even though it is not always recognized as such. For a child whose parents rank among the 'poorest of the poor', a straightforward attack of measles, influenza or diarrhoea often becomes a life-and-death struggle. Indeed malnutrition, together with parasites and infections (which collectively account for virtually all childhood deaths), stem from what we might call the 'social

The solution of sugar and salt which this Bangladeshi mother feeds her child has been hailed as potentially the most important medical advance of the century because it can correct the dehydration of diarrhoea, which kills 5 million children each year.

Left: In Africa, one child in three suffers from malnutrition, which turns commonplace diseases such as measles or influenza into killers.

ecology of poverty' – which means that these causes of morbidity and mortality can rarely be conquered through medical weapons alone.

Closely connected with malnutrition is diarrhoea, the most widespread and dangerous of the 'obvious' diseases in the Third World. What affluent-world citizens experience as an occasional inconvenience causes the deaths of at least five million developing-world children each year. Fortunately, diarrhoea can now be countered by a low-cost treatment of a simple sugar-and-salt drink, to rehydrate the body in the same manner as intravenously injected fluids. The price of this treatment, perfected way back in the 1960s, is a mere 10 US cents per dose – and for this trifling cost, we could cut diarrhoea-caused deaths by between 20 and 50 per cent.

As world population grows, resources dwindle. By the year 2000, the world's arable land (represented by the stalk of grain) will be cut by a third if present rates of land degradation continue, and productive tropical forest (symbolized by the trees) will be halved as the world population grows to 6 billion. Vast discrepancies in consumption divide the developed and the developing countries, aggravating the problems of scarce resources. One Swiss consumes as much as 40 Somalis.

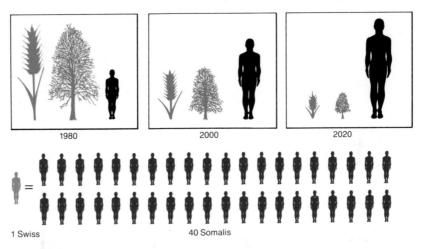

1980   2000   2020

1 Swiss = 40 Somalis

This recent breakthrough emphasizes the urgency of 'primary health care'. The strategy depends mainly on basic technologies and a few essential drugs, administered by community health workers, in contrast to the paraphernalia of 'hi-tec' hospitals with their few doctors. The total package need cost no more than an additional $12.50 per Third World citizen per year.

Were we to overcome malnutrition, we would drastically reduce the incidence of early death among children in the Third World. Whereas 99 out of 100 infants in the developed world celebrate their first birthday, and thereafter 999 out of 1000 celebrate their fifth birthday, the respective figures for the developing world are only about 80 and 700. Put another way, half of all Third World deaths occur in children under five years of age, compared to only 3 per cent or so of deaths in Western countries.

All in all, 15 million babies and small children die in the Third World each year, or more than 40 000 each day. Were we to reduce this massive mortality, readily avoidable as most of it is, longevity rates would instantly soar, and by the year 2000 we could be closer to making 70 years a universal norm. But as long as high mortality rates persist, high birth rates will also persist, with all that means for the population explosion (see p.55). Until parents feel absolutely assured that enough of their offspring will survive into adulthood, they will not reduce the number of children they wish to bear.

As for citizens in the developed world, they should accept that their yearnings for immortality will remain as futile as ever, and the centenarian is likely to remain a very rare creature. What is eminently possible, however, is to increase the quality of life, as opposed to the quantity, an altogether more desirable prospect anyway. We should surely be able to reach a golden goal where most people die after lives that remain vigorous to the end, expiring of what is said to have finally killed Wordsworth, that is, 'nothing serious'.

Greying of the population

However much long life is good for the individual, it can be costly for the community, in so far as an increasing number of old people means that the population will feature a disproportionate number of 'unproductive', i.e. non-working, citizens. In the United States at the start of this century, only one person in thirty was over the age of 65, but by 1970 the figure had risen to 1 in 9; by the year 2020, by the time today's teenagers reach middle age, it is projected to reach 1 in 5. At the same time, there is the

 % of people aged 65 years and over

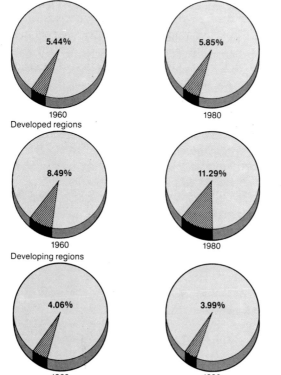

World totals

5.44% — 1960
5.85% — 1980
6.58% — 2000

Developed regions

8.49% — 1960
11.29% — 1980
13.04% — 2000

Developing regions

4.06% — 1960
3.99% — 1980
4.89% — 2000

Population pressures vary. As the Third World copes with a burgeoning young population, the developed world must accommodate growing numbers of unproductive elderly citizens (above).

The proportion of the world's population aged over 65 is increasing. But the increase is far more rapid in the developed countries than in the Third World (left).

phenomenon of the ageing of the aged, where the population aged 65 or over is the fastest-growing age group of all. Today the number of Americans over 65 is 27 million, a figure that will jump to around 50 million by the year 2020 as the majority of the baby-boom generation reach the status of 'old age'.

Of all those over 65 in North America and Western Europe today, almost two out of five suffer from some chronic physical or mental handicap. They thus place growing demands on the readiness of their fellow citizens to pay for their health care. As nation after nation encounters this phenomenon, we are going to have to make a basic shift in our perception. Rather than viewing the aged as rejects, we should re-invest in them as resources, mobilizing their experience and accumulated wisdom in the service of the rest of us.

Traditional diseases

The great success story of recent years has been the eradication of smallpox – or rather, near-eradication. The virus has been backed into a corner, to the extent that no human being suffers from the disease, and the organism survives only in a few flasks in laboratories. The 1967–80 campaign has been accomplished at a cost of just over $300 million, or the equivalent of five hours of the annual expenditure on armaments measured world-wide.

But we should also remember that viruses, including many pathogenic species, have been the sources of a number of momentous discoveries in biology during the past few decades. If we were to eliminate a single such species, we could eventually find that we have deprived ourselves of an important asset in our research on comparative biochemistry and genetics, or even for basic investigations into the nature and origin of life. Moreover, scientists suspect that the smallpox virus will assist our studies on antigenic relationships among a number of similar viruses, including the monkeypox, which are on the increase. If ever these smallpox-related viruses were seriously to threaten our health, the smallpox virus itself could, as a research model, prove important to us. Even more significant, the virus could help us to develop a 'recombinant' virus as a basis for an improved vaccine, along the lines of what has been achieved in our efforts against influenza.

Furthermore, our victory over smallpox could be replicated in the case of a long line of major diseases, including measles, polio, tetanus, whooping cough, diphtheria and tuberculosis. Mass immunization against these diseases can be accomplished at a cost of only $3 per child (only one child in ten has so far been immunized), or a total of $6 billion by the end of the century. To make the comparison again, this is only one-hundredth part of what is spent every year on instruments of death.

But we should move fast. Malaria, for instance, is making a comeback. In India alone, the number of reported cases slowly declined from a peak of 100 million in the early 1950s, to a mere 40 000 in 1962. But as almost 60 malaria-bearing strains of mosquito became resistant to chemical sprays, the number of cases soared to 50 million in 1978, with the result

Vaccination programmes, such as this one in Niger *(left)*, sponsored by WHO, could save some of the million or more children who die of malaria in Africa each year.

Below: The yellow fever mosquito, *Aedes Aegypti*, feeding off human blood.

that India's anti-malaria campaign today consumes more than half the nation's health budget. In many other countries too, there has been a 30-fold increase in malaria cases since 1970, so that the disease now afflicts at least 350 million people in more than 100 countries. In Africa, malaria kills at least one million youngsters each year.

Fortunately, we can turn to natural sources for weapons against malaria. Bark of the cinchona tree in Amazonia yields the alkaloid quinine, together with at least twenty other alkaloids, several of which can likewise be used against malaria (also as cardiac depressants and as anti-arrhythmic agents). So important has cinchona now become that botanochemicals from the tree are starting to represent a sizeable export item for certain tropical nations such as Kenya. Or we could turn to a new anti-malaria drug identified by the Chinese, from a plant called apiaceous wormwood, and known in China for more than a thousand years. It is being developed by the Academy of Traditional Chinese Medicine, in conjunction with the International Development Research Centre of Canada. According to scientists in both agencies, this could represent the first major drug breakthrough against malaria since the discovery of quinine.

New diseases

As long-standing ailments are elbowed off the stage, certain 'modern' diseases become more prominent, notably the so-called degenerative diseases that afflict older people, such as coronary disorders, strokes, hypertension, stress-related problems and cancers. Many afflictions appear to be genetically programmed, so the probability of disease rises with age, no matter how healthy a person's lifestyle may have been.

These modern diseases are all familiar to us. Lurking in the wings, however, are surely a number of other diseases that have remained latent in us. In other words, they are diseases to which many of us are susceptible, but do not fall victims as long as more established diseases hold sway. In fact, it is an emergent tenet of modern medicine that our battle against disease will never finally be won. As fast as we get on top of one set of maladies, a fresh category will take their place.

To illustrate the point, let us look at the instructive case of AIDS, or acquired immune deficiency syndrome. This disease has ostensibly been biding its time until it could exploit an upsurge in homosexual activities (plus intravenous use of illicit drugs): 7 out of 10 sufferers in the United States are homosexuals. The death rate of AIDS equals that of the worst epidemics in history, including bubonic plague, typhus and cholera. Most sufferers to date have died within two years of the disease being diagnosed; nobody with AIDS has been cured.

According to speculation by the WHO, AIDS originated in Africa, and was brought to the USA by Haitians who had lived and worked in Zaire. It spread to Europe both via the USA and from Africa direct.

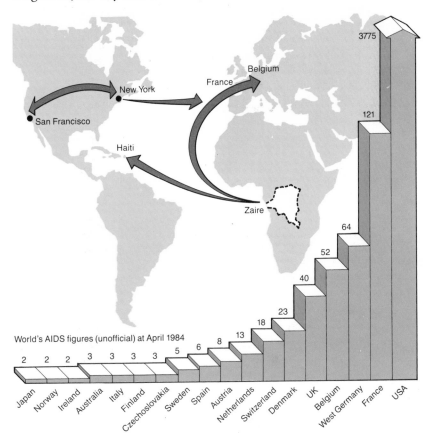

World's AIDS figures (unofficial) at April 1984

The disease has been reported from 33 countries, so it is becoming a widespread phenomenon. (So far there has been no news from India, China, and the Soviet bloc with their two billion people.) The rate of increase in these countries reveals an almost invariable doubling time of six to eight months. This means that the disease would, if unchecked, lead to more than 100 000 cases in the United States by the start of 1988, with 50 000 deaths in 1987, making that year worse than the worst years of the polio epidemic of the early 1950s, and representing about a 2 per cent increase in the US death rate. Recently, scientists in France and the United

States have gone some way toward identifying the virus that causes AIDS, but the real breakthrough – in terms of producing a vaccine – is unlikely to be made before the end of this decade at the earliest.

Environmental diseases

To counterbalance the emergence of new diseases, we are learning much more about the source of current widespread diseases. In particular, we are finding that almost all diseases are linked, in the broadest sense of the term, to the environment. While most people are susceptible to lung cancer through the 'latency effect', described earlier, non-smokers are very unlikely to contract it. But the high incidence of lung cancer among tobacco addicts in many countries, as of stomach cancer in Japan, and of liver cancer in Madagascar, suggests that between 60 and 90 per cent of cancers have environmental origins. Similar linkages can be postulated for a range of diseases. The better we understand this environmental dimension of disease, the sooner we shall be able to tackle it.

Chemical contaminants, for instance, are a suspected source of diverse cancers. Some 55 000 chemical compounds end up in natural ecosystems each year. This includes almost 500 million tons of pesticides, plus about 16 million tons of ammonia, 12 million tons of alkalis, and 4 million tons of acids. Of these chemicals, at least 2000 prove carcinogenic to laboratory animals (that is, when administered in chronic doses they cause cancers), and about 30 are demonstrably carcinogenic to humans. Many common food items contain at least one known carcinogen, notable candidates being barbecued meats together with other brown or burned foods, fatty products, spinach salad, mushrooms, sour cream and coffee and alcohol. As we gain insights into the dietary basis of cancers, so we shall be able to 'fine tune' our diets to avoid the 'big C'. Conversely, we should eat a broad variety of fruits, vegetables and grains for their anti-carcinogenic properties.

The dioxin disaster at Seveso, Italy, alerted the industrialized world to the dangers of highly toxic chemicals.

Tobacco

While we are less than certain about how far our diet is responsible for causing cancer, there is one environmental source that has been massively documented as a culprit – tobacco. According to the WHO, 'The control of cigarette smoking in developed countries could do more to develop health and prolong life than any other single action in the whole field of preventive medicine.' Yet consumers spend at least $100 billion each year to buy 4 trillion cigarettes, while governments of many political colours continue to subsidize tobacco production and sale. According to the American Cancer Society, the medical costs of smoking are at least $15 billion a year in the United States alone, to which can be added another $15 billion for lost productivity in the workforce through illness and premature death. The revenue collected by the US government from cigarette taxes amounts to only $6 billion a year.

True, cigarette sales in North America and in Western Europe are beginning to level off as the message spreads about the health toll – as more people learn that each cigarette they smoke shortens their lives by roughly the time it takes them to get their tobacco 'kick' from that one cigarette. Among adult males in North America, smoking dropped from well over half the population in 1965 to little more than one third in 1980, while among adult women, from a high of just over one third to about one quarter. Regrettably, there has been a slight increase in overall per capita cigarette consumption since 1970, due to the large numbers of teenage girls who take up the habit, partly in response to tobacco advertising that suggests that – of all things! – a woman who smokes is ultra-liberated.

But while the smoking curse is being steadily consigned to the ashpit of history in developed nations, cigarette corporations revel in their expanding markets in the Third World. In urban areas of Latin America, 45 per cent of men now smoke, and 18 per cent of women, both rates rising rapidly. Through advertising, smoking is represented as a mark of social status: at the University of Nigeria, almost three-quarters of male students are hooked on the habit. This means that as Third World countries finally conquer some of the great pandemic diseases that have plagued their communities for centuries, they are speedily taking on board a whole array of new diseases, notably lung cancer, coronary disorders and other health hazards that are aggravated, if not caused, by smoking.

As smoking declines in the West, Third World markets for tobacco are expanding. In Latin America, women are increasingly the targets of advertising.

Personal responsibility for health

Against this background of environmentally related disease, John Doe, citizen of the Western world, is increasingly recognizing that the person who is most responsible for his well-being is not his local doctor, but John Doe citizen himself. In nation after nation people's eating habits, as the shelves of supermarket chains show, reveal a shift away from fatty foods and other harmful items in our diet. More and more people are giving up cigarettes, and insisting that other people's habits shall not oblige them to engage in 'secondary smoking'. Non-smoking sections in trains and aeroplanes, restaurants and cinemas, are on the increase.

Left: Growing awareness of the need for fitness ensures a healthy turnout for amateur events such as this five-mile road race in Derbyshire, UK. Aerobic classes *(below)*, attended mostly by women, are part of the multi-billion-dollar health craze in the West.

Above all, there is a mass movement in several countries towards regular exercise. Professional physiologists now tell us that the premature dysfunction of an organ, whether heart, lung, muscle or joint, does not arise so much from over-use of the faculty, as from disuse. The body seems to 'rust out' rather than wear out.

At least a couple of times a week, then, one American in eight pulls on his or her jogging shoes, or heads for the tennis court, or puts in twenty lengths at the swimming pool. So keen are Americans on improved health through their own efforts that they now spend $7 billion a year on sports shoes, $3 billion on health foods, $3 billion on health clubs, and $6 billion on diet drinks.

This recent trend now supplies sufficient evidence for us – or rather, for the people who back their hunches with money, that is, life insurance experts – to assert that the 50-mile-a-week runner is working wonders for his cardiovascular system, while a person who can complete a marathon in less than three hours may well have reduced the chance of heart attack to almost zero.

Vegetarianism is catching on in the affluent West for a number of reasons, not all of them connected with health.

Holistic health

There is a broader dimension to this new phenomenon. Many people now practise 'holistic health', in the sense that they believe that all healing is, in some way or other, self-healing. They realize that the psyche and soma work hand in hand with each other: each contributes to the origin of disease, as it does to its treatment. They both help to maintain good health all-round. While there are plenty of ways to be sick, there are only a few ways to be healthy. Nobody needs to puzzle for long before figuring out some ground-rules on how to stay fit – fit to play, fit to work, fit to 'goof' around.

To express these concepts from another standpoint, people are coming to sense that disease is not only illness. Rather it is something like 'dis-ease', a disorder of the entire person, both physical and non-physical. Thus people are finding that, by their attitudes, they help to induce and foster disease – and by the same token, they help to stimulate cures and to sustain health thereafter. For example, individuals who believe that heart disease 'runs' in their families may well be prone, through behavioural patterns learned from their forebears, to practise a lifestyle that predisposes them to the disorder. When they put two and two together, they can adapt their lifestyle, perhaps with as much benefit as they would derive from a heart drug.

In short, we may soon accept that it is the very way we view ourselves and our ailments that is often the determining factor in both the cause and the course of our ailments. By extension, health – just as much as disease – will come to be perceived as a reflection of our lifestyles and our perceptions of ourselves. Again, we need to emphasize preventive rather than curative medicine.

Traditional medicine in the Third World

In point of fact, it is in this respect of holistic health that certain Third Worlders are perhaps ahead of Westerners – even though they will certainly not have heard of the word 'holistic'. They are unlikely-sounding candidates: medicine men, faith healers and other 'traditional doctors'. Not for nothing do they often insist that a patient undertake a cure within a context of the community, in order to cast out 'spells' and restore good feelings. This insight of tribal lore is being cautiously examined by a few, just a few, Western-trained professionals, who consider there may be more in it than meets the eye. Still more to the point, 'bush surgery' is being slowly incorporated into modern health systems by a number of Third World governments, including those of Tanzania, Ghana, Peru, Mexico, India and Thailand.

Moreover, the witch doctor is being brought in from the cold by virtue of his knowledge of herbal therapies. We have to thank traditional practitioners in India for reserpine, a bio-compound from the serpentine root that has served as a principal ingredient in anti-hypertensive drugs; and for vincristine, a potent anti-leukemia drug from alkaloids of the Madagascar periwinkle. The World Health Organization has mounted a task-force to find safer and more effective materials for contraceptive pills, to serve the needs of both women and men. The agency believes the best prospect lies with hundreds of plants found in tropical forests whose contraceptive powers have long been known to the peoples of Southern and South-East Asia.

The accumulated folklore of medicine men may eventually serve as an accredited source of health support for the bulk of Third World citizens.

A witch doctor of the Dinka tribe in Sudan. Traditional medicine, no longer viewed by the West as mere superstition, is coming under increasing scientific scrutiny.

Top left: A Chinese herb grower shows a team of medical workers how to identify medicinal herbs. *Top right:* One of the last *callawayas* (witch doctors) takes care of a patient in the Bolivian Andes. *Lower left:* Tibetan travelling doctors. Acupuncture *(lower right)* was one of the first forms of traditional medicine to attract the attention of Western scientists.

Few developing countries will be able to afford Western-style medicine for their entire populaces for decades to come. Their citizens must continue to depend upon their customary sources. If tribal healers can be upgraded into health auxiliaries, with their ancient crafts brought under regulation – with the good reinforced while the bad is rejected – they may come to serve a 'barefoot doctor' role along the lines of those who have provided basic health care for China's one billion people. It is primarily thanks to these village health wokers that life expectancy in China has now reached the astonishing level of 68 years.

Today there are fewer than 30 fully trained doctors per 100 000 people in the Third World, or one-sixth as many as in developed nations. A parallel disparity exists within many Third World countries: in Nairobi, there is one doctor to every 670 people but in Kenya's countryside only one to every 26 000.

Preventive vs curative medicine

The lack of super-skilled professionals should not matter too much, if the focus is to be on preventive rather than curative medicine. Preventive medicine, dealing with such issues as nutrition and environmental hygiene, can be undertaken by health support personnel after only a few months of training, by contrast with the six or eight years required by a fully fledged doctor.

As an example of preventive medicine on a grand scale, the UN Drinking Water Supply and Sanitation Decade of the 1980s seeks to eliminate the great scourges of water-borne diseases, such as typhoid, cholera, yellow fever and diarrhoea. The aim is to supply drinking water and sanitation facilities to the 1.5 billion people who do not have running water in their homes or any kind of toilet. This effort will cost about $30 billion a year or $80 million a day. Large as these sums appear, we can compare them with the global figures of $250 million a day spent on cigarettes, and the $1.4 billion a day on armaments. Were the campaign to succeed — the funding supplied hitherto has been derisory — it would achieve more than any other measure to cut back the grotesque mortality rate among Third World children, and thereby help cut back population growth rates.

Population growth and birth control

Population growth stems from the difference between death rates and birth rates. Health services are a central factor in both. The main cause of declining death rates, of course, lies with advances in health. But health is also often a precondition of falling birth rates, since, as was explained earlier, parents will not be persuaded to have fewer children until they are convinced that more of them will survive into adulthood. Family-planning programmes often succeed best when they are closely linked with the care of women and children, and acceptance of contraceptives is often greatest at post-natal clinics.

A family planning clinic in Lesotho. Breast-feeding is encouraged for reasons of health as well as to reduce the birth rate.

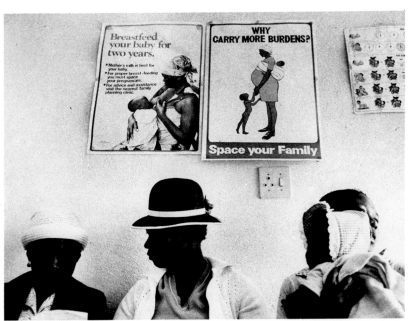

Plainly, however, many other factors are involved. While at one level population planning is a very public affair, at another level it is very private and personal. It is difficult to know just what are parents' motivations for particular family sizes. Fortunately we can now draw on a fair body of information. There is a clear, though far from conclusive, linkage with economic advancement. While we decry the large numbers of children that throng the Third World, we should remember that when Britain and the United States were developing countries a century ago, it was not unusual for parents to produce six or even eight offspring. Yet population growth remained around one per cent a year, since many children did not survive. As a measure of affluence started to take hold, so more offspring reached adulthood, and family size began to decline.

A century ago, families as large as this German one were the norm.

This 'demographic transition' – actually more of an economic transition – is an established concept. Hence, a related concept: 'Take care of the people and the population will take care of itself.' Hence, too, the startling success of birth-control programmes in middle-income countries of the Third World, notably Taiwan, South Korea, Hong Kong, Argentina and Chile, all of which have dropped below a 2 per cent rate of population growth, closely followed by Thailand, Malaysia and Brazil. Yet there is the anomalous experience of Cuba, Sri Lanka and Kerala state in India, where a low per capita GNP (gross national product) is matched by a fast-declining birth rate. This is due, so far as we can discern, to development policies of 'fair shares for all', with little extreme poverty – and with health-care services ensured at grass-roots level. So an enlightened community can be healthy without necessarily being wealthy – and it can be wise as regards its population prospects.

Whatever the factors that trigger declining birth rates, there is some good news on the population front. Little and late as it may be, it is much better than we hoped for in 1970. Asia (without Japan and China) is approaching the 2 per cent growth level, and Latin America has reduced its growth rate even further. Only black Africa remains above 3 per cent; worse, its rate is still rising, and several countries appear ready to follow the unfortunate example of Kenya in reaching a 4 per cent level. This means that Africa is not only over-populated right now (its people have grown steadily hungrier since 1970), but the 'youthful profile' to its demographic pyramid means that many potential parents of the future have already been born. Because of the phenomenon of 'population inertia' – a trend once established is difficult to change – Africa's population, now over half-a-billion, is projected to grow to around 2.6 billion by the time it stabilizes early in the twenty-second century. By

Chinese birth control propaganda. With a population of one billion, the Chinese have to be strict about enforcing the one-child-per-family rule.

contrast, Asia and Latin America are likely to approach zero growth rate a good deal earlier, with totals only a little over twice their present size.

The case of China is illuminating. Proclaiming that 'Of all things, people are the most precious', China does not want many more people than it has now. If all couples produce only two children from now on, the present total of one billion will expand to 1.8 billion before it stabilizes, due to the force of demographic momentum. So China's planners are pressing for the one-child family, and they use all manner of incentives – stick and carrot taxes, plus local-level social pressures – to achieve their goal.

A still more disciplined approach is employed by Singapore. While an almost entirely urbanized community of only 2.5 million people, Singapore has mobilized everything short of outright coercion in order to bring its rate down to 1.2 per cent.

Not that many governments feel ready to adopt the rigid discipline of Singapore's strategy. Yet at least a hundred nations that support family planning in principle leave much amiss in practice. Huge sectors of their populations are denied access to basic family-planning facilities : the 'hardware' is simply not available throughout the length and breadth of their lands. The immediate closing of this gap would reduce fertility in many countries by as much as one-third.

All in all, a world which added 13 million people in the year 1900 will add 90 million in the year 2000, and 75 million in 2025. If the pace of growth could be slowed, there would be many more resources to share around – food, energy, housing, schools, jobs and, above all, health services.

It is now clear that many people, in many different ways, will find they enjoy the sort of broadly defined health that the WHO aims for by the year 2000, and that many more will do so during the course of the next century. But it is also probable that millions of people in the Third World will continue to drag out an existence overshadowed by malnutrition and disease without the basic resources that make life worth living.

The world's food supply

MAGNUS PYKE

Enough to go round

The Food and Agriculture Organization (FAO) of the United Nations, founded in hope and enthusiasm at the end of World War II, was in its early years endowed with very articulate spokesmen who dramatized widespread concern over the world's food situation. This, along with excitement over recent findings in nutrition, led to a feeling that if the calculated intake of one dietary component or another – vitamin B, perhaps, or calcium or even protein – was less than the estimate of what was thought to be required, the community concerned should be officially numbered among the starving. It therefore became an article of doctrine that the so-called 'starving millions' constituted a significant and growing proportion of the world's population.

The first serious and reasoned dissent from this pessimistic point of view was voiced by Jean Mayer[1], who was at that time professor of nutrition at Harvard University. He made two important points. Firstly, that food is only one of the many commodities which are essential to the economic well-being of a community; secondly, that population density is by no means directly related (if at all) to an adequate food supply.

It may be justifiable to refer to the great city of Calcutta as an example of a place where over-population has led to an inadequate food supply, but it must also be recorded that the high-population–density band from Boston to Washington DC is one of the wealthiest and best fed in the United States. Nor is it reasonable to overlook heavily populated but prosperous Holland, Belgium, France and Great Britain, or even Hong Kong and Singapore.

Considering these points, Mayer, while accepting that there are still many people who are poor and underfed, concluded that there was (in 1964) no justification for the belief that there was a food crisis or that things were getting worse. On the contrary, agricultural statistics compared with population increase showed that a gradual increase in food supply per head of the world population was taking place.

Because human numbers are increasing, it does not automatically follow that people are running out of food. The *kind* of food that a particular community eats may change through force of circumstances. Nevertheless, throughout history, food supply – except in times of genuine crisis – has always kept pace with population numbers. It could even be argued that the increase in world population in modern times has been *because* of the increased food supply that accompanies increased prosperity. At the same time, some people always do better than others. Modern technology has not altered the truth of St John's statement that 'the poor always ye have with you'.

In considering the amount of food available, in terms of its calories and its proportion of protein, it is important to understand that people may live at a high or at a low level of nutrition. Prosperity is agreeable, and people if they could would choose to see their children plump, tall and forward for their age; hardship, however, unless it crosses the frontier into famine, does not necessarily do harm. Indeed, there is evidence that some measure of hardship when young may be associated with a lengthened life-span.

Meat or vegetables?

Of more direct relevance to a consideration of food supply, health and wealth – or its converse, poverty – is the often forgotten fact that the total tonnage of the world food commodities is influenced as much by likes and dislikes as by nutritional science. Up till the present – and, in my view, for the foreseeable future as well – it has been a general truth about human eating that *people like meat*. When they are prosperous and have money, they eat more meat; when they are poor, they eat less.

Statistics collected by the FAO show that when the wealth of nations expressed in terms of a standard currency (usually US dollars) per head of population is plotted on a graph against their intake of animal protein (meat, and fish and dairy products) the figures mostly fall along a smooth, rising curve. The richer a community is, the more meat its members eat.

Another way of expressing the same thing is to calculate our direct intake of vegetable foods (cereals, sugar, potatoes and the like) together with the plant food consumed by the animals we eat as meat and other animal products. When this is done, it becomes apparent that prosperous nations, such as the United States, New Zealand, and many of the European countries, eat – directly or indirectly – about eight times as much plant food as is eaten by poor people in Asia and Africa.

In terms of nutritional biochemistry and ice-cold logic (which are not the principles governing the real world) if prosperous nations gave up the meat they so much enjoy eating and obtained their nutritional needs instead from a simple diet of bread and beans, or rice and the occasional portion of dried fish, the food now used to raise livestock would become available to feed undernourished populations elsewhere.

There are two ways then of considering the adequacy of the world's food supply. We can ask if current supplies as they actually exist in different countries are adequate; or it can be calculated how much food *would* be available if prosperous communities reduced their consumption of meat and thus released for human consumption the tonnage of cereals

The Chinese are past masters at making a little meat go a long way. By contrast, meat eating, such as at barbecues *(below)* is a wasteful – and fattening – use of food resources.

and other commodities now used for animal fodder. The protein content of meat is only 5 to 10 per cent of that present in the food eaten by the animal from which the meat is derived. Similarly, five times more protein can be produced from a hectare of land planted to cereals than from the same area used to rear beef. The figure is doubled again if peas or beans are grown in place of grain. The world's human population eats (directly) only one-third as much vegetable protein as its herds of cattle.

Normally, the amount of animal food consumed by a community is proportional to the community's wealth. Here and there, however, minority groups are to be found who choose to eat a wholly or partly vegetarian diet. There are also people, in advanced industrial societies as well as in less sophisticated communities, who limit the amount of meat they eat because they hold the flesh of particular species to be taboo and not, therefore, fit to eat. Beef, pork, horse-meat, dogs, cats and many other sources of wholesome nourishment have been thus embargoed.

At the present time, existing vegetarian societies in the West are receiving some measure of reinforcement from those concerning themselves with animal rights. If it should happen in the future – although this is unlikely – that we all become vegetarians, the tonnage of food available for human consumption would become very much greater than it is. Nor need vegetarianism be total. Certain meat animals are economic to raise; sheep and goats can graze highland pastures or arid areas from which otherwise little or no human food could be obtained.

The numerous surveys of world food production and world population which have been made by such public bodies as the United Nations, the US Department of Agriculture and the UK Cabinet Office, and by diverse scholars and private organizations, have all highlighted the complexity of the so-called world food crisis. It is no easy task to assess the factors that decide whether people are likely to have enough to eat in the future. I have, perhaps, already written enough to illustrate the truth of the conclusions of a team at the University of Sussex when they wrote, in 1976, that 'All [the surveys] have one message in common: our inability to feed the world's population is not due to physical factors placing limitations on the total world food production. They also recognize that the causal factors in world hunger and malnutrition are the enormous economic, social and political problems associated with poverty.'[2]

It is difficult to estimate the area of land in the world used at present for the production of food, and it is doubly difficult to assess what additional areas, which are not farmed but which could be utilized for food production, will be available for any increased demand in the future. Such estimates as have been made by FAO, by United States advisory committees and by others imply that there are about 3 billion hectares (8 billion acres) which *could* be cultivated. Of this area, about half has been cultivated at one time or another. While investigators differ in some of their conclusions, all agree that only about half of the area of land which could without undue difficulty be used for food production is, in fact, so used.

Estimates of the amount of food that could be produced world-wide vary depending on a variety of factors, such as the weather, competitive uses for land and the problem of providing water. But they all show that so far as technical matters are concerned the world's food production could be doubled without any advancement in the technology that is already available in the 1980s.

The Common Agricultural Policy of the European Economic Community, which is a political and financial arrangement between the countries making up the Community, has dramatically demonstrated the degree to which food production can be influenced, quite apart from scientific and technical improvements in agriculture. When the economists of the EEC, in their efforts to adjust the money incomes of the farmers in the Community, have set the financial subsidy for one crop or another unduly high, it has repeatedly happened that farmers, spurred on by the possibility of financial reward, have produced an excess – the so-called butter mountain, for example – beyond what the Community can consume.

The 'Green Revolution'

In 1842, John Bennett Lawes showed that the yield of wheat per hectare could be increased if certain chemical elements were incorporated in the soil. He recorded that when 100 lb (45kg) of nitrogen, as nitrate of soda, was applied per hectare (2.5 acres), the yield of wheat increased by 30 bushels. In 1898, Sir William Crookes made use of these figures in his presidential address to the British Association for the Advancement of Science. Like his successors, he was concerned about world starvation. Unless the world's food supply could be increased by 1190 million bushels of wheat within 30 years – that is, by 1928 – he foresaw widespread starvation and distress. To achieve this goal, the seemingly unattainable amount of 12 million tons of nitrate of soda a year would need to be manufactured and applied to 65 million hectares (160 million acres) of land. In fact, within 15 years Fritz Haber and his colleagues in Germany had developed a process for the fixation of nitrogen from the atmosphere.

Alternative sources of protein: fried termites on sale in Bangladesh *(top)* and horsemeat, a staple in France.

By 1925, sufficient ammonia was being produced by the Haber process to supply Sir William Crookes' seemingly fantastic annual amount of 12 million tons of nitrogenous fertilizer twice over.

But the increase in crop yields – which was the beginning of what later became known as the Green Revolution – important as it was, was not brought about solely, or even principally, by these advances in fertilizer chemistry. It was in fact biological science which enabled the plant breeders and geneticists to produce new wheat varieties capable of growing in the vast, cold, dry areas where no crops at all could be produced before. At the same time, engineers designed and built great new machines which enabled grain to be cultivated and harvested much more efficiently than before.

In the 1840s, an observant Canadian farmer noticed a few ears of wheat in one of his fields that grew better than the rest of his crop. From this chance observation, the wheat variety Red Fife was developed. Later, Charles Saunders made more calculated observations which enabled him to select seedlings more vigorous and higher-yielding than the rest. By this procedure he isolated the variety Marquis. These two varieties, Red Fife and Marquis, proved to be well suited to prairie conditions and enabled wheat to be grown successfully much farther north and west than had previously been possible.

In 1916, however, when immense fields, covering almost the whole area of the plains of Manitoba, Saskatchewan and Alberta, were sown with Marquis, there came an epidemic of a fungus disease, stem rust. It was estimated that in one year alone 100 million bushels of wheat were lost. It became clear that the fungus had undergone a genetic change and had adapted itself to the changes in its environment, namely, life in association with Marquis wheat. The evidence for this grew stronger when, after the out-break in 1916, others followed. In 1927, 90 million bushels of wheat were lost; in 1935, the loss was 87 million bushels, and between 1925 and 1935 the total wheat loss due to stem rust in Manitoba and Saskatchewan was estimated at nearly 4000 million bushels.

No half measures: an American farmer of the 1930s fights flea-beetle with his 12-row bean sprayer.

Initially, no effective means of combating the fungus diseases of wheat was known. Chemical dips and sprays were unsuccessful. Soon, however, it became apparent that the means to defeat this threat to what we have come to call the Green Revolution also lay in the hands of plant breeders. And the solution was not any easy one. For example, it was discovered that there were some 130 different races of fungus that caused 'leaf rust' and over 200 causing the still more destructive stem rust. Nevertheless, although infected crops continued to occur much later, by 1924 research workers in the United States had succeeded in developing a variety of wheat resistant to stem rust. This strain was called Ceres and for a decade until 1935 it remained the most successful immune wheat in Canada. Then the fungus struck back and a strain of *P. graminis* capable of attacking Ceres wheat spread across the prairie farms, and the crops again succumbed. Again, the plant geneticists rose to the challenge and a further strain immune to stem rust was developed. This was called Thatcher, with which large acreages were sown. Thatcher, however, was not resistant to leaf rust, *P. triticina*. Then a further cross-bred strain, Regent, developed by Canadian scientists, was produced which was resistant to both leaf rust and stem rust.

The development of improved seed varieties in Canada and the United States over a period of years was mirrored in other parts of the world. The annual world wheat crop rose from about 125 million metric tons (tonnes) in the first decade of the twentieth century to almost 300 million tonnes in the early 1960s. It more than doubled in 50 years.

I have just described how in part this great increase was brought about. But towards the end of this period, the rate of increase accelerated still further. It was in 1944 that the Mexican International Maize and Wheat Improvement Centre was set up by the Mexican government. The advancement of science and the progress of plant genetics that had already taken place enabled the scientists in Mexico to identify with some precision the qualities in which new strains of cereals could be improved. In particular, they succeeded in increasing the yield of grain by restricting the energy expended by the cereal in growing long stalks. A further practical advantage of the new short-stemmed varieties was that ears of wheat and rice could safely be increased by the use of ample supplies of fertilizer without the danger of the upright plants falling flat under the weight of the grain. The phenomenon of 'lodging', which makes the crop impossible to harvest, is a constant danger when heavy yields of normal long-stemmed varieties are being grown.

Innovation and education

But the achievement of the Mexican International Maize and Wheat Improvement Centre was more than the research successes of its scientists. Its director, Dr Norman E. Borlaug, not only guided the scientific side of the research programme, but showed a remarkable talent for introducing the new varieties into what are often the deeply conservative farming methods of developing societies. This he did by insisting that the scientists themselves spent at least part of their time working with the very farmers whose problems their studies were designed to unravel. Largely due to these efforts, in Mexico the production of wheat rose from 1190 million tons in 1960 to 2100 million tons in 1970, and the country for the first time became self-sufficient in wheat.

Borlaug made similar provisions for the introduction of high-yielding short-stemmed wheat strains into countries outside Mexico. Centres were set up in Colombia, Nigeria, India and Pakistan. In the Philippines, the

International Rice Research Institute had as much success with rice as had been achieved elsewhere with wheat. Perhaps the most remarkable achievement has been recorded in India. By 1979, through the benefits attained by the adoption in the late 1960s of the genetic package that India accepted in the name of the Green Revolution, the country was becoming a major producer of cereals. During the four years from 1975 to 1979, bumper harvests were recorded. In 1978–9 for example, a record crop of 126 million tons was harvested, culminating in a government grain reserve of 26 million tons.

As a result, therefore, of the Green Revolution, we find India being in a position to supply food to Afghanistan, Bangladesh, Vietnam and even the Soviet Union. If this is the situation at the beginning of the 1980s, then the possibilities for the future look good. However, the President of the US Overseas Development Council, James Grant, has pointed out that even though the level of food production in India has already been raised by the adoption of the scientific advances of recent years, yields per hectare in that country are still low.[3] For the most important cereal, rice, about 2.5 tons per hectare (2.5 acres) are commonly harvested, compared with 7.5 tons in more highly developed countries, among which can be listed Taiwan and South Korea. Yet India possesses about the same area of arable land as the United States, much the same water resources (20 per cent of its farms under irrigation compared with 10 per cent in the USA) and a similar range of temperature. According to Grant, India could, therefore, be producing at least three times more grain per hectare than it is now doing. It needs to overcome, not technical or scientific constraints, but problems of organization and finance. This would increase the total output of the country from the current level of 120 million tons of grain to more than 300 million tons, and thereby outstrip the current US output of about 250 million tons.

Top: Maize damaged by beetles in the Amazon; *(above)* Triticale, a wheat and rye hybrid with a high resistance to disease.

Left: Scientific advances have boosted food production in India, but methods remain traditional.

Agricultural change

An aerial view of Varanasi, in India. India has as much arable land as the United States and could treble its food production.

Ever since the Industrial Revolution, the number of people working on the land in industrial societies has steadily and dramatically fallen, while the amount of food produced has increased. These trends have accelerated in recent years. For instance, the numbers of full-time farm workers in Great Britain fell between 1946 and 1976 from 695 000 to 213 000 while, during the same period, the number of farms diminished from 450 000 to 270 000; that is to say, the size of the average farm increased by about 40 per cent. Over the same period the average yields of wheat and potatoes increased from 2.41 and 17.5 tons per hectare (2.5 acres) to 4.97 and 31.6 tons per hectare respectively.[4]

Even though it has been generally assumed, both in communist countries with their emphasis on collective farms and in capitalist societies with their large, highly mechanized and heavily capitalized estates, that large farming units are more efficient than small family farms, evidence for this is by no means clear. There is even evidence to the contrary. In Western European countries, considerable emphasis is placed on small agricultural units where farmers have a strong motive to get the best out of their land. Similarly, in Hungary, under a communist system, a significant proportion of the total output of food is produced by individual private small-scale holdings. Nor is the efficiency of the collective farms invariably satisfactory.

Since the beginning of the century, when there was a demand for palm oil for the manufacture of an increasing tonnage of margarine, there has

been a trend towards the establishment of large-scale plantations of oil palms and the use of advanced technology in the extraction of the oil. It was as long ago as 1911 that Lord Leverhulme brought into existence La Société Anonyme des Huileries du Congo Belge in what is now Zaire, and in the years that followed large areas of land for palm plantations were cleared in Nigeria, the Cameroons and Ghana. Yet, in spite of the fact that adequately capitalized plantations permitted the culture of better varieties of palm trees, the application of proper amounts of scientifically selected fertilizers, more systematic harvesting methods and a regular supply of produce throughout the year, such systems have not found it easy to compete with producers operating on a family scale.[5] In periods of recession, the family producers can cut back their expenses by growing food rather than expending their efforts on harvesting a cash crop for a depressed market. This flexibility is not available to the plantation producer.

Top: Capital-intensive methods of grain harvesting in the USA. Small-scale harvesting French-style *(above).*

Although the small-scale grower may thus under appropriate circumstances produce food more efficiently than those operating a large collective farm, this may not invariably be so. For example, the splitting up of efficient, highly mechanized farms in a developing country newly freed from colonial rule is all too often followed by a disastrous fall in the tonnage of food previously grown on the same area of land.

The general weight of evidence seems to show that the system of agriculture – whether farms are large or small – is not crucial to the efficiency of food production. The three important factors are, firstly, the skill and commitment of the farmers, secondly, knowledge, and thirdly capital. Where improved seeds can be obtained, and where fertilizers and water are available and provision is on hand for tilling the land and harvesting the crop, good yields can be expected from small units, whether in Europe or Mexico, or from large units as far apart as Manitoba and the Soviet Ukraine.

I pointed out earlier that although technical and scientific innovations by which the yield of food from the land could be increased were important to the world's present and future food supply, the basic factors determining whether hunger and malnutrition occurred in one community or another were economic, social and political. For example, with fewer people controlling more land around the world, many small, poorer farmers have been driven from their traditional peasant holdings to the cities, where they become a burden to the community. At the same time, the high cost of fertilizer and pesticides has favoured the expansion of those farms that were rich to begin with. At their most extreme, the economic and political forces produced the grotesque paradox of Niger, during the years when the Sahel famine was at its height, actually increasing its food exports.

Above: The most primitive tools of all; this Dinka tribesman harvests groundnuts by hand.

Right: Children in Niger wait for relief supplies to add to their stocks of dried milk from Europe.

Nutritional alternatives

It was in 1869 that Hippolyte Mège Mouries took out a patent for what was to become margarine. Over the 114 years since then, margarine has become a major food product, a worthy substitute for butter and in certain respects its superior in nutritional value. The basic virtue of margarine is that, because it can be made in whole or in part from vegetable fats, it represents a more economical use than butter of the food crops from which it is derived. To produce butter the cows must inevitably consume much more feed than they return as the butter-fat from which butter is made.

There are lessons to be learned from the fact that more than a century elapsed between the beginnings of margarine and its present status as a widely used foodstuff. During this time, its aesthetic and dietetic qualities were gradually improved and people slowly became used to it and began to recognize its virtues. If the cost of food in general rises in the future, it seems safe to predict that margarine will be eaten in larger and larger quantities in those parts of the world where once butter was traditionally eaten.

In 1954, R. A. Boyer in the United States set out to do for meat what Mège Mouriès in France aimed to do for butter. In technical terms meat can be described as a system of woven or knitted protein fibres. If a substance has a meat-like texture, and is coloured and flavoured in a way characteristic of the various kinds of meat customarily eaten, then – the theory goes – it will be accepted as meat. In addition to its technical characteristics, however, meat plays an important social role. A 'cooked meal' is popularly interpreted as a combination of articles centred on meat and usually served hot. More subtle than this are the various taboos which, regardless of their antiquity, continue to exert their force in today's modern industrial societies and seem certain to to retain their force in the future. It is, therefore, hardly surprising that the so-called texturized vegetable protein (TVP) commonly made from soya beans has in its 30 years of existence so far failed to attain either the exact technical and aesthetic qualities of meat or its anthropological overtones. It remains to be seen whether a further 80 years will be needed for it to be accepted – as margarine has been for butter – as a valid substitute for meat and thus make possible the more efficient increased use of soya beans directly as human food. By eating soya beans like this the comparatively inefficient return obtained by feeding them first to livestock would be obviated.

There are various other ideas for the direct consumption by human beings of foodstuffs otherwise better suited for animals. Some limited success has been achieved with leaf protein, prepared by squeezing the juice out of selected leaves, heating the liquid and recovering the 'curd'. The product, however, is green and tends to have a slightly rank taste derived from the leaves from which it is made. Furthermore, it is unlike any food with which people are familiar in ordinary life. Nevertheless, it has attained some limited acceptance in India, and two international congresses have been held to discuss its merits.

Algae – the green scum on ponds is an example – has also been used as human food. Again, it is unlike any common article of diet. It also possesses a 'gag factor', which makes it disagreeable to eat. Krill is an abundant, small, marine, shrimp-like creature which forms the food of certain whales. Experiments, notably by the Japanese, have shown that it too can be used in limited amounts as human food. Whether it will become a significant article of diet in the future, however, seems doubtful.

Other suggestions for the future involve the conversion of non-edible raw materials into food. Waste effluent from paper-making has, for example, been used as a substrate for the propagation of yeast for use, when dried, as cattle or human food. Scientists have isolated other strains of yeast which are capable of being grown on hydocarbon fractions derived from petroleum. Dried material has been produced on a pilot-plant scale but, while modest success has been achieved in its use as animal feed, the economics of the process compared with the cost of soya-bean meal or dried milk are problematic. Similar material has been produced by propagating bacteria on methanol derived from natural gas.

The paradox of food considered as a source of nutrients on the one hand, and as an economic commodity comparable with motor cars or nylon shirts on the other, is sharply illustrated in the development of modern aquaculture as a source of food for tomorrow. Apart from simple systems of fish farming derived from medieval carp ponds, and the development of new fish species to be grown in flooded rice-paddy fields, the application of modern technology has had considerable success in the production of such highly esteemed, expensive species as trout, salmon, Dover sole and turbot. Within the next decade, commercial production of such fish will probably rise threefold. While this may be profitable, it does not represent any increase in the total food supply. On the contrary, since the feed given to fish in intensive fish farms is usually fish meal, the whole operation is basically a process for converting a larger amount of less desirable low-cost fish into a very much smaller amount of more desirable high-cost fish.

Possibilities for the future

Jonathan Swift, in the eighteenth century, wrote that 'whoever could make two ears of corn ... to grow on a spot of ground where only one grew before would deserve better of mankind ... than the whole race of politicians put together.' Modern knowledge, however, shows that Swift was unduly hard on politicians. Agricultural scientists and politicians (among whom I am prepared to include economists) are equally important.

Science applied to increase the yield of both crops and livestock has been strikingly successful in our own times. Nor can it be doubted that yields will continue to increase further in the future. For example, we seem to be on the verge of discovering how to fix nitrogen biologically for cereal crops rather than expend costly energy on the Haber process. Yet these crops, whether of meat or cereals, which science enables farmers to produce in plenty now and no doubt even more plentifully in the future, to cope with any foreseeable demand, will do little good to those who cannot afford to buy them.

Thus, while science is one half of the equation enabling us to produce the food we need for the world of the future, politics and economics, which are the other half, have yet to show that what can be produced can also be justly distributed.

References

1 *Nutrition Review* 22, 1964, p.353.
2 Rush, R., Mastrand P., Gribbin J., and McKerron G. *Nature* 261, 1976, p.181.
3 Agarwal A. *Nature* 281, 1979, p.250.
4 Winegarten A. *Proceedings of the Nutrition Society* 36, 1977, p.255.
5 Rowe J.W.F., *Primary commodities in international trade*, Cambridge University Press, Cambridge, 1965, p.223.

Chapter Three

ENVIRONMENT AND RESOURCES: IS EARTH OVER-EXPLOITED?

The answer Robin Clarke gives to the vital question he poses is 'no' – but a qualified 'no'. The danger signals are already there and we are beginning to heed them. But this may be too little, too late. How much damage has already been done by pollution, by over-fishing and even by clearing forests for crop cultivation is not fully known. The chains which bind all living things together are complicated, Clarke says, and the loss of one species can lead to the loss of other, dependent species. 'Ultimately', he warns, quoting Sir Peter Scott's memorable words, 'it is man that is the endangered species.'

Nigeria: burning off natural gas in the Niger delta.

Environment and resources: is Earth over-exploited?

ROBIN CLARKE

Since the Industrial Revolution the most important materials extracted from the earth's crust have been those that provide energy, of which coal was for a long time the most important of all. After World War II, however, its place was taken largely by oil and, more recently, to a lesser extent by natural gas. The world oil crisis of 1973 thus came as a great shock to the industrialized countries, serving notice on them that oil reserves would not last, and spreading panic at the prospect of future supplies being dictated by a few oil-rich countries.

So what does the future hold? The collapse of industrial societies wedded to the concept of limitless cheap energy? The emergence of new resources to replace those in short supply? Or the diversification and conservation of energy resources to power the growing service industries while the more demanding manufacturing industries are allowed to decline? Some experts believe that this last is the most likely course of development for the West in the years ahead; others disagree.

Coal, oil and gas

The industrial world now depends on four primary energy sources: oil, gas, coal (the fossil fuels) and nuclear energy. It will continue to do so for some time. But the future availability of each of these sources is very different. According to recent estimates, the supply of oil, if used at 1980 rates, will begin to fall short just before the turn of the century. Natural gas could be expected to last for 50 years, and coal should be available for another 230 years.

But these estimates must be interpreted with caution. They are based on proved, recoverable reserves of known quantity and quality. Yet new reserves are constantly being found. Up to 1973, proved reserves of gas and oil were growing rapidly. Between 1973 and 1979, however, they failed to keep pace with consumption, which grew at 4.1 per cent a year while new reserves grew at only 3.5 per cent a year. Since then, things appear to be improving, with new discoveries at least keeping pace with growth in consumption.

World energy consumption patterns could be very different in 2000 from what they were in 1983. Unless new reserves of oil and gas are found very soon, they will have to be used more sparingly. Coal, and possibly nuclear power, will increasingly be used as substitutes.

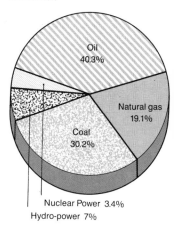

World energy consumption 1983

We are not talking here about an *absolute* reserve of any material in the crust – absolute reserves are far larger. Recoverable reserves are those which can be extracted at reasonable economic cost. As the price of a fuel increases, so more of a known reserve becomes economical to extract. There are, for example, huge deposits of oil contained in materials known as tar sands and shales, particularly in Canada. Although the technology exists for extracting useful fuels from these it is at present hopelessly uneconomic. If the day ever comes when these processes become truly economic, the proved reserves of oil will increase dramatically.

North Sea oil rig.

Nevertheless, it is clear that there is far more coal available than there is oil and gas. Over the medium term, say from the years 2000 to 2050, a widespread substitution of coal for oil and gas seems certain. In particular, more coal-fired power stations will be built and many oil-fired ones will go out of commission. Methods have also been developed for liquefying coal for use as an oil substitute in petrol. It should be noted that, in general, coal supplies are prolific in industrial nations but in very short supply in developing countries. The latter are likely to remain oil-dependent for much longer than the developed countries.

Nuclear energy

The future of nuclear energy remains uncertain. It currently provides about eight per cent of world electricity but its history has been chequered. From the building of the first power reactor in 1954 until 1973, the numbers of new reactors ordered each year rose sharply. Since then the number of new orders has fallen because of opposition based on the dangers of nuclear power and the threat it poses to the environment as well as a growing conviction that nuclear energy may never be as economic as was once promised.

Nuclear reactors depend on uranium for fuel. Though uranium is a common constituent of the earth's crust, it occurs only rarely in ores which are economic to exploit. In fact, recoverable reserves amount to only about 4 million tonnes (metric tons). Yet, it is estimated that if nuclear energy demand continued to grow as predicted, we would need 9 million tonnes by the year 2025. A nuclear power programme based on conventional thermal reactors would be very short-lived, not extending much beyond the turn of the century, because of the lack of uranium deposits.

There is, however, an alternative form of reactor, known as the breeder, which actually produces more nuclear fuel than it consumes. If the nuclear power industry is to have much of a future, the breeder reactor could be the answer. But the technology involved is much less developed than for present-day thermal reactors, and it is inherently, and probably unavoidably, much more dangerous. It does not take a great deal of wisdom to hazard the guess that the breeder reactor may never make it.

Above: 2 December 1942. The moment when the world's first nuclear reactor became self-sustaining – in a squash court at the University of Chicago.

Right: Alternative energy. Clockwise from top left: a domestic solar panel in Athens; a hydro-electric dam in Angola; a geothermal installation; a French fixed parabolic solar reflector; an American wind turbine generator.

Alternative energy forms

Much interest is currently focused on alternative energy forms: solar energy, wind energy, tidal power, wave energy, geothermal energy, biogas (fuel produced from animal and vegetable waste) and the production of alcohol fuel from crops such as sugar cane, something that is now done on a large scale in Brazil. Several countries, including Ireland, are once again planning wood-fired power stations.

Exactly what contribution these sources will make to the economy of the future is difficult to predict; compared to coal, however, none is likely to be globally significant. And by the time the bottom of the coal mine is in sight, it seems likely that nuclear fusion – a method of generating power in the same way as the sun – may be with us. If so, our energy problems will be solved for all time. Nuclear fusion would use as fuel hydrogen isotopes

that are obtainable from sea water, and their supply would last indefinitely. Furthermore, unlike the present generation of reactors, which are based on nuclear fission, a fusion reactor would produce no dangerous, radioactive waste.

But even if nuclear fusion does prove to be a long-term solution, it hardly solves the immediate energy problems, especially those of the developing countries. Having little or no coal, some of them at present are forced to spend as much as two-thirds of their foreign earnings on oil imports to fuel their domestic economies.

Their most feasible alternatives to oil are hydroelectric power – electrical energy generated by water power and wood energy. In 1979, 'hydropower' was providing 21.6 per cent of the world's electric supply. Some 75 per cent of all potential hydroelectric sites were in production in Europe and North America but the situation was radically different in Asia, Africa and Latin America. There only 43 per cent, 8 per cent and 47 per cent, respectively, of potential sites were in production. Furthermore, these figures account for only major sites. There is also considerable potential in developing countries for mini-hydropower, supplying energy at the village level where it is most needed. China has set a sterling example; in the past 20 years it has put into commission no less than 80 000 mini-hydropower units of an average size of only 70 kilowatts.

Other minerals

As well as energy-source minerals, substantial quantities of other minerals are extracted from the earth's crust to meet the needs of modern societies. Moreover, the situation for some of these appears to be even more critical than for energy resources. It was reliably estimated in 1977 that the known reserves of the following common metals were: aluminium, 53 years; copper, 30 years; lead, 29 years; zinc, 18 years; nickel, 42 years; and tin, 34 years. However, such figures can be grossly deceptive.

Open-cast mineral mine in Australia.

Minerals an average American will use during his or her lifetime		
Mineral	Weight	
	kg	lb
Sand and gravel	4091	9019
Stone	3864	8519
Cement	364	802
Clays	273	602
Iron and steel	545	1202
Aluminium	23	51
Copper	11	24
Lead	7	15
Zinc	7	15
Other metals	16	35

The message for the future?

Unlike the mineral energy resources these minerals are not, in theory, used up. Fossil fuels are consumed by burning them, but the uses we find for materials such as iron, copper, cobalt and aluminium do not alter the amount of these materials that is theoretically available. All these minerals can be recycled, and recycled endlessly, at some cost: as minerals become scarcer, so the economics of recycling change. Witness the now common bottle banks for recycling ordinary glass – a material which is, after all, made from the cheapest of all natural resources: sand.

The extent to which scrap metals are already recycled surprises many people. In the United Kindgom more than 60 per cent of all iron and lead used is recycled. So is about 30 per cent of all copper and aluminium. Over the coming decades, these figures will rise, and the number of materials which will be recycled will also grow. In this sense, we are not likely to run out of minerals. Future problems are more likely to be concerned with political issues such as the location of supplies of certain strategic materials such as titanium, which is used in the building of spacecraft and supersonic aircraft. The political roles of the superpowers become easier to understand when it is realized how dependent they are on imports of certain materials that are vital to national security. The United States, for instance, imports all its titanium, 97 per cent of its tantalite (used in the manufacture of electric light bulbs) and 94 per cent of its bauxite (aluminium ore).

However, over the next couple of decades a major new source of minerals is likely to come into production: the sea-bed, on which lies a great deal of copper, nickel, cobalt and manganese, particularly in the Pacific Ocean. Experts predicted in 1979 that the sea-bed could, by the mid-1980s, be supplying 12.3 per cent of world nickel, 14.0 per cent of manganese, 28.6 per cent of cobalt and 0.9 per cent of copper. Clearly, these estimates will not be fulfilled. The new Law of the Sea, which denies the right of individual nations to mine sea-bed resources without paying royalties to neighbouring countries, has delayed the industrial development of sea-bed mining because private companies have cut back their investment in technology for fear that profits to be made will turn out too small. But there is little doubt that sea-bed mining will be in full swing by the turn of the century.

Land cultivation

Currently, only about 11 per cent of the earth's land surface – some 1500 million hectares (3700 million acres) – is under any kind of cultivation. There would seem to be room for expansion. But there are problems, the main one being that much of the land is not well suited to the plough: 28 per cent of it is too dry, 23 per cent suffers from too much salt or other chemicals, 22 per cent has too little soil, 10 per cent is waterlogged and 6 per cent is permanently frozen.

This does not mean, of course, that none of this land can ever be used. Wet land can be drained, dry land irrigated. Even so, the world's potentially cultivable land is still limited to about 3000 million hectares (7500 million acres) – roughly double today's figure. In the developed countries, 77 per cent of land with potential is already in use, compared with only 36 per cent in the developing countries.

However, in the developing world, the situation can be expected to deteriorate rapidly over the next 20 years. While the developing countries as a whole can still triple the amount of land they cultivate, the lack of available land in some countries is already desperate: worst-off is South-East Asia, where 92 per cent of all the land that could ever be cultivated is already under the plough. South America, by contrast, is potentially well off: only 15 per cent of its cultivable land is yet in use.

How things will develop over the next 20 years has been studied in some detail by the Food and Agriculture Organization (FAO) of the United Nations. Out of 90 developing countries studied, the FAO found that in 17 of them, where half the total population currently lives, 90 per cent of potentially cultivable land is already in use. On average, there are currently 0.37 hectares (0.91 acres) of good land per head of population in the developing countries. By the year 2000, if current trends continue, there will be only 0.25 hectares (0.62 acres). By the end of the century, the FAO comments, 'shortage of land will become a critical constraint for about two-thirds of the population of the developing countries.'

This map shows all the cultivable land that might be brought into use in a world that was unaffected by political or economic competition.

Rice paddies in South Bali, Indonesia.

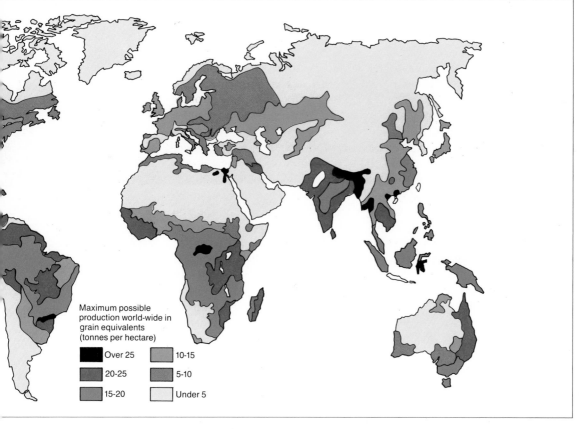

Maximum possible
production world-wide in
grain equivalents
(tonnes per hectare)

- ■ Over 25
- ▨ 20-25
- ▨ 15-20
- ▨ 10-15
- ▨ 5-10
- ▢ Under 5

By then, unless radical and unexpected improvements can be made, it seems certain that people will have to move from the highly populated regions into the less populated ones. This is already happening in Indonesia, where the government is moving farmers from Java to the relatively little-exploited neighbouring Sumatra. A similar movement of people is likely from the central highland plateau of Ethiopia in Africa. Of the developing regions, only South America is likely to escape severe pressure on agricultural land.

Loss of productive land

The amount of land in production is never static, however. Land degradation – due to building, toxification, waterlogging, salinization and soil erosion – is currently running at very high levels. At the present rate, something like one-third of all arable land could be lost to these causes by the end of the century. This figure is comparable with the amount of new land that could be brought into production over the same period. It seems we are running hard to stand still.

Much good cropland is built on or paved over every year. During the 1970s the developed countries destroyed 3 million hectares (7.5 million acres) of their best land in this way. Waterlogging and salinization – due almost entirely to bad land-management – takes a far bigger toll. In the mid-1970s, the FAO estimated that 952 million hectares (2.4 billion acres) of land were affected by salt. Every year about the same amount of land that is reclaimed and irrigated is lost through salinization and waterlogging. World-wide about one-fifth of the world's 200 million irrigated hectares (500 million acres) are either waterlogged, affected by salt, or both.

To these problems must be added those of soil erosion caused by wind and water. Both have reached frightening proportions. Wind erosion, of course, was responsible for the dust bowls of the 1930s in central United States. In one storm there in May 1934, 300 million tonnes of soil were lifted off the ground, carried an estimated 2500 kilometres (1500 miles), and deposited on the decks of ships 500 kilometres (300 miles) out in the Atlantic. The skies of New York were darkened for five hours. While the problems in the United States have lessened, they have grown severe elsewhere as attempts to use poor land for arable crops expose more and more unsuitable soil to the action of the wind. According to FAO figures, 22.4 per cent of land in Africa north of the equator, and 35.5 per cent of land in the Near East, are now affected by wind erosion.

Water erosion is also creating havoc in the developing countries, particularly where hillsides are brought under the plough in an effort to increase crop production. World-wide, every year about 25 000 million tonnes of soil are now being washed or blown off good land, to end up in the rivers, streams and seas of the world. About 30 per cent of India's 297 million hectares (734 million acres) of cropland is now affected by water erosion, and even in the United States soil loss from cropland still averages about 12 tonnes per hectare (5 tons per acre) a year. The US has lost one-third of its soil since farming began. The world as a whole has probably lost approaching 2 billion hectares (5 billion acres) – more than is currently in arable production.

FAO studies have revealed some alarming statistics about the future loss of production due to soil erosion. If no further soil conservation techniques were to be practised, it is estimated that the area of rain-fed cropland in the world would drop by 18 per cent between 1975 and the year 2000. However, because erosion decreases yield as well as actually destroying land, the production of rain-fed crops would fall by much more – by 29 per cent. This, of course, is not likely to happen, for some soil conservation work is already under way. Even so, to protect just a quarter of all farm land, and to provide adequate flood control on 20 million hectares (50 million acres) of land, would cost about $25 000 million by the end of the century.

Soil erosion is often an insidious process. While some land may be lost overnight during severe storms, what happens more often is that soil is gradually washed away, sometimes so slowly that the process is difficult to detect. Yields drop, and land that was once suitable for crops becomes capable of supporting only pasture. Eventually that pasture reverts to scrubland. In hot, arid areas, it is not long before the scrub becomes desert.

About one-third of the earth's land surface – some 4700 million hectares (8000 million acres) – is arid or semi-arid. About 3200 million

Dust storm in Agadez, Niger.

Sands of time: sand dunes advancing over pine woods.

hectares (8000 million acres), on which 80 million people struggle to make a living, are currently threatened with desertification. Every year 20 million hectares (45 million acres) of land deteriorate because of desertification to a point where it is no longer profitable to farm them. The cost of lost production has been estimated at $26 000 million a year, a figure which is roughly comparable to the GNP (gross national product) of Thailand. About 80 per cent of the world's cropland and rangeland in arid areas is now under threat of desertification. In the Sudan, the edge of the desert has advanced by about 100 kilometres (60 miles) in just 15 years.

The technical problems of recovering land from the desert's grip are not insuperable but it is expensive. A United Nations study has suggested that the cost of halting desertification in the developing countries over the next 20 years would amount to $2400 million annually, more than five times what is currently being spent. There are, as yet, few signs that the money that is needed is going to be found.

The problem of deserts is closely related to that of tree cover – chopping down trees in arid areas for fuelwood or to clear land for cultivation is one of the commonest causes of desertification. The same process is also removing much of the forest cover from the humid tropics. About 9 per cent of the earth's land area is forested and the tropical moist forests, which cover 40 per cent of land area in the tropics, are the most directly threatened. Recent statistics are alarming: between 1975 and 1980, 37 million hectares (90 million acres) of tropical forest were destroyed in Africa, 12.1 million in Asia and 18.4 million in Central and South America. At this rate more than 26 hectares (64 acres) of tropical forest are being destroyed every minute. While the future looks bleak, no one is sure whether current trends will continue. There are some signs that deforestation may already be slowing down. If not, nine countries will have destroyed all their closed (densely wooded) forest within 30 years and a further 13 countries will do so within about 50 years.

A desperate problem

This general situation reflects one of the world's most desperate problems: fuelwood shortage. About 2000 million people, nearly all of them in the developing countries, depend on fuelwood for their daily energy needs. This makes fuelwood the most commonly used energy source in the world. In fact, in the developing countries, 85 per cent of the wood that is cut is used for fuel – every man, woman and child there using an average of about half a cubic metre (over 17 cubic feet) of wood a year for cooking and heating.

There is no known substitute for fuelwood – nothing else is as cheap or as readily available. Solar power, biogas, wind energy, even kerosene and oil can be substituted to a small extent but the quantities of wood used are now so enormous – and are growing larger every day – that it is clear that the developing world will depend on trees for its domestic energy for a very long time to come.

However, the supply can no longer meet demand. In 1981 the FAO revealed that 96 million people were already unable to satisfy their

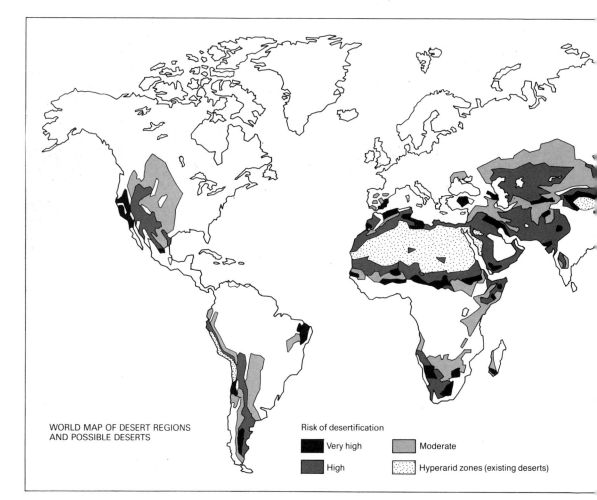

WORLD MAP OF DESERT REGIONS
AND POSSIBLE DESERTS

Risk of desertification

■ Very high   ▨ Moderate

▩ High   ⬚ Hyperarid zones (existing deserts)

minimum fuelwood needs for cooking and heating. A further 1052 million were in a 'deficit' situation, meeting their needs but only by consuming fuelwood faster than it was growing – they were, in fact, depleting their own reserves. Most of the shortages were experienced in the arid regions of Africa, in the mountainous regions of Asia, particularly the Himalayas, and on the Andean plateau in South America.

Fuel wood in Niger. The eucalyptus plantations now use a diesel-pumped irrigation system (above), though camels still transport the wood to market.

Map showing deserts and desertification potential due to deforestation and misuse of land.

By the end of the century, projections suggest, the situation will be much worse. By then, 2400 million people will either be unable to obtain the fuelwood they need or will be forced to consume wood faster than it can be grown. The world fuelwood shortage will amount to 960 million cubic metres (36 billion cubic feet) of wood a year – the energy equivalent of 240 million tonnes of oil. At today's prices, making that fuelwood deficit good by supplying oil would cost about $50 000 million a year – if so much oil were obtainable.

It is not, of course, inevitable that shortages of this magnitude will occur. But time is short, and trees grow slowly. The United Nations have estimated that the new plantations needed to prevent the fuelwood shortage by the end of the century would cost at least $1000 million a year – and this figure does not include the cost of building up the necessary forestry institutions in the developing countries, which would probably double the cost for the first 10 years of the programme. To achieve this objective would mean planting enough trees to provide a further 1000 million cubic metres (35 billion cubic feet) of wood a year in 20 years' time – the equivalent of several billion trees. It could be done, but only if the annual rate of planting were to increase fivefold.

Dependence on wood for fuel is a major cause of deforestation in Third World countries.

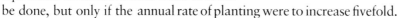

The ecological balance

Tree planting, in fact, can offer solutions to many other problems besides shortage of fuelwood. New trees, of the right type in the right place, can improve agricultural production, slow down desertification, provide fodder for animals and timber for building, reduce the rate of soil erosion and improve the lifestyle of rural communities. They also help to preserve the stock of genetic resources on which mankind is critically dependent.

No one knows exactly how many species of plants and animals exist on the planet: estimates vary from 3 to 10 million. So far, only about 1.5 million have ever been recorded, at least half of which are to be found in the tropical rain forests. In the African rain forests alone, more than 200 new species are being recorded every year.

The importance of all these species is difficult to overestimate. It is from them that all new strains and plant crops used by human beings are bred. For example, the varieties of wheat and other cereals we use are now changing every 5 to 15 years. They are bred to provide increased yield, resistance to disease and pests, better flavour and improved adaptability to new conditions of soil and climate. The parent material comes from the wild – and, if it did not exist, there would be no stock from which improvements could be made.

New products also depend to a large extent on the discovery of plants and animals with useful properties. In the United States the value of medicines which are derived from plant material is now approaching $3000 million a year. No one knows what may yet be discovered – another quinine, another form of rubber? The quaint armadillo, for example, has recently found an undreamt-of use. Because it is the only animal other than man known to catch leprosy in the wild, scientists have

Right: Reclaiming the desert; tree-planting in Abu Dhabi, UAE. *Below:* The armadillo – an unlikely ally in the fight against leprosy.

Above: The drug digitalis, extracted from the dried leaves of the foxglove, plays a vital role in the treatment of heart disease.

During the last quarter of this century the world population is likely to increase by more than a third. At the same time, the cultivated land available to sustain that population might fall by as much as a quarter.

been able to use it to develop a leprosy vaccine – though this work is still in the experimental stage.

Unhappily, the stock on which we can draw is being steadily diminished. About 2000 different kinds of vertebrate animals are in danger of extinction and so are 10 per cent of all flowering plants – nearly 25 000 species. In Europe and the Mediterranean no fewer than 115 of 145 indigenous cattle breeds are currently under threat of extinction. And, according to the FAO, 130 species of trees are now in need of protection.

Thus is the web of want completed. As pressure for land mounts, leading to erosion and deforestation, desertification and hunger, the very species on which human life ultimately depends are themselves depleted. So complicated are the chains which bind living things together that the loss of one species can easily lead to the loss of 20 or 30 other dependent species. The pool of genetic diversity is leaking away. Ultimately, as Sir Peter Scott has pointed out, it is man that is the endangered species.

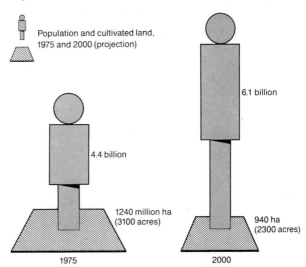

Population and cultivated land, 1975 and 2000 (projection)

6.1 billion

4.4 billion

1240 million ha (3100 acres)

940 ha (2300 acres)

1975

2000

Fresh water supply

Although three-quarters of the earth's surface is covered with water, only three per cent of that water is fresh. Even so, this amounts to about one per cent of a cubic kilometre (0.01 km^3 or 0.25 per cent of a cubic mile) – or some 10 million tonnes – of fresh water for every man, woman and child. Clearly, in no sense can we be running out of water in absolute terms.

But surprisingly little of this water can easily be used. An estimated 77.2 per cent of it is stored in ice-caps and glaciers, and a further 22.4 per cent is in the form of underground aquifers and soil moisture. That leaves only 0.4 per cent, of which one-tenth is atmospheric moisture. The rest is found in lakes and swamps (0.35 per cent) and in streams and rivers (less than 0.01 per cent). Together these are equivalent to 33 000 tonnes of fresh water per head of population.

Atmospheric moisture is produced during the hydrological cycle – an endless system for recycling and purifying water. Every year, 445 000 km^3 (107 000 cu. miles) of sea water, plus 71 000 km^3 (17 000 cu. miles) of surface water from the land, are evaporated by the sun and turned into atmospheric moisture. This in due course falls back to earth as rain or snow. But while most of the moisture came from the sea, much less will fall straight back into it. Only 412 000 km^3 (99 000 cu. miles) return directly to the oceans each year; meanwhile, 104 000 km^3 (25 000 cu. miles) of rain or snow fall on to the continents – 33 000 km^3 (8000 cu. miles) more than was evaporated from them. This surplus is what feeds the rivers and streams, and – because it returns eventually to the sea – it is called the continental run-off. Strictly speaking, this is the quantity of fresh water on earth which could be used by human beings without mining other water resources. It amounts to about 7000 tonnes of water per head of population per year.

In fact, much more than this is available if we take the trouble to recycle it. And, of course, we do. In many river basins in the world, water is used by one city after another as it passes downstream. In such places, there are not many glasses of water which have not been drunk before. There is, however, no need for water quality to suffer; modern methods of treatment are quite capable of producing water as clean as that produced by the hydrological system itself.

Distribution and pollution problems

From the user's point of view, however, there are two major problems. One is that the distribution of rainfall over the earth's surface is extremely uneven. And the other is the increasing pollution of the waters. Strangely, even though rainfall is so sparse in some arid regions, there are only two countries in the world where total annual average rainfall is less than average national water consumption. Nearly everyone could – given sufficient money and resources to collect it all – be self-sufficient in fresh water. Some countries are now increasing their fresh water supplies by desalinating sea water, mainly Abu Dhabi, Hong Kong, Kuwait, Sardinia and Saudi Arabia.

Water is used in one of three main ways: for domestic consumption, for industry and for agriculture. In 1980 the total amount of water used in the world was estimated at about 3000 km^3 (700 cu. miles) per year, a figure expected to reach 3750 km^3 (900 cu. miles) per year by 1985. This would be somewhat more than 10 per cent of total continental run-off. About 6 per cent is used domestically, 21 per cent by industry, and the rest – 73 per cent – by agriculture, almost all of it for irrigation.

Irrigating alfalfa for animal fodder, Utah, USA.

Very few of the planet's inhabitants have an unfailing supply of clean water on tap. Three out of five people in the developing countries – nearly 2000 million people – still do not have easy access to fresh water. In many places, people must either carry water long distances from the nearest river, or buy it (if they can afford to) from a water carrier. Either way, it may be polluted and unhealthy. Diarrhoea – the dirty water disease – is rife in developing countries, killing millions of people every year. And other diseases which result from poor water supplies abound.

The percentage of people with ready access to water is much lower in the countryside than in the cities, though the situation is slowly improving. However, a significant indicator of the plight of Third World cities is revealed by one alarming statistic: between 1970 and 1980 the proportion of people in towns and cities in developing countries who had some measure of sewage disposal actually declined – from 71 to 53 per cent.

The international aid organizations are trying to improve this situation. Yet between 1975 and 1980 (a period in which the United Nations held a major conference on the water supply problem) the number of people with no clean water to drink rose by 100 million. Partly as a result of this, the United Nations declared the present decade, 1981 to 1990, to be the International Drinking Water Supply and Sanitation Decade.

The aim for the decade is to give everyone in the world access to safe supplies of water and adequate sanitation by the year 1990. But by the time the decade began, hope that the target would be achieved was already

Clean drinking water – the world's most precious resource. *Top:* An open sewer in Calcutta; *(left)* long queues at the only water supply in the town of Tatki, Senegal; *(above)* bringing water back home from the nearest well, Korea.

fading. One reason for this was cost. In 1979 the level of spending on fresh water and sanitation was about $6000–$7000 million a year. To achieve the 1990 goal would mean increasing the level of spending by three to five times. Few authorities believe that this could now be achieved, even though the world currently spends at least three times as much on cigarettes and more than 17 times as much on arms. Many people now seem convinced that the basic right of every human being to ample, clean, fresh water will not even be achieved by the end of the century. But, as the figures above show, if this is the case it will be because our social and political systems are unable or unwilling to supply it, rather than because there is any shortage of water in absolute terms.

Pollution takes many forms

There is little doubt that the quality of water is beginning to suffer in many parts of the world. Water pollution is increasingly common and dangerous, and although the earth is provided with a natural water cleansing system of great efficiency, there are signs that it cannot any longer cope with the strain which human activity is putting on it.

The hydrological cycle purifies water by evaporating it. Because almost all pollutants evaporate at very much higher temperatures than water, the pollutants are left behind during evaporation. The result is that the evaporated water that eventually falls back to Earth as rain may be pure but the pollutants left behind become more concentrated.

Some of the pollutants may actually come down with the rain. Chemicals discharged by power stations into the atmosphere can turn the normally benevolent rainfall into showers of acid. This can have dramatic effects: buildings are corroded, forests are destroyed and lakes so acidified that all life in them dies (see page 94).

For the most part, though, the gradual build-up of pollutants in rivers and lakes has come about as a result of direct and deliberate discharges into them of industrial waste water, chemicals and sewage. Agriculture plays its part, too, as rain washes excess nitrogen fertilizers and pesticides straight into the waterways.

It was estimated not long ago that, world-wide, the incidence of minerals in 'surface' waters (rivers, lakes, oceans, etc.) has been increased by about 12 per cent over what would occur naturally. Yet despite growing awareness of the problem, little is being done to solve it. One reason is that, at the moment, purifying the water after it has become polluted – and before domestic use, for instance – is easier and cheaper than developing ways of cleaning up waste water before it is discharged. However, if the water is not filtered efficiently for human consumption, some pollutants may remain in it. The long-term effects these traces may have on health are not yet known. Nor, of course, is the effect on humans of eating animals which have had to drink polluted water.

One good measure of the pressure which is being put on clean water sources is the number of people in any country who rely for their domestic water on a treated water supply. In all the OECD (Organization for Economic Cooperation and Development) countries this number is rising.

At present it varies from less than 10 per cent in Belgium to more than 80 per cent in the United Kingdom. By the year 2000, it is safe to say, more people than ever will be drinking recycled water.

One thing which is critical to life in water is the oxygen supply. If quantities of organic material such as are found in untreated sewage are added to a river or lake, they will be broken down by micro-organisms in the water. This process uses up oxygen and in a deep, still lake other life may need that oxygen to sustain it. This is not the only way oxygen supplies may be depleted. If phosphates and nitrates enter the water, either from treated sewage or from agricultural fertilizers, they cause the growth of algae. When the algae die, they too are broken down, using up yet more oxygen. What then remains is a body of what is known as 'eutrophic' water – water in a very unhealthy state indeed.

Industrial waste waters are slightly easier to control. After it was discovered that waste waters from the paper and pulp industries were causing greatly increased levels of mercury in fish, some countries introduced legislation to prevent the use of mercury, or enforce filtering processes before discharge. Nevertheless, most of the world does not have controls; and even in countries where laws have been passed, the penalties for industrial pollution are often negligible. New effects of the build-up of metals and minerals in inland waters continue to be discovered.

While the industrial use of water is increasing fast – between 1965 and 1974 Japan's use of industrial water grew from 50 million m^3 (18 million cu. ft) a day to 120 million m^3 (42 million cu. ft) – more and more of it is being recycled. By the year 2000, nearly all major industries in the developed world are likely to be recycling their own water, drawing on fresh supplies only to compensate for evaporation and product loss. By then, the discharge of untreated water into public waterways is likely to be taxed in many countries, and standards established for the maximum permitted output of individual pollutants in industrial discharges.

It is now certain that cleaning-up operations can be remarkably effective. Fish have returned to the river Thames in London, for instance, after many years of absence. But such improvements increasingly require wise management and flexible attitudes. The issue of thermal pollution aptly illustrates the dilemma.

Thermal pollution is the name for what happens where cooling waters – such as those discharged by power stations – artificially raise the temperature in a river. New species of fish come to breed in the warmer waters. The oxygen level alters. These changes are not necessarily for the worse. But if, for some reason such as a power station temporarily shutting down, the water temperature suddenly returns to 'normal', millions of fish may die.

Ground water

Since mankind can and does rapidly pollute the available surface water, perhaps it is just as well that more than 20 per cent of the world's fresh water supplies are stored below the earth's surface, where it might be assumed they are safe from pollution. Unfortunately, this is not the case.

A hole drilled anywhere in the earth's surface will eventually strike water. How much water is found will depend on the area where the well is sunk. There are huge volumes of 'ground' water (water below the surface), and the water table marks their highest levels; where there are rivers and streams, the water table reaches up to the surface.

Although some of the deeper stores of ground water may be renewed only once in a few thousand years, ground water is never still. It flows out to the surface of the earth as springs or wells and is topped up from the surface, usually by rain, which gradually percolates through even to the lowest levels. Water from rivers, streams and lakes may also reach the lower stores of ground water – and it is these natural and essential interactions which pose the greatest threat to the purity of the ground water stores.

Some ground water which is found near the earth's surface may be entirely renewed in as little as a year. Here, the potential for pollution is obvious. A further problem is that when ground water is too rapidly exploited (faster than it is capable of being renewed), salt water or contaminated water may flow in to take the place of the pure water extracted. In some areas, too, the porous rocks below may dry out, causing unexpected ground subsidence at the surface.

But even if extraction is carefully controlled, pure water taken from an underground water store, or aquifer, may still be replaced by polluted water. When the rain percolates through the ground to top up aquifers below, it collects and carries with it minerals and salts which are present in the soil through which it passes. High concentrations of salts in ground water that reach the surface give rise to plenty of problems. If the water is used for irrigation, for example, it can cause soil salinity – a condition which gradually reduces the productivity of the land until eventually it becomes quite useless.

What effect the increasing exploitation of ground water resources will have, in terms of speeding up the natural cycle of replenishment, is unknown. What is certain, though, is that if pollution reaches the deep, slowly replenished stores of ground water, the contamination might as well be regarded as permanent.

For the time being, ground water is still fairly safe and pure. This is especially important considering how few people in the world have access to safe drinking water supplies.

'The oceans have no outlet'

'Man today,' Thor Heyerdahl said recently, 'overestimates the size of the oceans and underestimates their importance for life on this planet. If you stop polluting a lake or a river the pollutants will run out and clean rain will come in; but the oceans have no outlet.'

One way of measuring ocean pollution is to monitor the levels of mercury and other elements in the bodies of mussels. Many fish are able to concentrate metals such as mercury in their bodies, and in the past this has caused illness and death among people who have eaten fish caught in polluted coastal waters. Nowadays, it is hoped, monitoring can warn of danger spots before widespread food poisoning can result. In some countries, controlling the output of industrial waste water with a high mercury content has reduced the amount of mercury flowing into the sea. But to be really effective, tighter controls will need to be applied throughout the world in coming years.

Ocean pollution comes not only from the land but also from ships at sea. Nuclear wastes, oil 'washings', unwanted chemical weapons – all are disposed of in the seas. Fortunately, since 1975 the dumping of wastes at sea has been outlawed in the Convention on the Prevention of Marine Pollution, but not all nations are yet party to it. A number of other treaties now cover different aspects of marine pollution. Their importance is likely to grow over the next two decades.

There are plenty of substances in the sea these days which are there as a result of human activities. What effect they may have in the long term is simply not known. Certainly it is understood now that the oceans absorb large quantities of carbon dioxide – and just as well, perhaps, since we are producing more and more of it by burning fossil fuels at ever-increasing rates. It seems possible that the seas may also absorb trace metals and chemicals from the atmosphere. Radioactive material has been found in the oceans as a result of nuclear weapons testing and nuclear power production. DDT has been found in some of the quietest and most remote ocean areas.

The fight against ocean pollution: members of the Greenpeace organization try to stop the dumping of radioactive waste in the Atlantic.

Oil pollution

One form of pollution about which widespread concern will again emerge before the end of the century is oil pollution – first dramatically brought to the public's attention by the wreck of the *Torrey Canyon* in the English Channel in 1966. Some 550 000 barrels of oil were spilled, wrecking beaches and killing thousands of birds. But in 1978 the *Amoco Cadiz* was wrecked off France and 2 million barrels spilled. During 1970–8, there were 46 major oil spills at sea in which 8 million barrels of oil were lost. In 1981 it was estimated that oil discharges at sea due to shipping amounted to 1.5 million tonnes a year, of which 27 per cent was caused by accidents.

Oil pollution at sea is growing steadily worse and seems likely to continue to do so for the rest of the century – partly because both the rate of oil transport and exploration will increase, but also because public fears about oil pollution have – for the moment – been allayed. Several reports have recently pointed out that no oil spill has effected lasting damage to the environment – the most that has happened is that some beaches have had to be cleaned up, some sea birds have been lost and, in one or two cases, local oyster and shellfish industries have been affected. No one has succeeded in linking declining fisheries with oil spills, and statistics have been produced to show how 'cheap' oil spills are compared to the size of the industry involved.

The true cost of oil: *(right)* the half-submerged wreck of the tanker *Amoco Cadiz* in 1978. The resulting oil-spill devastated 60 kilometres (nearly 40 miles) of coastline. *Below:* Cleaning up on the Brittany coast, after an oil-spill from the tanker *Tanio* in 1980.

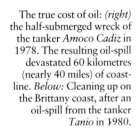

Nevertheless, the clean-up costs of the *Amoco Cadiz* and *Tanio* wrecks amounted to about $100 million. The cost of cleaning up oil discharged at sea can amount to several thousand dollars per tonne, the highest recorded figure being $7500. However, as an OECD report has made clear, the costs to OECD countries of oil spills is relatively modest: $675 per tonne spilled, the equivalent of $0.1 per tonne of oil carried at sea, a figure which is insignificant compared to the cost of the oil ($230 per tonne). The average cost of oil spills in France between 1967 and 1980 was 1.5 francs per person per year – and in most other countries it was even lower (just over one penny per person per year in the United Kingdom).

While this kind of data may make a splendid justification for the oil industry, it should have given us pause before now. The amount of oil which ends up in the oceans is huge, and growing bigger. We do not know what its long-term effects are and we cannot guess how long it will be before a really major oil spill ruins a whole tourist industry, a whole fishery or even a whole sea. The chances of one of these things happening before the end of the century are high.

Learning the lesson

The idea that the seas are enormous and cannot be affected by dumping waste materials into them has been proved clearly false in closed seas such as the Mediterranean. There, with no tide, the water is renewed only every 80 to 100 years. The waters are intensively polluted by industry, by ships, by agriculture and by sewage from the hundred million tourists who visit the region each year. Some 120 coastal cities flush their sewage into the sea, 85 per cent of it untreated. A recent survey showed that one-quarter of all the beaches there were dangerously filthy and that 96 per cent of all oysters and mussels were grown in polluted water, and would be unfit for consumption unless cooked. A major stumbling block to any improvement has been the large number of countries (some of them mutually

A dying forest in West Germany – is acid rain the cause?

hostile) that would need to cooperate if any plans for improvement were to be made.

For the Mediterranean the problem is at least on the way to being solved, thanks to the initiative of the United Nations Environment Programme's Regional Seas Programme. Today, 84 laboratories from 16 Mediterranean countries are working together to try to stem the flow of rubbish into the sea which is known as 'the cradle of civilization'. Agreements to cooperate in cleaning up the seas have also been made for almost all the seriously polluted semi-enclosed seas around the world, including the Caribbean, the Red Sea and the sea around Kuwait. The lessons learned as these waters are monitored may be the example which will allow the deeper oceans to escape serious contamination.

Fish – a vital resource

Fish play an important role in world diet; in 1976 more than 70 million tonnes of fish provided 18 per cent of the animal protein consumed world-wide. The FAO has predicted that demand will double by the end of the century,

It is very unlikely that this demand will be met. Traditionally, the sea has belonged to everyone and to no-one, and fishing has not, as a result, always been a well-managed operation. Now, however, as the new Law of the Sea takes effect, more than a hundred nations have claimed authority over their 'exclusive economic zones', extending for 200 nautical miles from their coasts. It is thought that restriction of fishing rights in this way will allow better management of the world's fisheries. In effect, if bigger catches are wanted, fish stocks need to be conserved and looked after almost in the way that farmers manage their livestock. The World Conservation Strategy has estimated that if fish stocks had not been so severely damaged by over-fishing, the world catch in 1980 could have been 15 to 20 million tonnes higher than it actually was.

Although some figures still represent the annual fish catch as steadily increasing – or at least remaining constant – these are misleading. The truth is that the catch includes more non-commercial fish than previously, and that the quality of the fish caught is lower than it used to be. For example, in 1970 herring, sardine, anchovy, cod and haddock accounted for 32 per cent of the world catch; by 1975, they accounted for only 25 per cent of it. The case of the herring is the most dramatic: in 1962, herring made up 33.3 per cent of the world catch; by 1976, it was reduced to only 7.2 per cent.

Clearly, the stocks have been over-fished; fish have been taken from the sea in such numbers as to stop them from breeding at their optimum rate. Just how easily a fish population can be over-exploited was illustrated in the early 1970s by the almost complete collapse of the huge anchovy fishery off Peru, from 12 million tonnes in 1970 to only 4 million tonnes in 1972. It has since recovered somewhat, but has not yet reached former levels.

If, by wise management, fish stocks are allowed to build up again and the numbers taken are strictly controlled, the Food and Agriculture Organization believes that production of conventional, readily market-able fish could be increased to 84.7 million tonnes by 1990 and to 92.5 million tonnes by the turn of the century. Even so, this is not expected to be enough to satisfy demand. Total global fish production is estimated at only 240 million tonnes a year, of which traditional species account for 100 million tonnes a year. There is little room for manoeuvre in the future.

Research is under way, therefore, to identify species of fish which have not previously been exploited but which might be commercially successful. At the moment, krill is the favourite, with estimates of the potential catch ranging as high as 60 million tonnes a year. But with krill, as with other fish, care must be exercised. Krill is the major food of five species of great whale – some of them endangered – and of many other sea creatures. Mankind's voracious demands for food from the sea must be

Freshly caught Antarctic krill.

tempered with good sense and wise management because it is impossible to predict the long-term effects of destroying the livelihoods of other species.

The fish and the oceans have not yet been ruined by the often thoughtless uses they have been put to. A few warning signals exist, but it is possible that the awareness which has, as a result, been promoted will encourage their future protection.

Dangers to the atmosphere

There are three major threats to the earth's atmosphere: acid rain, carbon dioxide accumulation and ozone layer damage. During the next 15 years, many of the doubts and unknowns surrounding these dangers are likely to be resolved. We shall discover, for instance, whether the carbon dioxide released when fossil fuels are burned has already altered, or is likely to alter, the Earth's climate. We should know whether the use of chemicals called freons was stopped in time to prevent them punching a hole in the ozone layer, and admitting dangerous ultraviolet radiation onto the Earth below. But we already know that acid rain has caused damage totalling thousands of millions of pounds, as well as killing all life in many thousands of lakes, in Europe and North America.

In recent years, rain as acid as vinegar has fallen on the earth: a storm in Pitlochry, Scotland, on 10 April 1974 produced rain with a pH value of 2.4, almost exactly the acidity of vinegar. Generally, rain is now 5 to 30 times more acidic than it was before the Industrial Revolution; in places, it can be 100 to 1000 times more acidic.

Exporting acid rain

Acid rain is caused by the presence of sulphur and nitrogen oxides in the air. These chemicals are produced in huge amounts when fossil fuels are burned in power stations, and to a lesser extent by car exhausts. Ironically, attempts to disperse local pollution have, in the past 20 years, led to increasing international acid rain pollution, in which the waste products of one country land on the buildings, fields and lakes of another.

Building power stations and smelting works with taller and taller chimneys, so that the waste products are thrown high up into the atmosphere, has indeed greatly reduced local pollution. But what goes up must come down. Eventually, after travelling hundreds or even thousands of kilometres, the oxides form sulphuric and nitric acids which, dissolved in rain or snow, fall back to the ground and do substantial damage.

Scandinavia has beeen particularly badly affected, suffering from acid rain which originates from power stations all over northern Europe. Ten per cent of Sweden's lakes no longer contain any fish at all; and more than double that number – 20 000 lakes – are known to have been seriously damaged by acid rain. Norway has been almost as badly hit, and the results in Canada of pollution from the United States are also serious. There, 140 lakes are without fish and 1000 more are damaged; another 48 000 are expected to be at risk over the next decade.

Since the problem was internationally acknowledged in 1972 a number of solutions have been tried. Neutralizing acid lakes by treating them with lime has been partially successful but, to keep acidity down, more and more lime has had to be used. The amount of lime needed to keep agricultural land from becoming too acidic has also increased sharply in many countries.

What goes up, must come down: pollution from a Merseyside power station.

Damage to lakes and their fish is not the only effect of acid rain. Buildings as far apart as Cologne Cathedral and the Acropolis in Athens are crumbling as acid rain eats into their fabric. Railway lines in Poland have, in some places, been so badly pitted that speed limits of 40 km/h (25 m.p.h.) have had to be imposed. The latest, and perhaps most worrying, possibility is that acid rain is killing off Europe's forests. In the past few years, huge areas of forest in West Germany have been found to be dead or dying; it is feared the cause may be acid rain which, by leaching away salts in the soil, can expose plants to high levels of toxic metals.

In the longer term, the only solution will be to reduce sulphur emissions. Awareness of the problem together with new air pollution laws is already going some way to producing slight reductions – but energy policies are expected to become increasingly reliant on coal as a major fuel, which in turn is likely to increase the levels of sulphur being released, and reverse the downward trend. The problem of acid rain, in other words, is not only one for the present: all the indications are that the situation will get worse in the future, and current attempts to reduce sulphur emissions may be completely swamped as coal comes back into vogue as the preferred fuel later this century.

Desulphurization systems can be installed in power stations, but they are not cheap. International legislation aimed at controlling the problem, and promoting cooperation among polluted and polluting countries, has long been debated. In Europe, in 1983, a step forward was achieved when 31 countries voluntarily agreed to try to reduce air pollution. But solving the acid rain problem is greatly complicated by its international dimension. This inevitable international involvement in a common resource, the atmosphere, is also a feature of the other major threats to it, the problems of the ozone layer and of carbon dioxide.

Ozone layer depletion

It is now clear that the ozone layer is essential for the survival of life on earth. High up in the stratosphere, it absorbs most of the ultraviolet radiation emitted by the sun and so protects us from its harmful effects. If the ozone layer were to be reduced, and more ultraviolet radiation allowed to reach the surface of the earth, the effects might be drastic. Skin cancer and eye diseases would increase, and plant growth would be affected. The yields of cereal crops all over the world might be reduced. But the full implications are still not known.

A number of human activities down here on Earth is now threatening the stability of the ozone layer. Nitrogen fertilizer, used in increasing quantities, might have an effect on it. Supersonic airliners could also interfere with it – but it seems less likely now than it did a decade ago that enough of them will operate to make any significant difference.

The most serious threat currently stems from the use of aerosol sprays. The propellants used in these, known as chlorofluorocarbons (CFCs), can cause the ozone molecule to break down. To what extent ozone is already being destroyed is not accurately known. It has been estimated that, if CFCs continue to be used at the same rate as they were in the late 1970s, the ozone layer would eventually be depleted by 10 per cent.

A one per cent reduction in the ozone layer could result in as much as a three per cent increase in the amount of ultraviolet radiation which reaches the surface of the earth. The US National Academy of Sciences has calculated that this would lead to a two per cent increase in the incidence of skin cancer in human beings.

Although monitoring of the levels of ozone present in the stratosphere is now being attempted, conclusive information will not be available quickly enough to allow any destruction to be halted before it has an effect. Therefore it obviously makes sense to limit the quantities of CFCs being manufactured, and a campaign to achieve this was begun in 1982 by the

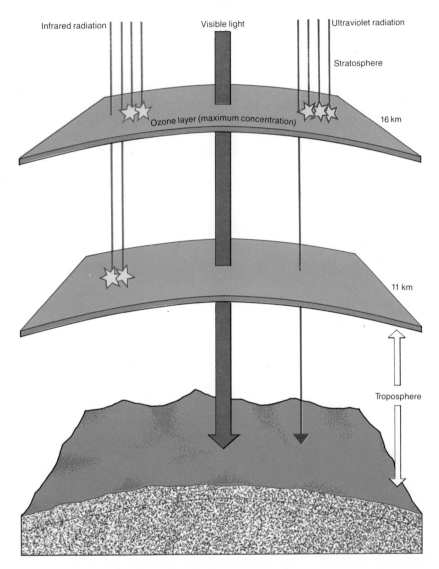

Infrared radiation   Visible light   Ultraviolet radiation

Stratosphere

Ozone layer (maximum concentration)   16 km

11 km

Troposphere

Diagram showing how the ozone layer screens out much of the incoming ultraviolet radiation – and some infrared rays – before it reaches the lower regions of the earth's atmosphere (troposphere).

United Nations Environment Programme. Several nations have already begun to reduce their use and production of CFCs. But whether these actions will be enough to avert possible catastrophe by the end of the century remains to be seen.

The 'greenhouse effect'

The greatest worry of all is the increasing level of carbon dioxide in the atmosphere. Carbon dioxide is involved in a natural cycle between the land, the oceans and the atmosphere, but when fossil fuels are burned, carbon which has been laid down over thousands of years is released very rapidly, disrupting the natural balance.

Each year, as a result of burning fossil fuels, 5000 million tonnes of carbon are released into the atmosphere, and at least half of it stays there.

Since 1900, the level of carbon dioxide in the atmosphere has increased by at least 15 per cent. It has been calculated that if the world's consumption of fossil fuels were to continue to rise by 4 per cent each year until the end of the century, by the year 2000 the atmospheric concentration of carbon dioxide would reach levels at least 30 per cent higher than those which were present before the Industrial Revolution. The removal of the earth's ground cover, from tropical forests and from areas which have now been turned into desert, is also adding to the effect by drastically reducing the number of plants that absorb carbon dioxide.

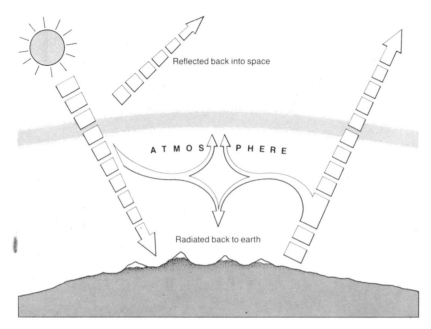

Reflected back into space

ATMOS PHERE

Radiated back to earth

The 'greenhouse effect'. Most of the incoming solar radiation is reflected back by the earth's atmosphere or is absorbed by it. Less than half reaches the earth's surface. This is later radiated back into the atmosphere, which re-radiates some of the heat energy back to earth again.

The most important result of this increase of carbon dioxide levels in the atmosphere is likely to be a change in climate. Indeed, this may already be happening.

The earth's temperature is maintained by a delicate system in which the amount of energy the earth absorbs from the sun exactly balances that which it radiates back into space. Carbon dioxide plays a key role in this, acting rather like a pane of glass in a greenhouse. It lets the sun's heat through, but traps infrared radiation, so that not all the heat escapes back through the atmosphere. Most experts believe that the net effect of the extra carbon dioxide in the atmosphere will be a warmer earth.

By the middle of the twenty-first century carbon dioxide levels in the atmosphere are expected to have doubled. It is predicted that this will produce an increase in the average global temperature – now 15°C (59°F) – of about 3°C (5°F). This may not sound a lot; but it is the kind of temperature difference which has in the past made the difference between ice ages and ice-free ages.

Such a drastic alteration in weather patterns could have profound economic and political effects – most notably by reducing the grain harvest in North America. At the same time, it seems likely that many other parts of the world would be able to increase their agricultural production – perhaps shifting the balance of power towards the developing countries. If the increased temperatures were sufficient to melt the polar ice sheets, flooding could result from higher sea levels, with possibly disastrous consequences for coastal cities.

By the end of the century more accurate models of the possible effects of the carbon dioxide problem will be available. Although some of the predicted effects may well be beneficial, calculating the overall effect of even relatively small temperature changes on the earth is no easy matter. But it is one which could be vitally important. We are, in effect, now engaged in a gigantic geophysical experiment with the earth, juggling our need for more energy against the risks of altering the climate. How long we can go on playing this game of cosmic roulette remains to be seen – but certainly by the year 2000 we should know whether the climate has already altered, and by how much more it is likely to do so. The odds now are that the earth will be a distinctly warmer place in the twenty-first century than it was in the twentieth.

Chapter Four

THE POWER BUSINESS: WHO RUNS THINGS?

Today, all speculation about the future is overshadowed by renewed fear at the prospect of nuclear war. In examining recent changes and likely developments in geopolitics and superpower strategy, Dan Smith emphasizes the very real dangers as the United States attempts to re-assert its role as world leader. But the nightmare of global conflict may obscure a more insidious threat – to civil liberties and human rights. Duncan Campbell traces the precarious growth of international guarantees of individual freedoms – and considers the new problems posed by the increasingly sophisticated technology of control and surveillance.

One more 'local' war that rarely makes international headlines. Members of the Eritrean People's Liberation Front – one of the guerrilla groups fighting for independence from the Soviet-backed government of Ethiopia.

International politics

DAN SMITH

The modern political era began in the wake of World War II, with three great changes in the distribution of world power which established the political pattern of the following years. The great European empires entered their terminal phase. The United States became a global superpower, extending its economic and political influence through most of the world. The Soviet Union established control of Eastern Europe, moved out of its pre-war isolation and began to increase its own world role.

The political pattern initiated then put most countries into one of three groups. In the first group are most of the advanced capitalist countries, in military-political alliances with the United States as the leading power. Then there are the state-socialist countries, dominated by the Soviet Union. And there are the others, the majority, competed over by the two power blocs for allies, influence, raw materials and markets. The pattern is defined by confrontation between the power blocs, and by gross disparities of wealth and power between these two on the one hand and the rest of the world on the other. These dividing lines of world politics are usually called (with little respect for geographical accuracy) East–West and North–South. Only a few countries have been able to stand aside from that pattern.

It is a pattern in which the United States has been the pre-eminent world power. The Soviet Union was commonly described as a superpower long before its influence, political reach or military strength was remotely comparable on a world scale to the United States'. It achieved that position towards the end of the 1960s. But although it is now rivalled as a military superpower, the United States has had an economic and political weight in world affairs which is quite without parallel.

What happened in the early 1980s was that the post-1945 pattern of world power entered a period of crisis in which the potential exists for profound transformations. Crucially, this crisis reflects the relative decline of US power. The possibility of change makes this decade and the next simultaneously exciting, hopeful and dangerous.

American troops using defoliants in Vietnam.

A violent peace

The political pattern of the modern era has provided no great stability. Including civil and border conflicts, there have been about 300 wars since 1945[1]. Reliable figures do not exist to add up the total of people killed, maimed and displaced in these wars. Alongside undiminished armed conflict there has been an intensely armed peace – the permanent East–West military confrontation which has kept Europe as two heavily armed camps and amassed unprecedented and constantly escalating levels of destructive power. Permanent preparations for war entail the permanent risk of nuclear conflagration. There is now a real possibility that such a conflict would extinguish all human life[2].

But actual warfare since 1945 has been concentrated in the Third World. Many of these wars attended the demise of the European empires or reflected its unfolding consequences. Wars of national independence hastened imperial withdrawal, often to be succeeded by further wars over the nature and distribution of post-colonial power. The wars in Vietnam and in South-East Asia generally fit these categories, as do those in Southern Africa. Others do not. Israel's wars since its foundation in 1948 reflect not the conditions of imperial withdrawal, but the consequences of Israel's implantation in a hostile context. The current wars in Central America grow from oppostion to national governments, not colonial administrations.

A feature of many of the wars is the active participation of outside powers as suppliers, advisers or combatants. Often, one form of participation has led to another, as in the case of the US war in Vietnam or the Soviet war in Afghanistan. Tendrils from East–West confrontation thus intertwine with the complex problems of Third World countries. As most obviously in the 1980s in Central America, East–West politics are imposed on regional issues and conflicts.

None of this is new. Nor are all instances of it merely a cloak with which to hide other motives for political or military intervention. This can and does happen, on both sides – although it is often hard to know how cynical

Soviet troops enter Kabul, Afghanistan, in December 1979.

is the brandishing of the Soviet (or American) bogey. But more importantly, East–West confrontation has always included the Third World. When guerrilla forces or established states challenge Western interests in the Third World, the Soviet Union is virtually the only source of needed aid and support. For Western states and corporations to have a free hand in the Third World, keeping Soviet influence out has always been important.

Soviet support for guerrillas and states opposing Western interests seems to have been provided opportunistically and even rather haphazardly. Not all such forces have received Soviet aid. When provided, it has usually been rather limited and occasionally subject to a complete cut-off, as in the Greek civil war in the 1940s and the Eritrean war for independence from Ethiopia in the 1970s. The Soviet Union's motive seems to be to compete for influence on the world stage. In part, this may simply reflect a desire for international prestige. More basically, it reflects determination never to risk a re-run of its isolation in the 1920s and 1930s. It may also derive from an interest in keeping the West so busy that it cannot challenge Soviet power in Eastern Europe or the Soviet Union itself. These are relatively limited ambitions, pursued with fairly modest success. The Soviet Union has a bad track record of holding on to client states. The vast majority of the world's states remain essentially Western in their political and economic orientation.

Conflicting advice: *(top)* US 'advisers' in El Salvador; *(above)* Cubans in Angola.

While expenditure on foreign aid has risen only gradually since 1968, military spending over the same period has shot up.

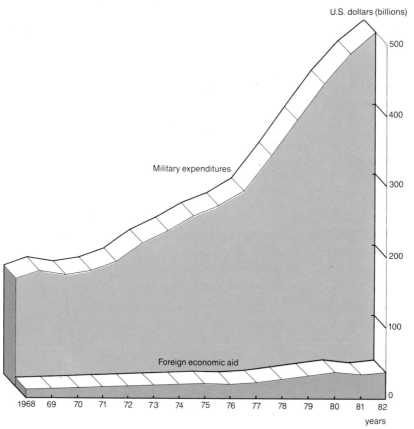

U.S. dollars (billions)

Military expenditures

Foreign economic aid

500

400

300

200

100

0

1968 69 70 71 72 73 74 75 76 77 78 79 80 81 82

years

Neo-colonialism

Grossly unequal divisions of wealth and power remain a major characteristic of world politics. Consumerist societies in the advanced capitalist countries contrast sharply with Third World countries suffering from famine, widespread malnutrition, the persistence of curable diseases, crippling lack of clean water, medical and social services. No less sharp is the contrast between that poverty and misery and the great wealth expended on armed forces as instruments of power. According to one estimate, a 10-year programme to meet essential food and health needs in the poorer countries could be funded by diverting less than 5 per cent a year of world military spending (70 per cent of which is accounted for by the US and Soviet blocs).[3]

These contrasts cannot be ignored. They may be qualified by noting that there is still poverty in rich countries, while rich elites hold sway in poor countries. But these qualifications simply expand our understanding of a world full of inequities.

The fundamental inequities concern not only wealth but also its travelling companion, power. By itself, political independence from the declining European empires failed to solve the problems of poverty and powerlessness. Political independence could not guarantee economic independence, let alone prosperity or social justice, and strictly

Respective shares of world-wide military expenditure.

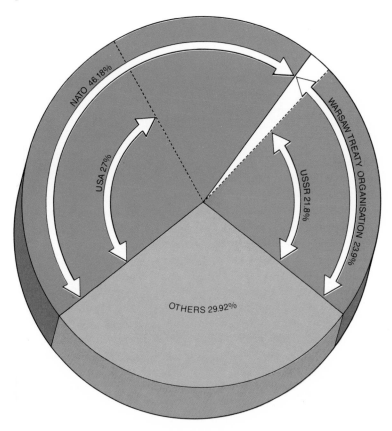

circumscribed economic independence meant that political independence was often more formal than real.

Social and economic development in post-colonial countries has remained largely dependent on external forces. Before independence, the external forces were primarily the metropolitan states and their local colonial administrations; after it, they are primarily multinational corporations and international agencies such as the International Monetary Fund and World Bank. By serving and representing these interests, a small national elite can grow wealthy and remain powerful in the midst of abounding poverty. But that domestic power depends on continued subservience to foreign interests. De-colonization was thus, for the most part, merely an introduction to neo-colonization, a new form of subjugation in which, as ever, some profited while most were deprived. But this neo-colonialism is not an issue only among those states which have emerged from colonial status since 1945. It remains a major issue in Latin America, whence the Spanish and Portuguese empires long since departed, and in the Middle East, where the Ottoman empire was broken at the end of World War I. Subordination to foreign interests is no less real simply because there is no colonial administration.

One effect of all this is to internationalize domestic politics. Efforts to get more equitable distributions of wealth and power within countries are initially directed against the local ruling elites. But in consequence they also challenge the foreign interests upholding and upheld by these elites. It is in the wake of this challenge that the imposition of East–West politics occurs, as Western states move to support the positions of Western corporations. But in the 1970s, deeply felt inhibitions in the United States against foreign military adventures restricted the scope for further interventionism.

Arms, investment and independence

The North–South order is not only challenged by groups which initially seek to overthrow local elites. In some countries, it is the ruling elites themselves who have made the challenge. The outstanding examples are among the oil-exporting states, who have used their oil wealth to purchase arms, prestige and influence. More ambiguous examples can be found among those countries, especially in Latin America and Asia, where there has been significant industrialization. This has usually come about as a result of foreign investment attracted by low labour costs and high labour discipline, both normally enforced by repression of trade union organization. These countries have become so attractive to foreign investors, and so necessary in the planning of multinational corporations, that the situation of dependence on foreign investment has to some extent changed to one of interdependence. Foreign-financed industrialization may also serve as a basis on which to build a country's domestic industry and investment with a possible longer-term gain in independence.

These states have begun to challenge the North–South order, though without changing their essentially Western international orientation. Increasingly, degrees of mutual dependence are replacing a simple

International status symbol: a French Mirage jet on display at the Farnborough Air Show, UK.

relationship of dominance and dependence. The power of the 'North' has thus become less encompassing in the 'South'. But this challenge remains limited, in two respects.

Firstly, the increased purchase of arms as a symbol and instrument of greater independence is double-edged. It enmeshes the importing states in a web of technical needs which tie them to the exporters. Those states which seek to gain further independence by developing local arms industries have to begin by producing equipment designed in the supplying countries. If they go beyond that stage to designing their own equipment, they then risk dependence on an international export market in order to make their production financially viable. In that market, the terms are set primarily by the United States and the Soviet Union, which together account for about 70 per cent of world arms exports. Even without the direct use of armed force, the international military order is an insidious means for the North to ensnare the South.

Secondly, from a global perspective, greater independence for some ruling elites has only touched the surface of the North–South problem. Countries less rich in natural resources vital to advanced industrial states cannot follow the oil states' example. For the mixed blessing of foreign investments, they must depend on decisions by entities totally outside their control. For a programme of altruistic aid able to meet basic needs they await apparently unlikely changes of heart and priorities among the richer countries. For most of them, to turn to the Soviet Union is to turn to a limited source of aid and to court Western displeasure. To take a more autonomous development path such as that charted out of necessity by China would require enormous internal upheaval, with the probability of civil war and perhaps even foreign intervention.

Although its terms are changing, the North–South problem persists.

The new cold war

In the early 1980s, opinion polls in Western Europe and North America revealed an extraordinary lack of confidence in the future. Majorities expected a nuclear war to occur. At the same time, nuclear disarmament movements became major political forces in most Western European countries.

This upsurge of concern and activism was, at a general level, a response to dangerously deteriorating East–West relations. The relative calm of the period of *détente* beginning in the late 1960s was replaced at the end of the 1970s by a new Cold War.

Where did the new Cold War come from? In the West, the orthodox explanation blames it all on the Soviet Union for its steady military build-up (often wildly exaggerated) in the 1970s, for its invasion of Afghanistan in December 1979 and for its general activities in the Third World. Not surprisingly, in the Soviet Union all the blame is placed on the West: for the United States' bid to regain nuclear superiority and recommence military interventions in the Third World, for NATO's 1979 decision to deploy US cruise and Pershing II missiles in Western Europe and for the increase in military spending, led by the USA, in the late 1970s.

'Protest and survive': a nuclear disarmament rally in London.

Both explanations say the other fellow did it. Neither is convincing.

Partly, the new Cold War is a matter of self-reproduction. *Détente* did not affect the basic East–West antagonism or change its terms in the Third World or reduce military confrontation. The Soviet Union sharply increased its nuclear arsenal in the second half of the 1970s, following a sharp increase by the United States in the first half. The US military effort slackened in the mid-1970s, mostly as a result of the scaling down after withdrawal from Vietnam. Throughout *détente* the entrenched power of the military and arms industries on both sides remained untouched. The momentum of new weapons' development and production that they have established, and the ambient hostility, suspicion and insecurity they require to sustain that momentum, worked against the achievement of major arms' reductions and a lasting improvement in East–West relations.

But the new Cold War is only partly a matter of self-reproduction. The first Cold War, beginning after World War II and lasting into the 1950s, was the midwife to a new distribution of world power. It allowed Stalin to seal Eastern Europe off against Western influence and establish Soviet dominance there. It enabled the United States to draw clear lines of global political conflict and establish its hegemony over a far wider area. It entered the era of its great power – world policeman, strategic guarantor of its allies' security, underwriter of the world financial and trading system.

The decline of US hegemony

The new Cold War has occurred at the point when that system of US power is breaking down. High military spending associated with the roles of world policeman and strategic guarantor weakened the US economy. The other advanced capitalist states experienced faster economic growth and emerged as major economic and commercial rivals. The war in Vietnam intensified the strain on the US economy and ended in a humiliation which threatened the credibility of the policing role as well as tarnishing the United States' international image. The strength of the dollar declined through the stresses of being the world's major trading currency; the dollar-based financial system collapsed in 1973. The challenge of the oil-exporting states, with major price-rises beginning in 1974, was followed by growing disputes with Western European states and Japan over how to handle gathering economic recession and a host of other issues. At the same time, the United States was experiencing the 'Vietnam syndrome' – a reluctance after the failure in Vietnam to be involved in foreign military intervention – which lasted until the invasion of Grenada in 1983.

Throughout the 1970s, the United States underwent a relative but marked economic decline together with a relative loss of political leadership, which was reflected in relations with the other advanced capitalist states as well as with the Third World. On the other hand, while the Soviet Union has also had severe problems, they are not of this scale.

Lech Walesa and other members of Solidarity's Coordinating Committee in October 1980, when the movement had 6 million members. A year later martial law was introduced and Solidarity was outlawed.

Successive Soviet leaderships have been unable to develop agriculture to the point where the country is self-sufficient in food, or to galvanize an increasingly sluggish economy. Imposition of military dictatorship was required to repress the challenge of the *Solidarność* movement in Poland, and there are rumblings of discontent elsewhere in Eastern Europe. To cement its newly gained influence in Afghanistan, the Soviet Union has entered a costly and protracted war. Soviet gains in the Third World during the 1970s were at least off-set by losses, and China remains a hostile neighbour. But none of this has challenged the Soviet power within its sphere of influence in the way that US power has been challenged within its much larger sphere.

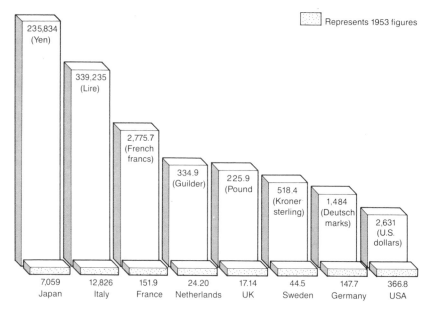

235,834 (Yen)
339,235 (Lire)
2,775.7 (French francs)
334.9 (Guilder)
225.9 (Pound)
518.4 (Kroner sterling)
1,484 (Deutsch marks)
2,631 (U.S. dollars)

7,059	12,826	151.9	24.20	17.14	44.5	147.7	366.8
Japan	Italy	France	Netherlands	UK	Sweden	Germany	USA

The pursuit of Cold War policies by the United States, and the associated high military spending, have slowed up her economic growth as compared with major West European states and Japan.

Facing these problems in early 1979, a major article in *Business Week*, the leading US magazine for corporate opinion, diagnosed a 'crisis of the decay of power'.[4] The article argued that US power could be restored by stressing its strategic leadership over its allies. While relative economic and political decline were real, strategic pre-eminence remained. US leadership could be re-asserted by increasing military spending and forcefully encouraging allies to follow suit. In turn, this would help to create the conditions in which domestic economic strength could be restored.

To carry this programme through, a focal shift in the perception of real challenges to US power was required. The main challenges came from US allies and the Third World. To overcome them it would be necessary to stress the threat from the Soviet Union and the need for uniting against it. The Soviet Union does indeed pose a threat to the United States and its allies, both because its missiles are pointed at them and because it competes for influence in the Third World. Of the problems faced by the United States in the late 1970s, however, the Soviet *political* threat was (and remains) secondary. But to solve the problems, it would have to be seen as the primary feature. To an extraordinary degree, that *Business Week* article mapped out the course followed by the United States in the last two years of the Carter administration and even more vigorously by the Reagan administration.

Apart from the aspect of self-production, which is not unimportant, the new Cold War is a product of the United States' response to its relative decline. Despite the illegality of the Soviet invasion of Afghanistan and the brutality of the ensuing war, that action was not the cause of the new Cold War, but merely a convenient peg on which to hang it. The Soviet Union has, however, responded with predictable hostility and its own sharpened anti-American rhetoric to counter the United States' renewed anti-Soviet attacks. And in so doing, it has managed to justify the perception of the new Cold War in the West.

Nuclear strategies

The onset of the new Cold War marks out a period of crisis in world politics. It is a crisis in the genuine sense – at least potentially, a turning point. At stake is the distribution of power in world affairs. Can the United States re-establish political leadership among advanced capitalist countries? Will the South increase its independence from the North?

One thing that seems certain is that the United States will continue to try to re-assert global leadership. The alternative is the graceful acceptance of orderly decline. US political culture is ill-equipped for that. The urge to be 'number one' is too strong.

There is some basis for supposing the effort could be successful. While transatlantic disputes show little sign of slackening, the Western European states have re-affirmed their acceptance of US strategic leadership by welcoming the deployment of the cruise and Pershing II missiles in the face of massive popular opposition. If they are unable to develop an alternative solution to economic and political crisis, they may go further and accept reduced independence as a necessary cost of finding a new international stability. They might even cooperate, as junior partners, in the role of world policeman, thus reducing the costs to the United States of maintaining this role and making it easier for them to get domestic support for military intervention overseas. All this would lead, in somewhat modified form, to re-establishing the pattern of world politics since 1945.

However, for this to happen Western European states would have to reverse their political and economic trajectories, which, virtually ever since US-financed reconstruction of their domestic economies began after World War II, have been away from dependence on the United States. Moreover, although Third World states which bolt from the US camp can be coerced back into line, the more insidious challenge to the North–South order posed by essentially pro-Western ruling elites cannot be dealt with so directly. For them to cooperate in the loss of their relative independence would be another major reversal of direction. The major trends among the advanced capitalist states and important Third World

Hiroshima, 1982. Young Japanese theatrically commemorate the destruction of the city on 6 August 1945.

Nevada desert, 1983. An underground nuclear test.

countries have been undermining US power. Trends of such weight are not easily reversed.

Overall, a complete US return to former heights of power seems unlikely. What we cannot know but may fear are the costs that the effort to re-scale the peaks of power will impose. They could well be severe, especially in the Third World. As frustration accumulates and builds on the hostility and insecurity of the new Cold War, they might even culminate in nuclear conflict.

The prospect of nuclear war is not unrealistic. Western (primarily US) nuclear strategy deals not just with the threat of nuclear retaliation as a deterrent to nuclear aggression, but with more sophisticated concepts of limiting and prevailing in nuclear war. It accepts the possibility of using nuclear weapons before the other side has done so; indeed, NATO strategy in Europe is based on that. With their increased accuracy as technology has advanced, nuclear weapons are seen as having the potential for precise and discriminating use. This is something of a return to traditional ideas about the political use of armed force, applied now to nuclear weapons. The Soviet Union never really departed from such ideas, although in recent years its leaders have declared a nuclear war would be unwinnable by either side.

What matters is not just what each superpower thinks about the potential use of its own arsenal, but what it fears about the other side. Each provides enough evidence for the other, hostile and suspicious, to fear the worst. In their competition for influence in the Third World, it is not inconceivable that the United States' and the Soviet Union's forces could directly confront each other, probably at a relatively low level. At that point, both sides might refuse to back down for fear of the wider political costs. Either side, fearing the worst from the other, might then conclude that a nuclear attack was bound to be launched against it and decide to strike pre-emptively.

It is not pleasant to consider such a prospect, but it is necessary. The world is in a very dangerous situation. Even if the roots of East–West confrontation remain unassailable, limited and short-term measures to dispel at least the worst of the nuclear peril are urgently needed.

A new pattern?

If neither a nuclear war nor the reassertion of US power is in store, it is most likely that the next two decades will be dominated by the slow dissolution of the political pattern that has prevailed since 1945. It is unlikely that another power could take the United States' place. Despite its military strength, the Soviet Union is not a candidate for this role: its political influence, economic strength and ideological pull are all too weak. It would remain a major power, but unable to fill any power vacuum the United States might leave behind it.

The United States would, in fact, remain the most powerful among the advanced capitalist states, but would no longer be the clear leader. Japan would be a major economic world power and important as a regional political force. Western European states might cohere into a major entity in world politics, but they have many disputes among themselves to resolve first. If they managed it, they might provide something of a balancing force between East and West.

In the Third World, declining US power could provide more space for countries to develop more independently. They would still face massive problems and need foreign investors, but the constricting fear of military intervention and economic isolation might slacken. Combined with developments among the advanced capitalist countries, this could strengthen the role of the non-aligned states – those which refuse to take sides with either the United States or the Soviet Union – and move world politics away from the dominance of the East–West issue. In turn, this could be the basis for major military reductions, releasing resources for, among other things, strengthened aid programmes to the poorest countries.

This optimism, however, should immediately be qualified. Gloomier outcomes are also possible. Third World regional powers may arise, ready to use military force to assert regional dominance. A more independent and united Western Europe might shrug off US leadership but could remain strongly anti-Soviet and emerge as a new nuclear bloc. With China outside the US camp but still virulently hostile to the Soviet Union, a single East–West confrontation would have fractured into several such confrontations while the North–South problem would have become the North–South–South problem. The political pattern would have altered just as basically as in our more optimistic scenario, but the result would not be much more desirable than the pattern which is now threatened with breakdown.

Because politics never stands still, we know there will be changes across the next couple of decades. And because of the current crisis, we know they will be major changes. What we cannot know, because politics is a human affair, is whether those changes will be for better or worse, whether catastrophe will devour us or whether the divisions and inequities of the world will at last begin to break down.

References

1 This figure is taken from *The War Atlas* by Michael Kidron and Dan Smith (London, Pan, 1983; New York, Simon & Schuster, 1983); see Maps 2 to 4.
2 The most eloquent description of this grim possibility is in *The Fate of the Earth* by Jonathan Schell (New York, Knopf, 1982; London, Pan, 1982). Since its publication further research into effects of a nuclear war has produced the concept of a 'nuclear winter' – prolonged darkness and a sharp drop in temperatures caused by smoke and dust blocking out the sun, with catastrophic effects on food production.
3 The estimate is taken from *North–South: A Programme for Survival*, the report of the Independent Commission on International Development Issues, commonly known as the Brandt Commission (London, Pan, 1980).
4 'The Decline of US Power', *Business Week*, 12 March 1979.

Liberty and law

DUNCAN CAMPBELL

Although human societies and civilizations have through history adopted legal codes requiring respect for the rights and liberties of the citizen, the idea of internationally enforceable human rights is new to the twentieth century. By the end of the century, barely 50 years will have passed during which individual citizens have been offered the right to challenge, internationally, their national government and to have international bodies rule on their human rights and fundamental freedoms.

By the year 2000, new international courts and investigating authorities will have been established to enforce human rights. In the twenty-first century, the idea that human rights are fundamental to civilization and good government will become more firmly implanted, both through the consolidation and extension of international law and by becoming the accepted standard of civilized behaviour, nationally and internationally.

But the history of the first three-quarters of the twentieth century can give little confidence that abuses, even gross abuses, of human rights will not continue for many years to come. Greater international vigilance is still required. During the 1970s, for example, the governments of even some relatively advanced societies actively or passively sanctioned such grotesque activities as the systematic killing of political adversaries. Such countries included Kampuchea, India, Argentina, Uganda, Chile, El Salvador, and Guatemala. One government, in Libya, repeatedly and openly proclaimed its plans to kill political opponents living abroad in exile. The plan was put into practice on at least 15 occasions.

Such human rights abuses are often hard to prove, and evidence as to the identity of the perpetrators scanty. Good evidence of government involvement in such state crimes as the 'disappeared' political opponents of the former Argentine government may emerge only belatedly – perhaps after a radical change of government. International campaigns for human rights will become far more effective in future when leading nations adopt more impartial standards in identifying and publicizing abuses. More often than not, governments like those of the Soviet Union, the United States and the United Kingdom systematically and selectively highlight human rights abuses in certain countries for their own political ends, while ignoring or condoning violations of fundamental rights conducted by allied or friendly countries.

Buenos Aires, 1983. A demonstration by the mothers of the *desaparecidos* – opponents of the Argentinian junta who had 'disappeared', in a country which claimed it had no political prisoners.

International law

Ironically, the almost revolutionary idea that sovereign national governments should submit to international jurisdiction concerning their duties towards the citizen arose from recent acts of barbarism in which every human right was systematically desecrated. Just as the United States Constitution, which provides US citizens with relatively powerful protection for their individual rights, was born in a war of liberation against colonial Britain, so the United Nations Universal Declaration of Human Rights was born from popular revulsion at the atrocities committed by Nazi Germany and the Axis during World War II. The aftermath of war, and in particular the evidence of Nazi pogroms, created powerful international determination that such conduct should in the future be condemned, constrained, and prohibited – and thus so far as possible prevented altogether.

When the invading Vietnamese armies toppled the Khmer Rouge government of Kampuchea, in 1979, they disclosed evidence of genocide. Twelve graves out of 129 found on this site near Phnom Penh were opened; they contained an average of 280 bodies.

The UN Universal Declaration on Human Rights was adopted in 1948. The Declaration requires the member nations of the UN to uphold human rights and fundamental freedoms. Article 1 of the United Nations charter, on which moves to strengthen human rights will continue to be based in the future, avows that:

The Purposes of the United Nations are to achieve international cooperation in ... promoting and encouraging respect for human rights and for fundamental freedoms for all, without distinction as to race, sex, or religion.

Following the Declaration, regional treaties between member nations have created new international courts and investigating and reporting commissions. The first such treaty was the European Convention for the Protection of Human Rights, which came into effect in 1953. The Convention led to the establishment of the European Court of Human Rights, and the European Commission on Human Rights, both of which are based at Strasbourg, France, the seat of the Council of Europe.

Top: The International
Court of Justice in session at
The Hague, 1979; *(left)*
prisoners in a Nazi con-
centration camp in World
War II; *(right)* early nineteenth-century American
notice advertising a slave
auction.

Other regions of the world followed the example of the Council of
Europe. The Organization of American States adopted the American
Convention on Human Rights in 1969; it came into force in 1978. The
Inter-American Commission on Human Rights is sited in Washington
DC, while the Inter-American Court of Human Rights is in San José,
Costa Rica. By the year 2000, Africa too will have its Charter on Human
and People's Rights, which was adopted in 1981 by the Organization of
African Unity. The OAU's treaty had, in 1984, still to enter into force.
When it does, the OAU will establish an African Commission on Human
and People's Rights, which will have powers similar to its European
counterpart at Strasbourg.

As well as these and other major regional charters and conventions,
there have been a succession of minor conventions dedicated to enforcing
specific important human rights. The earliest such conventions (in 1926)
outlawed slavery internationally. More recent, specific declarations have
dealt with stateless persons, discrimination against and the political rights
of women, apartheid, and labour law – including equal pay legislation and
the rights of trades unions to bargain on behalf of their member workers.

The Helsinki accords

Major regions of the world where the international regulation of human rights will still be in its infancy in the year 2000 are Asia and the socialist or communist states of Eastern Europe. The human rights movement did make considerable apparent progress in the Soviet Union and its aligned nations between 1973 and 1975, after Eastern and Western nations had gathered at Helsinki, Finland during the Conference on Security and Cooperation in Europe. All European nations, excluding Albania, but including additionally the United States and Canada, signed the Helsinki Final Act of August 1975. Under the Final Act, the contracting governments undertook to 'respect human rights and fundamental freedoms, including the freedom of thought, conscience, religion or belief, for all without distinctions as to race, sex, language, or religion'. The human rights provisions also included a guarantee of the 'effective exercise of civil, political, economic, social, cultural and other rights'.

An important and novel feature of the Helsinki accords was the undertaking by each government to publish the Final Act and 'make it known as widely as possible' amongst their peoples. In many countries, this was the first occasion that international laws and agreements on human rights had received any publicity. Inside the Soviet Union, several groups were set up to monitor the government's observance of the provisions of the Helsinki Final Act. But the Helsinki accords were specifically declared not to be an international treaty, and were therefore not international law.

The beneficial effects of the Helsinki accords on human rights in Eastern Europe were neutralized by the worsening East–West tension of the late 1970s and early 1980s, and by the undermining of the spirit of *détente*, which had originally brought together the Helsinki Conference participants. The Helsinki Final Act had included many other provisions

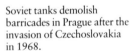

Soviet tanks demolish barricades in Prague after the invasion of Czechoslovakia in 1968.

concerning defence, security and disarmament, as well as human rights. Inevitably, as *détente* dwindled, some participants asserted that growing external threats to their national security required the harsher administration of internal security laws. Another provision of the accords, mentioned by the Soviet Union when its human rights record has come under attack, stresses that governments should not attempt to interfere in each other's internal affairs.

The practical effect of the loss of *détente* has been to remove the protection of the Helsinki declarations from human rights activists in Eastern Europe. Unofficial Helsinki monitoring groups were set up in the Soviet Union; but by 1982, the Moscow group had disbanded itself after most of its members had been accused of 'anti-Soviet' offences.

Détente, with all its value for human rights, has not disappeared from the future political agenda. The Helsinki Final Act provided for a continuing review, and future conferences. One such review took place in Madrid in 1980. By the end of the century, if the pendulum of international relations has not swung back to restore some of the spirit of Helsinki, there will be graver matters for humanity to fear than the lack of social progress in human rights.

Amnesty International

Although there is near universal respect for principles of human rights and liberty as the cornerstone of civilization, many governments are in practice far from respecting fundamental rights. Since the United Nations charter was proclaimed in December 1948 as a 'common standard for all peoples and all nations', many signatories have nevertheless continued to hold unfair trials, to detain political prisoners, to inflict cruel, inhuman or degrading treatments or punishments on prisoners, and to exercise systems of discrimination based on race, religion, sex, or political belief. Some states are known to have routinely executed political opponents without trial.

An international monitoring group, Amnesty International, was established in 1961 to highlight the most severe abuses of human rights, and in particular to campaign against unfair political imprisonment, torture, political killings and the imposition of death penalties. Few countries – including Western states priding themselves on liberal and democratic traditions – are excluded from criticism in the reports which Amnesty prepares every year.

Surveying the state of human rights in 1982, for example, Amnesty International reported complaints against every government in Europe, except for Austria and the Scandinavian and Benelux countries. There were complaints against the United States, as well as every Latin American country and many Caribbean states, including Cuba. No Asian, Arabic or African state of any size was exempt from documented complaints of human rights abuses, except for countries such as Oman and other Gulf African states who had refused to allow external enquiries into their internal affairs.

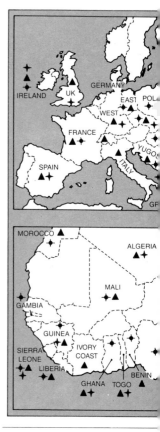

In the future, the need to investigate and report how national governments treat their citizens will not disappear. The need will grow. The importance of international human rights law is, however, increasingly recognized, and new treaties being negotiated during the 1980s improve the prospects for human rights at the turn of the century. But like any of the fruits of civilization, human rights will be gravely at risk if economic slump or collapse, or military confrontation and war, rearrange the priorities of government activity and human affairs.

World government and human rights

The internationalist idealism which swept many nations in the first two decades of the existence of the United Nations was blunted and dissipated during the 1970s and early 1980s. The world, it was recognized, could not be turned into a single, peaceful utopia overnight. With a gloomy realism induced by economic slump came also the realization that a single world government, or any single 'perfect' vision of the future, was by its very nature totalitarian. No single utopia for all can be designed or even conceived, and the value of plurality – multiple, different and sometimes conflicting centres of power in a single society – came to be recognized as a guarantee of, and not a threat to, freedom. Because of these complications and others, the idea of world government will not appear on the

As this map shows, there are very few countries in the world that are not guilty of some fundamental breach of human rights.

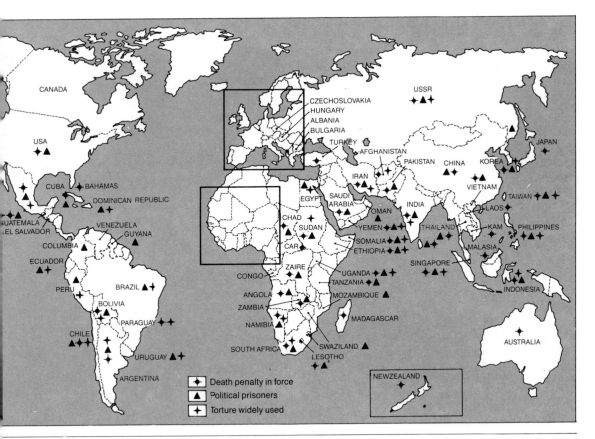

international political agenda during the late twentieth century and early twenty-first century, despite the 'predictions' of science fiction writers and other soothsayers.

World government is no longer an issue, not least because the importance of maintaining diverse cultural and ethnic traditions is now widely recognized. African nations in particular are increasingly rejecting the dominance of Western culture as a residue of their colonial periods under European rule. In fact, the idea of world government only came to the fore because there had been, about the middle of the twentieth century, a near consensus in European and North American countries over desirable values and government systems. But the values of this consensus were not necessarily widely shared outside the countries concerned.

In the same spirit, it is sometimes claimed that Western nations, deploying Judaeo-Christian ethics and moral standards, have invented the concept of human rights and then sought to impose these principles on countries with quite different ethical and moral traditions. Unlike objections to the idea of world government, however, this argument is quite ill-founded. In every nation, irrespective of its cultural traditions, there are at the present and will be in the future legal codes which identify the dignity and integrity of each person, and which recognize common goals of freedom from persecution and unjust oppression. Moreover, the United Nations Declaration, which sets out these human rights and fundamental freedoms, has been endorsed by almost every nation on the globe.

Signs of apartheid: *(top left)* a township in the black 'homeland' of Bophuthat-swana, South Africa; *(top right)* municipal notice warning blacks to keep off an all-white beach. *Above:* American medallists giving the Black Power salute at the 1968 Olympics.

Press freedom

Although the rights of individual men and women have thus come to enjoy a growing prominence, there are also international agreements and new demands to come which concern other rights, allied to such fundamental principles as freedom of thought, freedom of speech, and freedom of association. Among such rights are commonly identified the principle that men and women should be treated equally by society; that workers' rights to free association in a trade or labour union or similar body should be respected; and that there should be freedom of the press. But the consensus about the meaning of press freedom will alter during the 1980s and 1990s. An international row about press freedom which began in the 1970s well illustrates how the granting of equal freedoms and rights, in a world where the distribution of wealth, power and resources is far from equal, may produce a situation that is far from free.

Third World countries have long felt particularly strongly that international news media – especially radio, television and reporting services based in Europe and the United States – reflect cultural domination by the West. The vision of a world coming together culturally and economically under Western influence had begun to fade and crack by the late 1960s, leaving a strong contrast between developing countries' economic expectations and the performance which their weak economies could actually achieve. The growth of satellite broadcasting systems by the end of the century also boded ill for cultural independence, unless international agreement was reached on how international communications should be governed.

Because the output of Western international news and communications media naturally tends to reflect the outlook of the Western developed countries, Third World governments have sought to establish a 'New International Information Order'. The idea was widely discussed at UNESCO conferences during the 1970s. At a key meeting in Nairobi in 1976, there was a heated confrontation between representatives of Western countries and those from developing countries. The Third World side wanted to introduce controls on the operations of international media organizations, which Western countries claimed threatened press freedom and the free flow of information. Instead, Western governments offered financial support to develop journalism and strong media institutions in the Third World. The boom in international communications during the last two decades of the twentieth century will provide a continuing focus for the conflict of interests that led to the proclamation of the New International Information Order.

Freedom of information

Other developments which have been intended to reinforce democratic and human rights will only slowly be adopted in less developed countries in the coming decades. These include the concept of personal privacy, and the idea of freedom of information. The right to privacy is enshrined in Article 12 of the United Nations Declaration:

No-one shall be subjected to arbitrary interference with his privacy, family, home or correspondence ...

In some countries, like the United States, a written constitution or Bill of Rights has long provided guarantees of this kind to the individual citizen. In contrast, countries such as the United Kingdom, where there is no written constitution, offer citizens no legally enforceable right to privacy.

'Freedom of information' laws are more concerned with the collective right of a people to supervise the activities of government than with individual rights. Such laws have been introduced in the Scandinavian countries (especially Sweden), Canada, Australia, New Zealand, the United States, the Netherlands, Austria, France, and some of the *Länder* (provinces) of the Federal Republic of Germany. Under freedom of information legislation, civil servants have to make available to the public all government information which is not covered by specified categories of exemption.

The idea of freedom of information first became powerful in the United States in the 1960s, and again during the Watergate era. Most other countries created their freedom of information laws during the 1970s. This right is now recognized as desirable in many other democracies, and many new or strengthened freedom of information laws can be expected to be passed by the start of the twenty-first century.

Sexual equality

The rights proclaimed in the United Nations Declaration and other treaties fall short of establishing peoples' rights to equal treatment before the law irrespective of sexual attitude or orientation, as well as of their gender, although this is now a popular concern in Western states. In any case, until the 1960s, only notional acknowledgement was generally given to the principle of equal rights for women. Even in many advanced countries in the 1970s and 1980s, women still face discrimination in practice in employment and other opportunities.

But rapid and effective progress has been made and will be made in this area of human rights. It was not until the 1970s, following the famous Stonewell riot in New York (when city police had attacked homosexual men), that the principle of equal rights irrespective of sexuality came on to the political agenda, with the birth of the gay rights movement. Although homosexuality was legal in many countries before that time, gay men and women have come late to the arena of human rights and fundamental freedoms, and in most countries have to make considerable progress before they too have secured equal rights.

Sexual politics: the opening of the gay 'Olympics' in California.

The technology of repression

Growing international sensitivity to human rights issues has led the developed countries to adapt and change historical methods used by police or paramilitary forces to keep public order. Whereas in the eighteenth and nineteenth centuries in many European countries armed troops and police units regularly used lethal violence to suppress riots or other disorder, by the middle of the twentieth century such action was universally abhorred. Yet during the students' and workers' disturbances of the 1960s, and again with the anti-nuclear power and anti-nuclear weapons movements in Western countries, democratic states increasingly have sought to find 'acceptable' means of imposing non-lethal violence. The Federal Republic of Germany and the United States in particular have widely employed such devices as water cannons, marking dyes, as well as using choking gases to contain crowds. In the developing world, national governments have usually felt less compelled to find or use such exotic, low-violence means of suppressing disturbances.

The British government has developed many anti-riot gases, known as CN, CS, DM or CR. All cause nausea, vomiting, and choking, but do not kill their victims. The British Army has also pioneered the successive use of (wooden) 'baton rounds' and rubber and plastic bullets, with which troops can confront rioters, particularly in the conflict in Northern Ireland. On many occasions, however, such weapons have in fact been lethal in effect, or caused serious injury, and their employment has been internationally criticized.

Security companies and law-enforcement agencies will nevertheless continue to develop new and more exotic means of suppressing riots and demonstrations while reducing as far as possible the apparent level of violence employed. This is an important feature – and one which will grow in significance – as public opinion has been shown to respond quickly to televised confrontations.

In the Western democracies, nuclear power and nuclear weapons have for two decades generally attracted the greatest, most widespread popular protests of any cause, testing not just the restraints these states may deploy to contain freedom of expression, but also the democratic mechanisms which should make government responsive to popular causes. *De facto*, these protests have become – West Germany is a particularly good example – the testing ground for new technologies of repression ranging from electronic surveillance to anti-riot equipment.

The search for new techniques of riot control in the 1990s and beyond will include research on hallucinogenic and incapacitating gases, and on electronic psychological devices, such as a proposal made in Britain and the United States for a 'photic driver' – a powerful sound- and light-emitting machine intended to induce giddiness and a lack of coordination. So-called 'instant banana peel' chemicals have been invented, designed to disrupt crowds by creating a slippery surface underneath them. Some manufacturers are seeking to develop an alternative 'instant jungle' spray, intended to make movement difficult.

Surveillance

Anti-nuclear groups in Western countries have frequently been the target of secret intelligence-gathering activities. In the United States, local and state police forces operate an intelligence centre which coordinates police information on anti-nuclear activists with intelligence from private investigators working for nuclear power corporations. In 1975, the United States government's Nuclear Regulatory Commission examined the dangers to Americans' civil rights and liberties posed by an intensified national nuclear programme, including the circulation of increasing amounts of plutonium, and warned that:

The possibility of surveillance is probably the most severe civil liberties effect of a plutonium recycle decision. The surveillance would act at all times; it would not be restricted to emergency situations. It could have significant chilling effects on First Amendment discussion, particularly in the nuclear area.

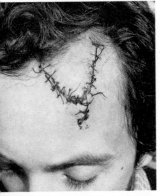

Street politics: the victim of a plastic bullet fired by the Royal Ulster Constabulary; *(below)* French CRS riot police using tear gas grenades against student demonstrators in Paris.

In the United Kingdom, similar fears about the quality of life in the late twentieth and early twenty-first centuries were expressed by a Royal Commission led by leading physicist Lord Flowers. His report warned that the future would involve:

Secret surveillance of members of the public and possibly of employees who may make 'undesirable' contacts. The activities might include the use of informers, infiltrators, wiretapping, checking on bank accounts and the opening of mail . . .

In the extreme circumstances created by nuclear terrorism, accidents, or the threat of war, citizens of all countries face the loss of the right to free speech. The opportunity to say 'no' to war might only be exercised at the gravest risk to life and liberty. After a nuclear attack, it goes without saying that there would be neither civilization nor civil rights. Democracy and the rule of law would be over for the duration, supplanted for those who do survive, by the law of the jungle. In a wrecked world where the existence of human life itself might lie in the balance for decades, no time period could be suggested during which mankind might slowly crawl back to pre-holocaust democracy and civilized standards.

Capital punishment

During the latter part of the twentieth century, governments around the world increasingly recognized that a judicial punishment of death was incompatible with human dignity and respect. There was enormous progress, which is expected to continue, between the 1950s – when all but a few states allowed the death penalty to be used routinely – and the 1980s, when over 40 states had either completely outlawed judicial executions, or limited them to exceptionally grave acts such as war crimes. Although the death penalty is legal everywhere else, the judiciary of many other states, in practice, never impose death sentences. Nevertheless, around the world in the 1980s, about 2000 people every year are known to have been sentenced to death or executed.

In some countries, inventive technology, such as death pills, has increasingly been sought in order to make judicial execution more dignified or painless. But such 'advances' have usually been rejected. Other electronic methods of punishment have been proposed, particularly in the United States. 'Law and order' groups have urged that technological control systems rather than socially-based remedies be applied to criminals. The most widely publicized scheme, which came under consideration during the early 1980s, involved implanting radio monitoring devices in convicts, so that they might be set free under surveillance, and confined to particular areas – rather than sent to jail.

Computers and control

In more-developed countries, personal databanks on computer are increasingly being seen as a future threat to privacy and liberty, unless suitable legal controls are applied to their use. This was recognized, for example, by the Council of Europe in 1981 when it drafted a new Convention on Data Protection to supplement the European Convention on Human Rights. In many countries, not just in Europe, the novel *Nineteen Eighty-Four* created a powerful concern for personal privacy – and in particular for its protection from encroachment by centralized systems of surveillance and supervision, such as data-processing machinery.

It is unlikely that any country will attempt to introduce a real 'central computer'. This is not the direction in which computer developments now lead. But in most countries linkages are continually being formed, for example between computers holding personal medical information, tax and financial details, social security and employment records, police criminal records, and security and intelligence information, including political data. The threats of unregulated computer surveillance are that:

Information in an official file may be collected by underhand or improper means, or without consent;

Information may be unnecessary for or irrelevant to the purpose for which it is collected;

Information may be false, inaccurate, out-of-date, irrelevant, misleading or incomplete;

Information from official files may be leaked to or tapped by unauthorized persons;

Information given for one purpose may be transferred to an entirely different use, without knowledge or consent.

Without safeguards, the future threat may be severe. An American specialist on privacy, attorney John Shattuck of the American Civil Liberties Union, claimed during the 1970s US debate on privacy and freedom of information that:

Power may come out of the barrel of a gun, but far more power comes out of a computer or databank, particularly if the information in it relates to people who do not know that it has been collected or cannot challenge its accuracy or use . . .

Shattuck analysed the conflict between the need to collect personal information to support essential social services, and the danger that such information, in another guise, transferred elsewhere without consent, provides an insidious and powerful means of exerting social control.

Computer databanks will make an increasing impact on the democratic political process itself. In major elections in Western democracies political parties have begun to make effective and politically powerful use of computers. 'Direct mail' political campaigning techniques, using computers to manage frequent communications to a party's supporters, were imported into Europe from the United States in the early 1980s. American politicians had been pleased with the success of the technique. Direct mail techniques can be extended to support and fund lobby organizations on controversial political issues; 'target' groups to support a selected issue can easily be found and automatically selected. Ironically, one of the first successful targets of such a campaign was a distinguished American Senator, Frank Church, who had led investigations after Watergate into US intelligence agencies. He lost his seat when a direct mail campaign was organized against him. Church had reported with particular alarm on the dangers and technological potency of intelligence-surveillance activities. He particularly noted the immense computer power of the United States National Security Agency, which widely monitors international communications, and warned in 1975 that it 'at any time could be turned around on the American people ... The capacity is there to make tyranny total.'

Tapping and bugging

In most countries, civil liberty is threatened less by sophisticated surveillance technology *per se* than by the lack of legal controls and political constraints which govern the use of surveillance methods and devices. For some time to come, government use of the less recognized or exotic forms of political surveillance – snoopers, agents and informers – will be much more common than complex electronic techniques. The present technological threat to liberty therefore comes only indirectly from the availability, at low cost, of microcomputers and machine intelligence – although that threat will develop markedly by the year 2000. But a telescreen (as in *Nineteen Eighty-Four*) or a telephone tap in every home is neither a necessary nor an effective means of keeping an entire population under control.

The US National Security Agency base at Menwith Hill near Harrogate, UK, used for tapping international telephone lines passing through Britain.

The greatest danger to liberty from political surveillance generally arises in military or other dictatorships, where state security bodies tend either to have or to take for themselves wide extra-judicial powers. In more democratic countries, sufficient flexibility in the enforcement of legal or extra-legal sanctions or punishments may also enable a purportedly 'neutral' legal code to operate selectively against political activity thought to be undesirable or unacceptable by the government. Both technical devices and surveillance agencies and agents fit neatly into this framework.

Systems like telephone tapping are used far less than many people fear, but more than most governments are prepared publicly to admit. At present, the need for surveillance agencies to employ human listeners to transcribe tapped conversations makes widespread surveillance prohibitively expensive. Increasingly, however, computers are able to identify and interpret speech – although it is not likely to be until the next century that this capability will have been extended to the wide variety of accents, dialects, speech patterns and even languages that an automatic telephone tapping device would have to cope with.

But in time, voice recognition technology will greatly reduce the cost of tapping phones. Similarly, although some electronic listening 'bugs' are capable of remarkable eavesdropping performances, secret police forces and security agencies find that these devices are nevertheless only worth using in operations of such importance that the complexity of planting and using a bug is justified. A new danger in the twenty-first century will be development of automatic complex picture and face recognition capabilities by advanced computers, enabling much more elaborate and extensive video surveillance devices to be brought into use.

Policing the global village

Computers thus pose a growing threat, which both requires and has received attention in the international law of human rights. As social administration comes to rely on computers and automatic data-processing support, so the information pool that may be tapped for sensitive personal information is growing. In the United States, the mere fact that government agencies *may* be gathering or storing information about particular types of person has in the past been held by the Supreme Court to have a 'chilling' effect on political liberty and constitutional rights, and therefore to be unlawful. No specific adverse effect need be proved.

International courts, such as the European Court of Human Rights at Strasbourg, have reviewed national telephone tapping practices by governments such as Britain and Germany. However, there has been no review of the practice by intelligence agencies – particularly the US National Security Agency and Britain's GCHQ (General Communications Headquarters) – of intercepting all international telephone calls, telex messages and telegrams. All international written messages, such as telex, have been automatically intercepted, processed and analysed by intelligence agency computers since the 1960s – and vast new computer systems are being installed to keep pace with the growth in global communications.

That growth in communications has helped create new standards of human rights and civil liberties in the international community and will continue to do so in the future. The global village will not be the homogeneous government system once predicted – but it will be increasingly difficult for human rights abuses to be perpetrated in secret. Governments cannot live on their own, but increasingly, too, individuals and peoples may lose their right and opportunity to live alone, undisturbed. The price of material prosperity and a stronger international system of law through most of the world may inevitably be some loss of personal as well as national independence.

Chapter Five

WAR AND PEACE

As in so many other spheres, technology has revolutionized weapons and warfare. While – inevitably – the nuclear debate is always uppermost when we consider war in the future, the implications of the development of 'conventional' offensive and defensive weapons and of computer-controlled intelligence gathering systems are no less startling. Frank Barnaby looks at what the technology has produced and is expected to produce before the end of the century and how this is affecting our expectations in current and future conflicts.

Martin Walker looks in depth at one aspect of war – terrorism or freedom-fighting or guerrilla warfare depending on your standpoint – which is as old as governments and which will continue into the year 2000 and beyond.

French soldiers with tactical nuclear weapon *Pluton*.

The technology of warfare

FRANK BARNABY

New military technology is advancing at such an unprecedented rate that it, more than any other factor, will dictate the shape of the battlefield of the future. Developments in micro-electronics have transformed nuclear weapons and their supporting technologies as well as conventional offensive and defensive weapons and their supporting technologies.

We can be sure that future war will use organizations and techniques radically different from those used by the military in the 1970s and early '80s. There will, of course, be resistance to change: military men are reluctant to modify familiar tactics and ministries of defence are notorious for their intertia. Nevertheless, the momentum of military technology is so forceful that it will break through such barriers relatively quickly. In addition there are powerful vested interests – military, industrial, academic and bureaucratic – pressing political leaders to agree to the deployment of all weapons developed by military scientists.

The increasing risk of nuclear war

The most far-reaching technological advances in nuclear weapons are those which improve the accuracy, reliability and targeting flexibility of nuclear-weapons systems. Already, both the United States and the Soviet Union have improved their land-based intercontinental ballistic missile forces to such an extent that they are now aimed at small military nuclear targets. These missiles are consequently seen to be more suitable for *fighting* a nuclear war than for *deterring* one.

Nuclear deterrence, until recently the official nuclear strategy of both sides, is based on the threat of mutually assured destruction, that is, the enemy will not attack you if he knows that you will destroy most of his cities and industries in retaliation. Paradoxically, such deterrence is workable only with inaccurate nuclear weapons. Once the weapons become accurate enough to destroy the other side's nuclear forces, the enemy will assume that they are aimed at those forces rather than at his cities, which then cease to be hostages. Policies of deterrence by mutually assured destruction must then give way to fighting policies, based on the destruction of the other side's military forces.

Currently, land-based ballistic missiles are accurate enough to be nuclear-war fighting weapons. Submarine-launched ballistic missiles (SLBMs) are not. The navies are, therefore, still operating a policy of nuclear deterrence by mutually assured destruction, with their missiles targeted on the enemy's cities. Both sides are, however, improving the accuracy of their SLBMs, so that within five years or so, these weapons will be accurate enough to be aimed at enemy military nuclear targets. Superpower nuclear policies will then be purely nuclear-war fighting policies.

Many believe that dropping the policies of deterrence and adopting nuclear-war fighting policies will considerably increase the risk of a full-scale nuclear war. These people argue that a particularly dangerous situation will arise if significant numbers of tactical nuclear-war fighting weapons (i.e. those employed in systems such as ground-, air- and

Pershing II medium-range nuclear missiles at an assembly site in the United States – destined for deployment in Europe.

submarine-launched cruise missiles, anti-aircraft, air-to-air ground missiles and so on) are deployed in Europe at the same time as strategic nuclear-war fighting weapons are deployed in the United States and the Soviet Union. Strategic nuclear weapons have a range of 6000 kilometres or more (about 4000 miles). The deployment of tactical weapons means that they will be integrated into the army at low levels of military command. A war in Europe would then almost certainly escalate into a nuclear war (military tactics cannot be changed radically once a war has begun) and the military will make the necessary psychological adjustment into believing that a nuclear war is 'fightable and winnable', and that a limited and protracted nuclear war is possible.

In the technology that backs nuclear-war fighting weapons, the most important developments are being made in anti-submarine warfare

An example of modern air-strike power: USAF McDonnell Douglas F-15 fighter armed with an Asat missile.

systems, anti-ballistic missile systems, and anti-satellite warfare systems. Strategic nuclear submarines are much less vulnerable to sudden attack (first strike) than land-based strategic forces. It is not possible for one side to detect and destroy instantaneously all the other side's strategic nuclear submarines; and even the most optimistic military planner will assume that some enemy missiles will escape his attack. Few scientists believe that in the foreseeable future it will be possible to develop an anti-ballistic missile capable of destroying *all* the enemy warheads fired in a full-scale attack. Each side, after all, has deployed over 7000 warheads on their ballistic missiles. This is why both sides are working on anti-ballistic missile systems, mainly based in high-energy lasers in space capable of

The dangerous equilibrium maintained by the superpowers with their ever increasing nuclear arsenals will come under growing strain as more and more states develop a nuclear capability.

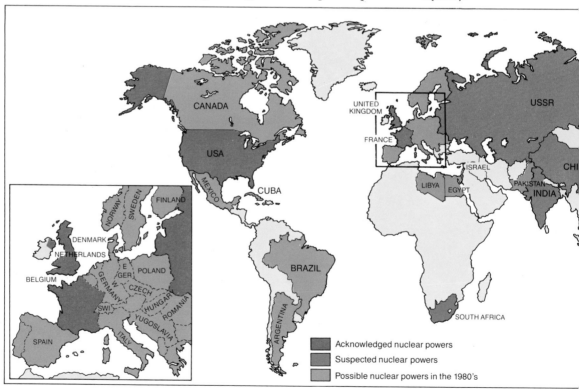

Acknowledged nuclear powers

Suspected nuclear powers

Possible nuclear powers in the 1980's

dealing with a few hundred warheads. The first move in a first strike would be to destroy the enemy's reconnaissance and early-warning satellites, his 'eyes and ears' in space. Both sides are actively developing systems to do just that.

If successful anti-submarine, anti-ballistc missile and anti-satellite warfare techniques become available in, say, 10 or 15 years, the side that has them may well perceive that it has a first-strike capability and would gain a big advantage in making a surprise nuclear attack. Nuclear-war fighting strategies would then give way to nuclear-war *winning* strategies. This change would again significantly increase the probability of a nuclear world war.

The effort being put into developing and deploying nuclear-war fighting weapons and technologies can be judged by the amount of money being spent. The United States for example, plans to spend the staggering sum of $450 000 million between 1983 and 1988. Many experts believe that the very magnitude of the effort devoted to developing nuclear-war winning strategies virtually guarantees its success.

There is also an increasing danger of nuclear war by accident or miscalculation. But the greatest risk may well be that of an unintended nuclear war following an international crisis. In fact, most experts believe that the greatest danger we face is that a conflict in a Third World region (most probably the Middle East) may begin as a conventional war, escalate to a local nuclear war, and then spread to Europe, where it would start as a conventional war, rapidly become a tactical nuclear war, and finally escalate to a strategic nuclear war between the superpowers in which all, or most, of the 50 000 or so warheads in the US and Soviet nuclear arsenals are used.

The more nuclear-weapon powers there are, the more likely it is that this scenario will occur. The spread of nuclear weapons to new countries is, therefore, as dangerous for world security as the superpower nuclear arms race.

Few suggest that either superpower will come to believe that a nuclear strike is necessarily a good option for it. But, at a time of acute international crisis, one side, particularly if it believes it has a first-strike capability and the other does not, may perceive that, of all the options available to it, the best might be a pre-emptive nuclear attack. Under these circumstances it is hard to see how the temptation to strike first could be resisted, even if only to prevent the other side from getting a first-strike capability too.

The conventional battlefield

Conventional warfare is also being transformed, not just by micro-electronics but also by developments in other areas of military technology including more efficient fuels and greater engine efficiency; improved resistance to electronic and other counter-measures; smaller and lighter weapons; smaller weapon-delivery systems; greater adaptability of weapon-firing platforms on land and at sea; the use of new materials, particularly alloys; better armour; and so on.

JAPAN

REA

VAN

PHILIPPINES

Most battles can be broken down into four distinct stages. Attacking enemy forces are located and identified; information about them is used to decide how to deal with them; appropriate weapons are chosen and fired at enemy forces; and, finally, the damage done to the enemy is assessed and the sequence repeated if necessary. Each of these four stages has been revolutionized by advances in weapons technology and in intelligence-gathering. One of the most startling developments in modern warfare is the vast amount of information generated by sensors and other devices before and during a battle. The human mind is unable to handle this amount of data effectively and much of it has to be automated. Hence the importance of improving one's own computerized command, control and communications systems and of being able to disrupt similar systems used by the enemy.

In future battles, enemy forces will be located and tracked (even in their own territory) in 'real time'. Commanders will essentially follow the battle as it happens using television monitors in their command posts. Information about enemy forces will be collected by reconnaissance satellites, remotely-piloted vehicles (unmanned aircraft), and a variety of sensors planted in the ground. It will then be transmitted to central computers for analysis.

It is already possible to construct an effective electronic border around one's territory – the Israelis have recently done so along the Lebanese

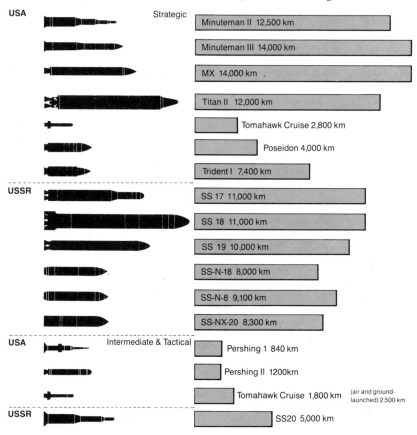

How they compare across the East–West divide. A line up of the major US and Soviet nuclear missiles, giving their respective ranges.

Israeli remotely-piloted
vehicle (RPV).

border. A whole range of ground sensors – sensitive to light, sound, magnetic fields, pressure, infrared radiation, chemicals and so on – are available for this purpose. They can be implanted by hand in peacetime, fired in by artillery or dropped by aircraft. The most common types of sensors pick up the seismic disturbances in the ground produced by the movements of people or vehicles. When used with acoustic and chemical sensors, seismic sensors can distinguish between tractors, tanks and people and thus identify the nature of enemy forces. Their location can be determined by arranging the sensors in a grid of known coordinates.

Static ground sensors are useful for monitoring a border. But there is much military interest in 'imaging' devices, such as television cameras, either in fixed positions, along a border, say, or carried by remotely-piloted vehicles. The advantage is that imaging devices transmit information live.

Remotely-piloted vehicles (RPVs) will play a big role in future warfare. They are cheap enough to make their use in large numbers feasible. Their potential was dramatically demonstrated by the Israelis in the Lebanon where they were used both for reconnaissance and for combat missions such as targeting artillery fire. The vehicles carried TV cameras aimed and focused by operators on the ground who were able to observe vehicles on the streets of Beirut or to track (for example) helicopters in flight. The Israelis also used RPVs to fly close to Syrian surface-to-air batteries to monitor the frequencies of the radars associated with them. They then used this information to neutralize the missiles.

Because they carry no crew, RPVs can be made very small and be submitted to very high accelerations. Their size gives them a small radar cross-section, making them hard to detect and destroy, particularly when flying at high altitudes. The need to fly over hostile territory can, in any case, be much reduced by the use of side-looking radar which can scan wide areas of enemy territory when the aircraft is flying within the confines of its own border.

Weapons systems which need humans to fly or drive them are expensive because of the need to protect the people from an evermore hostile environment. It is also very costly to train highly skilled professionals to operate them.

As events in the Falkland Islands and in the Middle East have recently shown, modern warfare relies more and more on missiles which are becoming increasingly 'smarter'. The preference will be for missiles with automatic homing devices which, once launched, seek out and destroy their targets without further external help. They use sensors operating on the far infrared and radio frequencies. Increasingly, millimetre-waves able to penetrate atmospheres polluted with dust, smoke, haze, fog, and so on will be used for missile guidance. Future high-technology warfare will be fought in virtually all weathers and in all environments.

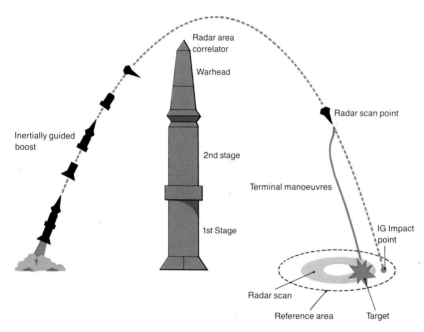

Pershing II. The missile is rocket-launched by the first stage, and the second stage releases the warhead. As the warhead approaches the target area, a radar scanner identifies the precise target. The warhead deviates from its natural trajectory and is guided home to strike with deadly accuracy.

These missile developments are a major part of what the American scientist Daniel Deudney has described in a recent paper for the Washington-based Worldwatch Institute as the 'transparency revolution'. Advances in information technologies have, he says, 'created a rudimentary planetary nervous system, fragments of a planetary cybernetic'. Deudney argues convincingly that central to the transparency revolution is the militarization of yet another 'natural feature of the planet lying beyond the effective sovereignty of the nation-state' — the electromagnetic spectrum.

He points out that worldwide military reconnaissance, command, control and communications systems have formed a 'planetary-scale web of electronic intelligence that alters the potency of weapons as well as the incentives for using them'. The emphasis in warfare is shifting from the destructive power of weapons to the ability to detect and target the enemy's forces and to 'hide and communicate with one's own'. Deudney believes that future warfare will no longer be a 'traditional struggle between offensive and defensive military force' but rather 'a competition between the visible and the hidden – between transparency and stealth'.

Does the 'transparency revolution' favour offence or defence? Many experts believe that it favours defence to such an extent that major offensive weapons (battle tanks, long-range combat aircraft and warships) are, or soon will be, obsolete, because of the development of defensive missiles of deadly accuracy.

Take, for example, anti-tank missiles now under development. The missile is designed to engage in a short time a number of enemy tanks spread over a wide area. When enemy tanks are detected by side-looking radar, a missile is launched from the ground by a signal from an RPV. The radar guides the missile into position above the tank formation, the nose

Laser guided missiles in action: *(top and above)* US Army Copperhead anti-tank missile homes in and strikes its target; *(right)* Hellfire missile being launched from a US Army helicopter.

of the main missile opens and releases a number of smaller missiles, or submunitions. Each submunition can scan the area underneath it with a sensor which seeks out a tank and guides the submunition downwards. It then fires a small high-speed projectile into the turret, the weakest part of a tank. If one main missile carries 20 submunitions and it takes, on average, two submunitions to destroy one tank, then each missile could destroy 10 tanks. A main battle tank costs today at least $3 million so one anti-tank missile could destroy about $30 million-worth of tanks. A government would think twice about invading territory defended by such missiles.

Future missiles of this type will be virtually fully automated, as are the US Patriot anti-aircraft missiles, now being deployed in Europe. Patriots' radar can track many aircraft at the same time to give early warning of an air attack. It can fire a Patriot missile at the appropriate moment and guide it in flight to its target. The system can cope with a number of engagements simultaneously and the whole operation is largely automated.

Soviet T.72 tank, with a range of about 500 kilometres (over 300 miles) and a top speed of nearly 100 km/h (60 mph).

Although recent and foreseeable military technologies have produced very effective defensive weapons, they have also produced a number of conventional weapons of great destructive power. Some NATO military personnel see these as a way of reducing reliance on the early use of tactical nuclear weapons. The Airland Battle concept, for example, calls for the use of long-range conventional weapons to strike deep inside enemy territory; such as the Improved Lance missile which can carry a 600-kg (1300-lb) warhead containing as many as 800 unguided bomblets, each of which produces many metal fragments. A warhead of this type would be lethal over a large area and would decimate, for example, infantry or soft-topped lorries carrying infantry.

Similar weapons are being developed to attack enemy air bases. In one, several hundred bomblets are carried in one casing which, when dropped over an enemy airfield, opens to release them. Two types of bomblets are carried: one is able to penetrate the concrete surface of runways and explode at a depth to create a fair-sized crater; the other is provided with a delayed action fuse, timed to explode, booby-trap fashion, when personnel are likely to be repairing the damaged runway. These explosions keep the runway out of use for as long as possible.

These new, extremely destructive offensive weapons, known as area-denial weapons, will make conventional warfare potentially as destructive as nuclear warfare, within the area of their use. For example, just one of the proposed Total Air Base Attack System missiles would be sufficient to wipe out a major enemy airbase, including all support facilities. The possible number of combinations of launchers, warheads, sensors, and so on, for long-range area-denial weapons is very large.

Electronic warfare

In future warfare, the 'electronic order of battle' will be a crucial factor. The development of new offensive and defensive weapons based on a variety of sensors has stimulated a never-ending electronic arms race for counter-measures, counter-counter-measures, and so on. Electronic intelligence, a new espionage activity called Elint, is a vast and costly enterprise using global land, sea and air information-gathering operations, as well as satellites. The knowledge gathered by Elint is used to develop appropriate electronic counter-measures to frustrate the enemy's weapon systems.

The military in advanced countries are becoming increasingly dependent on space for their activities. Since 1957, the United States and the Soviet Union have launched about 2000 military satellites, about three-quarters of all those in orbit. Future warfare will depend on the information they supply through photographic and electronic reconnaissance, on early-warning of attack, navigation, communications, weather forecasting and geodesy (surveying the earth). This is not to imply that future wars will actually be fought in space but that space activities will make war on earth more effective and more destructive, and perhaps more likely.

The future of war

What can we conclude about the nature of future armed conflict? The pattern over the past twenty years or so has been one of increasingly frequent conflict, particularly in the Third World. There is no reason to believe that this frequency will decrease in the near future.

In mid-1984 the United States successfully tested a new anti-ballistic missile system. An interceptor rocket, equipped with a metal framework, destroyed a Minuteman III ICBM on impact.

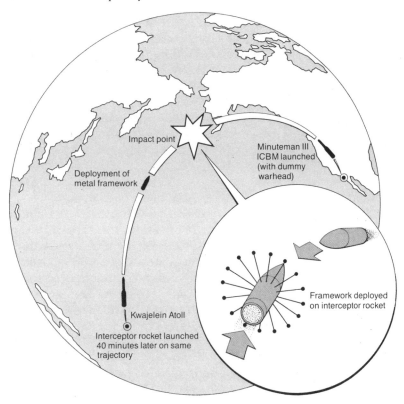

Impact point

Minuteman III ICBM launched (with dummy warhead)

Deployment of metal framework

Kwajelein Atoll

Interceptor rocket launched 40 minutes later on same trajectory

Framework deployed on interceptor rocket

The nature of conflict will, however, vary according to how industrialized are the countries concerned. As we have seen, military technological developments are automating the battlefield. We cannot predict where this process will end but we do know that future soldiers will be highly skilled technicians operating computerized equipment rather than traditional infantrymen. In theory, the battlefield could become completely automated. An area on each side of the border could be evacuated and the war might then consist of one side invading this territory with robot-driven tanks and remotely-piloted aircraft; the other side would attack these weapons with missiles, chosen and fired by computer.

All this is feasible in the foreseeable future certainly. But how would victory be defined? Would we still demand that blood is spilled? Or will wars be lost or won on economic grounds, with victory going to the side that keeps up the automated battle the longest? If so, are we heading for economies kept on a permanent war footing, and the total militarization of society?

A costly US Navy Nimitz-class aircraft carrier. In the future, will its power be more symbolic than real?

In the technological arms race, the two superpowers have far outstripped their nearest rivals, the French, the British, the West Germans and the Chinese. Only the superpowers can afford a worldwide military communications network, and only they can afford to operate vast navies in all the world's oceans, including aircraft-carrier battle groups. Although these enormously expensive juggernauts are so vulnerable as now to be virtually useless in war, the superpowers keep them to project their power in peacetime to back up their foreign policy. In the future the use of military muscle to threaten smaller countries may well become routine.

The superpowers are likely, in any case, to become increasingly involved in conflicts in the Third World through competition for key strategic raw materials such as oil and minerals. In addition, they or their allies provide almost all the weapons used in Third World conflicts. They essentially become the guarantors of the survival of their arms-clients and would lose credibility if they failed to prevent a client from being beaten in war.

Predictions about the nature of future war are complicated by changing attitudes to national security. It is becoming increasingly realized that there are major threats to 'social and political values' over and above external military threats of territorial invasion and occupation. Non-military threats to security will include economic crises, threats to the environment, shortages of important raw materials, and increasing populations. In particular, North–South tension may well become a more important international factor than East–West tension.

Once again, predictions are difficult. Increasing political and social unrest in the rich countries due to the consequences of low economic growth, and worsening poverty, rapidly increasing urbanization and unbearable population pressures in the poor countries, are the very circumstances under which nations may resort to war. Political leaders may choose to use military action to divert people's attention from domestic crises. Populations may even demand that the politicians go to war to secure scarce raw materials.

Future uncertainties about the risks and outcomes of high-technology wars are likely to be reflected in increased sub-national violence, including terrorism and urban guerilla fighting (this topic is dealt with later in the chapter by Martin Walker). A major factor here will be the role of non-renewable resources, such as forests, grasslands, agricultural lands, fish stocks and water. Population pressures will put great stress on these resources in many Third World countries; more and more people will be forced out of rural areas. Greater urbanization and poverty will generate violence, political unrest and terrorism.

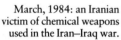

March, 1984: an Iranian victim of chemical weapons used in the Iran–Iraq war.

All in all, given foreseeable developments in nuclear weapons, chemical weapons, and conventional offensive weapons, the world is likely to become more insecure as time goes on. The superpowers now seem to be locked in a race for a first-strike nuclear capability. More and more countries are acquiring the capability and the fissile material to produce nuclear weapons. Although, however, the general picture of future war is a depressing one, there are reasons for cautious optimism. Military technology has made available weapons and their supporting technologies which favour defence. Advancing weapons technology is making the weapons of invasion obsolete. Defence of one's territory can be made effective and cheap without relying on offensive weapons. As we have seen, a tank can be put out of action effectively, in adverse weather and battlefield conditions, by an anti-tank missile costing only a fraction of the cost of the tank.

Non-nuclear defence

Given the new possibilities for effective defence, there is currently much discussion of alternative, less threatening and less expensive defence policies than those presently pursued, particularly for NATO countries in Europe. One such alternative is non-nuclear, non-provocative defence, the

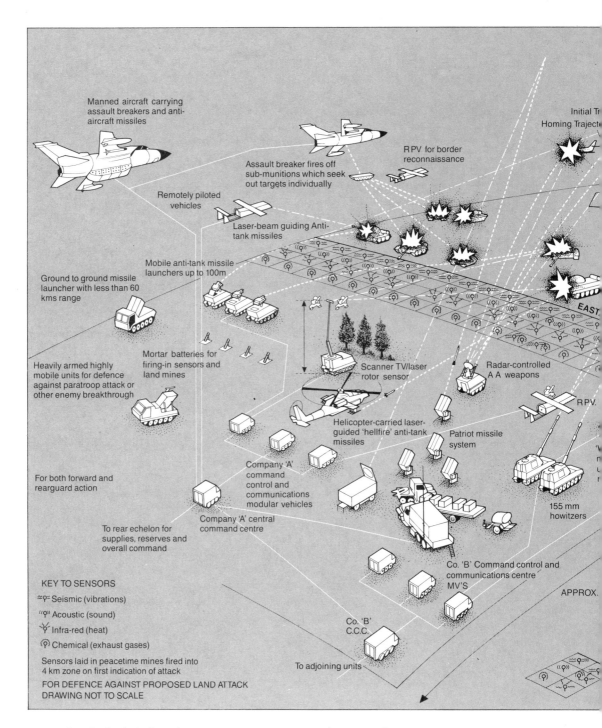

principle of which is that the size, weapons, training, logistics, doctrine, operational manuals, war games, manoeuvres, and so on, of the armed forces are so arranged that they are seen in their totality to be incapable of offence but capable instead of a credible defence without reliance on nuclear weapons. Self-defence is allowed for and preparations made in

Satellite scans general
area for early warning

DIRECTION OF WARSAW
CONVENTIONAL ATTACK

Laser beam

4 km minefield
and pre-laid
sensors

'Blowpipe' hand
held AA missile
for low flying
aircraft

2 kms m/cycle
& infantry missile
launchers AA &
A.tank

n up to show aiming points etc, before
hostilities and fed into computers for
e location. Contact by fibre-optics or
es.

A possible scheme for the
deployment of a non-
nuclear, non-provocative
defence system.

such a way that surrounding countries or rival power blocs would not feel threatened.

Advocates of non-nuclear, non-provocative defence for European countries argue that its adoption would remove one of the factors driving the East—West arms race. If the military posture of one side is demonstrably defensive, the 'hawks' on the other side would find it much more difficult to justify new weapons for self-protection.

The military in smaller countries may in the future be deployed in the following way. A defence zone, some 40 kilometres (25 miles) deep, would be prepared along the border. This zone would be saturated with all kinds of sensors, a vast network of underground fibre-glass cables for communications and numerous positions for troops to take cover. The zone would be monitored by remotely-piloted vehicles, and possibly by reconnaissance satellites. Details of the zone would be fed into computers so that any hostile troop or tank movements could be located, tracked and destroyed by pre-planned fire. The military forces would be equipped with a judicious mixture of the most effective anti-tank, anti-aircraft and anti-ship missiles and artillery. Command, control, communications, and intelligence systems would be mainly computerized but decentralized so as not to provide an easy target. Highly mobile squads of troops armed with defensive weapons of high fire-power, mainly missiles, would attack any enemy forces which broke through the forward defence zone and troops would be dispersed to deter attack by airborne forces and to defend coastal areas.

The armed forces of countries adopting this sort of defence policy would have no main battle tanks, long-range combat aircraft, or warships. Combat aircraft would be confined mainly to single-role interceptors, and naval ships to fast missile patrol boats and diesel submarines for coastal defence. The ranges of missiles would be limited to those required to bombard the defence zone; maximum ranges would be about 80 kilometres (50 miles).

Countries other than the superpowers will be encouraged to move towards defensive deterrents by the sheer cost of offensive weapons. Already, only the superpowers can afford long-range multi-role combat aircraft, large warships, and the latest main battle tanks in numbers which make strategic sense. The next generation of offensive weapons will, of course, be even more costly. In the 1990s, therefore, the armed forces of the smaller powers will be increasingly supplied with defensive weapons. Chemical and biological weapons, however, can be produced cheaply and easily by small countries, and in militarily significant quantities. In 1984 Iraq used mustard gas against Iran, and the USA was preparing new types of nerve gas munitions.

The capability to produce weapons of mass destruction – nuclear, chemical and biological – is spreading to more and more countries. The planet, and even outer space, is being increasingly militarized. The superpower nuclear arms race is out of political control. We seem to be drifting to nuclear catastrophe. But more and more people are realizing the dangers of future wars. Perhaps the pressure of public opinion may yet force politicians to move back from the brink.

Terrorism

MARTIN WALKER

'Treason doth never prosper: what's the reason?/For if it prosper, none dare call it treason' quipped Sir John Harington four centuries ago. The same can be said for terrorism. One person's terror is another's legitimate tactic in a political struggle. Moreover, terrorism works. It is a tried and tested method by which small and determined groups can impose their political will upon society.

The question is to define legitimacy. The German government of 1942 condemned acts of sabotage and murder in its occupied European territories as terrorism. In Britain and the United States these terrorists were hailed as freedom-fighters, the valiant resistance against Nazi oppression. Depending on your viewpoint, terrorists or freedom-fighters were partially or wholly responsible for bringing about Ireland's independence in 1922; for liberating Algeria from the French in 1962; for the independence of Cyprus in 1960; Kenya in 1963; and so on. And should the Palestinians regain their homeland and a conventional government, they will be hailed as fighters in the people's cause.

Victorious freedom-fighters? The IRA in the streets of Dublin, 1922.

Terrorism is not simply a feature of the modern world. It is as old as governments. The Jewish struggle against the Romans, Henry V· at Harfleur, the Thirty Years' War and the Spanish guerrilla war against Napoleon all saw campaigns of terror. St Thomas Aquinas and John Locke were prepared to condone a terrorist tactic such as assassination of a tyrant.

And terrorism is unlikely ever to go away. Indeed it is far more likely to spread beyond its traditional arena of politics and into the spheres of organized crime, commercial competition and economics. Political terrorists and conventional criminals can be interchangeable. Al Capone's protection rackets, like organized crime in the present day, depended on terrorizing people into cooperation. Today's organized crime is a multinational industry with worldwide offices, and its facilities for moving and laundering large sums of money around the globe offer almost perfect cover for terrorists. The first act of what could be called commercial terrorism took place in 1982 when poison was secreted in jars of headache pills, killing consumers across the United States, and provoking an economic crisis for the manufacturer, the giant Johnson & Johnson corporation. And in Jamaica in 1980, terrorism was used as an act of economic warfare; gun-battles in the streets drove away the tourists whose foreign exchange had sustained the Jamaican economy.

It may just be a matter of time before the first nuclear weapon is exploded by a terrorist. It has been a feature of terrorism throughout history that it keeps up with the latest available technology and puts it to tactical use. In the nineteenth century, the Irish used bombs in London, and the Russians who assassinated Tsar Alexander VI made use of the latest invention, dynamite. A distinctive feature of terrorism in the 1970s was the use it made of the availability of international travel. Aircraft and airports themselves became targets. Sophisticated electronics allowed bombs to be remote-controlled. Nationalist terrorists fighting their liberation campaign in Rhodesia-Zimbabwe shot down airliners with

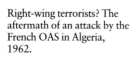
Right-wing terrorists? The aftermath of an attack by the French OAS in Algeria, 1962.

anti-aircraft missiles. If the technology is available, the terrorist will use it. And there is no shortage of nuclear warheads in the modern world. The technology of building an atom bomb is not beyond the capacity of an intelligent science graduate.

Direct and indirect terrorism

In the last 100 years, terrorism has evolved two quite distinct strategies: there is direct terrorism, striking at the very symbols of government or repression, killing the tsar, the chief of police, the general, the landowner; and there is indirect terrorism, striking not at the leaders but at the society they are charged to protect. Ironically, the more effective a government is at protecting its own leaders, the more attractive does indirect terrorism become. If the tsar is too well guarded, then strike at his relatives, or his innocent subjects to point to his regime's weakness, creating a crisis of security and provoking him into imposing more and more security, which will in itself provoke more unrest among the population.

There is nothing new about this ideology of terrorism. Indeed, its intellectual fathers were men of the nineteenth century – Bakunin, Nechayev, Most and Sorel – who glorified violence in a political cause. Bakunin wrote: 'The urge to destroy is also the urge to create.' Nechayev, in his essay 'The Catechism of the Revolutionary', took the argument further:

The revolutionary is a lost man; he has no interests of his own, no feelings, no habits, no belongings. Everything in him is absorbed by a single, exclusive idea, one thought, one passion – the Revolution. He will be an implacable enemy of this world; and if he continues to live in it, it must be only in order to destroy it.

It is a striking feature of nineteenth-century terrorism that its intellectual fathers were anarchists, men who did not believe in political parties, or in promoting their ideas through conventional politics. And because they

Above: Andreas Baader and Ulrike Meinhof, leaders of the German anarchist group which was active in the 1970s.

The passenger lounge at Lod Airport in Israel, 1972, following an attack by pro-Palestinian terrorists.

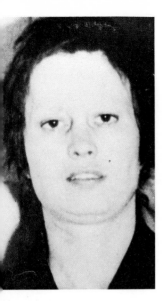

lacked political parties and organization, they had no orthodox levers with which to bring about social change. Terrorism was therefore the tactic of the politically weak and it was intended to *shock* society into change.

The terrorism of the twentieth century is rather different, often seen as one more tactic to bring about a political cause that was already being promoted through a formal political party. Al-Fatah was the military wing of the political movement the PLO (Palestine Liberation Organization). Menachem Begin, the terrorist of 1946, was acting as the military arm of a Jewish political movement which wanted the British out of Palestine, to be replaced by the state of Israel. And it is a strking feature of modern terrorist groups such as Baader-Meinhof in Germany or the Japanese Red Army, that they did not follow the ideology of Nechayev and commit acts of terror in their own country solely to shock those societies into change; they also put their members and their skills at the service of the political cause of Palestine, as if they felt they needed the cloak of moral justification that such a cause might bring.

While Nechayev was writing, the nations of nineteenth-century Europe were building their colonial empires. And much of the history of our own century has turned on the wars to drive the European colonizers out. Such wars of national liberation, in Algeria, in Ireland or Cyprus or Zimbabwe or Vietnam, gave at least a degree of justification to the tactic of terror. But the language and ideology and glorification of violence of the twentieth-century terrorist thinkers uncannily echoed the style of Nechayev. Frantz Fanon, of Algeria's National Liberation Front, wrote: 'Violence is a cleansing force. It frees the native from his inferiority complex and from his despair and inaction; it makes him fearless and restores his self-respect.' And this in turn was paralleled by Menachem Begin, writing in his own history of the anti-British campaign: 'Out of blood and fire and tears and ashes a new specimen of human being was born, a specimen completely unknown to the world for over 1800 years, the *Fighting Jew*' (his emphasis).

Terrorism since the 1970s

The anguish of governments at the wave of terrorism that emerged in the 1970s was caused not only by horror at the violence. It was caused also by governments' fear for their monopoly of violence. There is a tacit acceptance that governments have a special licence to run secret services, to engage in acts of assassination and terror, to make war upon enemy civilians, to damage their crops, bomb their bridges and dams and canals, to blockade and starve them. The distinctive feature of the 1970s' terrorism was that non-governmental organizations were muscling in upon the tactics that governments had thought were reserved for themselves. Ironically, without the backing of legitimate governments, terrorists would find it more difficult to flourish. The government of Colonel Gadafy of Libya, for example, has given sanctuary, finance and weapons to terrorists ranging from the IRA, to Carlos the Jackal, to George Habbash's Peoples' Front for the Liberation of Palestine.

We can in fact trace back the terrorist wave of the 1970s to a conference held in Havana in 1966 under the auspices of the Cuban government. It was called 'The First Conference of Solidarity of the People of Africa, Asia and Latin America' (or the 'Tricontinental' for short). Delegates attended from 82 countries, and the Soviet Union sent a team of 40. Che Guevara, then fighting his doomed guerrilla war in Bolivia, was named President of Honour, and sent to the Tricontinental his celebrated call for 'two, three, many Vietnams'. The Cuban government set up its training camps for Third World guerrillas, and Carlos the Jackal attended one where he was trained under a system devised and supervised by General Viktor Semyonov of the Soviet KGB; Carlos then went on to Moscow's Lumumba University for further training. Veterans of this conference convened another meeting at Baddawi refugee camp in the Lebanon in May 1972.

Some experts on terrorism have argued that every significant terror group of the 1970s can be traced back to Soviet training, funds or support. And Soviet commentators have pointed out that several terrorist groups can also be traced back to the American CIA. Certainly, in 1982, three supporters of the IRA who went on trial in the United States for smuggling guns to Northern Ireland were acquitted by the court after they said that they had worked with the knowledge, approval and assistance of the CIA. And the CIA protestations of innocence in the case of their own former executive Ed Wilson, who ran a terrorist training school for Colonel Gadafy in Libya, were not altogether convincing. It would be remarkable if the intelligence agencies of the world's two major powers were not keeping in close touch with terrorist groups. The classic way of defeating terrorism is to infiltrate it, to take over its purse strings and supply chain, to dominate it and either snuff it out or point it in another direction. Ed Wilson's defence was that he became Gadafy's supplier and training organizer with CIA approval. Perhaps. This is a clouded world and full of double agents. But it is certain that traces of the CIA, the KGB, the French SDECE, Israel's Mossad and the intelligence agencies of an endless list of countries run through the history of modern terrorism as blue veins run through cheese.

'Carlos the Jackal', photographed at Algiers Airport in 1975.

Most vulnerable to terrorism is the open society of a liberal democracy, where the free media permit the deployment of terrorism as theatre; even defeats become media spectaculars. The police siege of and assault on the Japanese United Red Army group at Karuizawa in February 1972 was watched live on TV by 92.2 per cent of Japanese viewers, the rating recorded. Media publicity lent a glamour, and perhaps a disproportionate credibility, to the terrorist strikes. And the security forces themselves learned to take advantage of a glamour of their own, most notably in the SAS assault on the terrorists holding London's Iranian Embassy hostage in 1980.

Terrorists have skilfully taken advantage of other vulnerabilities in open societies, playing upon the humanitarian nerves of governments that would pay a large ransom, surrender prisoners or give free TV-time to guerrilla groups, rather than risk human lives. Such terrorists set governments a dilemma: if they gave in to demands, the terrorists

Anti-terrorist action: the British government used the SAS to storm the Iranian Embassy in London in 1980 after a siege lasting six days.

flourished; if they hardened their hearts, increased their security measures, introduced detention without trial and special courts (as the British did in Ulster), then the terrorists could make propaganda about the repressive nature of the regime.

The Red Brigades of Italy and the Baader-Meinhof gang in Germany were able to provoke the state into stern measures, but they were not then able to mobilize mass support for the state's overthrow. But, in the process, they had dealt a shrewd blow at the legitimacy of the state. The Italian and German and British governments all introduced new legislation in the 1970s that gave the police very much wider powers of surveillance, arrest and detention. These protective measures began an insidious process of driving a wedge between the state and the people it was supposed to represent. Groups who campaign for civil liberties themselves became suspected of subversion. The terrorists had injected a poison into the bloodstream of the state, even in their defeat. And those tough new laws will stay. Searches at airports, searches in the street, phone-tapping and arbitrary arrest had become commonplace tools of democratic government by 1980. The implications are ugly.

In a closed society like the Soviet Union, terrorist groups are denied the weapon of publicity. But they, or even milder dissident groups, could provoke the kind of KGB crackdown, the intensification of security measures, which involved a major propaganda defeat for Moscow. Just as Nechayev's disciples provoked tsarist Russia into the kind of authoritarian over-reaction which bred more opposition, so in 1970 the Tupamaros guerrillas of Uruguay launched a terrorist campaign which ended with the collapse of Uruguayan democracy and the introduction of repressive military rule. The process was given an ugly twist in the Argentine, where the AAA death squads of the police and the army became terrorists on their own account, killing many opponents of the regime and provoking street battles and a state of siege which then was used to justify even more repression. It became a vicious spiral of terror and counter-terror, more repression and more discontent, a government without public support, whose only justification was its own security. And in South Africa, in the Philippines and South Korea – and less visibly in communist countries – this kind of vicious spiral has built up a momentum which has carried into the 1980s and probably beyond.

The continuance of terrorism

There remain a number of obvious candidate causes for terrorism around the world. In 1982, the Vietnamese refugees, the boat people, began to establish and recruit their own liberation groups, aimed at the Vietnamese empire that stretched across South-East Asia. The growing Muslim population of the Soviet Union, and dissident nationalist groups among the Crimean Tartars and the Ukrainians, had their own motives for challenging the Muscovite empire. The growing Spanish-speaking population of the United States, vulnerable to both sides of the long war between Fidel Castro's government and the US-based Cuban exiles, could also prove fertile ground. And in Northern Ireland, the Basque country, the Middle East, South Africa and Latin America, the wars go on, with terrorism just another tactic.

But the evidence of the 1970s, after the Tricontinental meeting and the Baddawi camp conference, was that terrorist groups helped each other, made tactical alliances and provided cross-funding, weapons, identity papers and protection. A terrorist international has a momentum of its own, a bureaucracy and even a tradition.

Against this, the defences that governments can erect are not impressive. The US-Cuban agreement has stopped the spate of hijackings to Havana, and the mutual opening of the French, British and German databanks has made it harder for terrorists to cross the once open frontiers of Europe. But while there are political causes with community support, there will be

Celebrated victim of terrorism: Alda Moro, pictured shortly after his capture by the Italian Red Brigades, in 1978, at whose hands he met his death.

Palestinian guerrilla, dressed in black and armed with a rocket launcher, prepares to go into action.

freedom-fighters, or terrorists, using as targets, as victims, the very people in whose name the terrorists' war is being fought. So they are faced with the old dilemma about whether or not the ends justify the means. There is a broad, if grudging, acceptance of the idea that governments are licensed to use vicious means for decent ends. Measured by results, few wars are worthwhile, but governments continue to fight them and citizens to volunteer. And plainly, the very embrace of vicious means changes the nature of the government or the individual who employs them. The British government is an alarmingly more powerful and potentially repressive system since it began fighting the IRA than it was in the 1960s. And the evidence of the careers of Menachem Begin and Fidel Castro suggests that the men who embrace terror themselves pay a fearsome price when they achieve power. And they exact an even higher price from others. Terrorism pollutes its practitioners, and brutalizes the governments who fight it. And both kill and maim innocent people along the way.

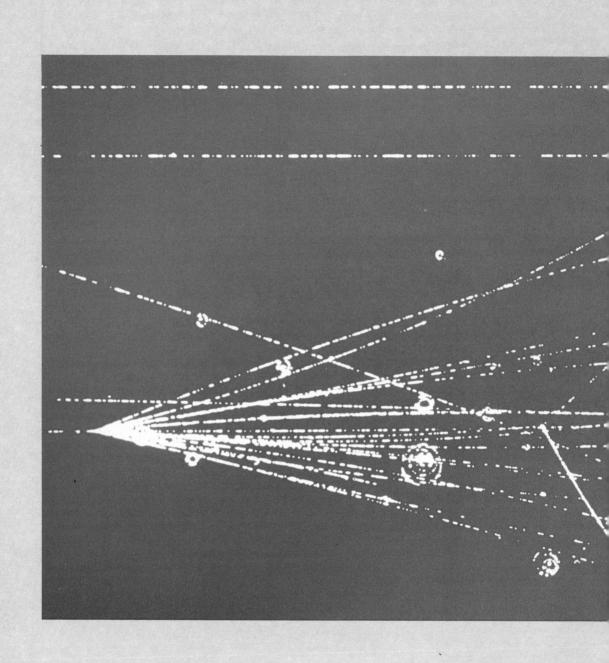

Chapter Six
SCIENCE, TECHNOLOGY AND THE CHANGING WORLD

In this chapter on the applications of science, Duncan Campbell outlines the changes taking place as a result of new insights into the nature of the physical world – from fundamental particles to 'star wars' technology and outer space. Science is not neutral, Campbell argues, and its role in the future will be viewed differently from how it is viewed today.

One of the greatest areas of technological advance has been transport. Mick Hamer considers how transport has developed and plots its future course of development. High-technology magnetic levitation trains, he argues, will take their place alongside rehabilitated forms of transport such as propeller planes, airships and trams.

The frontiers of physics: particle tracks in a liquid hydrogen bubble chamber. The kinks show the points at which particles were located, decayed or underwent collisions. Particles carrying no electrical charge leave no tracks.

The physical world: future insights

Duncan Campbell

During the second half of the twentieth century, nothing has changed the human world more fundamentally than the discoveries and application of science and technology. But by the end of the century, the role of science and technology in society will also have changed dramatically. Modern science was received in a mood of great optimism and certain faith, but has since slowly lost its glamour, its certainty and sureness of touch. Self-doubt among the scientific community and, elsewhere, an explicitly anti-technological (if not always anti-scientific) humanism have been born and will not disappear. By the year 2000, pure scientific research may be regarded as one of many cultural and aesthetic activities, not as an absolute good and priority of itself. Science may indeed become art. Will its concepts and methods change, and if they do, why will these changes have come about?

In the 1940s, in the aftermath of World War II, the potency of organized science and its achievements seemed limitless. Redirecting energy and inspiration from harnessing the power of nature to the machinery of war, the scientific class was set to provide humankind with the tools for a new and harmonious millenium. Even by the mid-1950s, there seemed little reason for the public to question their general faith in scientists and scientific endeavour. In the Western countries, applied science promised rapid advances in transport, in communications, in energy supplies and in production methods. In the developing world, the pursuit of scientific and technological research offered the chance of autonomous progress to the newly independent nations. Science appeared to be a magic wand which would solve theoretical and practical problems for the benefit of all, building economic strength and providing material happiness.

'Big science' and technology's tarnished image

The first change of the 1960s was the development of 'big science'. To keep pace in astronomy and fundamental physical research, increasingly large and costly projects were necessary. Technological applications, from space satellites and their launchers to huge nuclear projects and supersonic transport aircraft, also became more sophisticated and more costly. For the researchers giant particle accelerators, radio telescopes and the space race itself were the glamorous money-getting projects of the decade. But even larger amounts were poured into military research and devoted to the assembly of ever-greater and more widespread nuclear stockpiles, or applied to finding other new or exotic methods of projecting military power. The image of science and technology tarnished, partly through the poor performance of many large technological projects, such as supersonic transport and nuclear power; partly through increasing awareness of environmental pollution and other adverse side-effects of technological progress; and partly through the re-awakening in a wider public of that horror that many physicists experienced when the first atom bombs were detonated over Japanese cities. Science in the 1960s was not delivering the golden age foreseen in the aftermath of war. Most of the fundamental human problems of hunger, disease and poverty seemed as far from solution then as they ever had been.

Science and technology are not directionless. Discovery and development are achieved in the fields where effort is applied. In the closing years of the twentieth century, great progress will be made in learning about the world, and in comprehending limitations to the application of knowledge. A century of scientific progress had also demonstrated that skills and knowledge are not merely acquired at random from some cosmic pool, but that scientific advances and technological progress are most often – although not invariably – won when the human investment of time and effort is at its highest. This realization had led to two sorts of criticism about the direction of scientific research. Governments increasingly ask, particularly at times of economic stringency, that research should be 'relevant' to manufacturing industry and the political needs of a national economy. Critics of society's defects charge that the failure of science to relieve human plight arises precisely because of such pressures. Social, political or industrial criteria do dictate the types of scientific knowledge that are available. With the technological advances expected by the twenty-first century, the gap between richer and poorer nations will widen – adding force to the criticism that historians may make, that much twentieth-century technology was misdirected. They may criticize the vast preponderance of intellectual skill and financial investment which advanced nations had directed towards military research and production, at heavy cost to productive industry, the underprivileged groups and impoverished countries.

Theories of matter and the universe

In the basic physical sciences, theories of matter and the universe initially made great progress after World War II. Great effort went into atomic and nuclear physics, and an array of 'fundamental' nuclear particles other than the familiar proton, neutron and electron were discovered. But for almost 20 years, particle physics stagnated on masses of empirical data, for which no adequate or sufficient theoretical physical explanation was forthcoming. New particles and nuclear reactions were observed and charted copiously and comprehensively. It was not until the mid-1970s, when the once exotic-looking theories explaining the new particles began to seem plausible, that meaning was restored to the inner core of physics. The new theories quickly came to seem unchallengeable. By the 1980s, theoretical progress in physics was fast and forward-looking, predicting new states of matter to be researched over the coming decades.

The ultimate goal of fundamental physics is a single 'unified' theory of nature and natural forces. Four fundamental forces are known – gravity, electromagnetic force, and 'weak' and 'strong' nuclear forces. Gravity is the least powerful force but is nevertheless the most familiar. Electromagnetic forces between electric charges are also well known to most people. The other two forces operate inside atomic nuclei; although fundamental, their effect is complicated and unfamiliar. The strong force holds together the atomic nucleus; without it, the positively charged protons would repel each other and prevent the formation of nuclei, and atoms and molecules (and humankind) could not exist. The weak force is involved in other nuclear reactions, including some causing radioactive emissions.

Fundamental particle research

The particle researchers' basic tool in investigating the structure of matter is the beam accelerator. Research physicists are continually trying to look inside the structure of atoms and nuclei. It is only by producing highly energetic collisions of particles and nuclei that what is inside the nucleus may be observed – by examining what flies out when particles collide. The first accelerators used proton beams, fired at stationary targets. In static accelerators, powerful electric voltages are used to accelerate the beam to high energies. In the cyclotron, alternating magnetic fields accelerate the beam around a loop, so that the beam can acquire extra energy before striking its target. Most recently, beam 'storage rings' and 'colliding beam' accelerators have been built. In storage-ring experiments, beams of electrons or protons, and positrons or antiprotons (the respective antiparticles), are created and then stored in evacuated circular tubes, held in place by powerful magnets. The particle and antiparticle beams are then steered into highly energetic head-on collisions. The first such storage rings were built in France and Italy.

Quarks herald a renaissance

Research into fundamental particles has finally paid off, producing almost a new renaissance in fundamental physics. The renaissance has centred on a new class of particle – the quark. First proposed by theoretical physicists in 1964, quarks were in the 1980s still thought to be 'fundamental' particles, the simplest and most basic form of matter, without inner structure. Only one other group of particles, called leptons, are also thought to be structureless, fundamental particles. However, unlike leptons – which are free particles – quarks are always found bound in groups, making up protons, neutrons and other rarer nuclear particles. Inevitably, of course, theoreticians wonder if eventually they may find that the quarks and leptons are themselves assembled from smaller particles still.

In the first decade after they had been named, quarks, despite the elegance and logical appeal of theories which described them, appeared merely to be clever mathematical artefacts that did not really exist. Although with each passing year the quark theory seemed better and better able to describe the properties of nuclear particles, no one was ever able to see a single quark alone to prove that it did have a separate existence as an identifiable particle. This was still the case in 1984.

If there was a renaissance day, it was in November 1974, when two separate groups of American physicists, from California and New York, announced that they had discovered a vitally important new type of fundamental particle, the ψ (psi) meson. Like all rare and exotic nuclear particles, the ψ meson only briefly existed before decaying into other, more common, particles. But it was very heavy, with a mass more than three times that of a proton, the building block of atomic nuclei. The fact that such a particle should exist at all had been a direct and precise prediction of quark theory; the discovery of the new meson thus gave the theory great credibility.

The existence of the ψ meson in fact showed that there were four sorts of quark, as many had suspected, and not just three. Quarks therefore paralleled the better-known set of four leptons, which included the electron, the everyday particle of physics and chemistry.

Bringing together the physical forces which operate at the atomic level is an important step towards a unified theory of physical forces. Quarks interact to produce the so-called 'strong' force which binds protons and neutrons together as atomic nuclei. The measure of this force is a new quark property, called colour. In order to explain and measure this force, a theory called Quantum Chromodynamics (QCD) was evolved. QCD is very similar in its structure to Quantum Electrodynamics, a highly

Tunnel for the Super Proton Synchrotron at the CERN research plant.

successful theory which has unified the familiar properties of electrical charge with the behaviour of light and other electromagnetic radiation, and with quantum theory. There is great hope that all three nuclear interactions – the weak force, the strong force, and the electromagnetic force – may soon be brought together in one theory, perhaps within a decade. Physicists call this possibility 'grand unification'. One aspect of grand unification that will be confirmed or disproved by the end of the century is the suggestion that all three fundamental forces would have been indistinguishable from each other in extreme circumstances such as existed at the beginning of the universe.

The electromagnetic interaction between electrons which orbit round each atomic nucleus has created the whole of chemistry and biology. In turn, the quarks and their strong or 'colour' interactions create atomic nuclei and nuclear particles, which are the building blocks of physics. By 1984, it was known that there were definitely four, almost certainly five, and probably six different types of quark. Three of these, called the 'up', 'down' and 'strange' quarks, had been predicted by 1970. The ψ meson seen in 1974 was the first evidence for the existence of the fourth quark, called 'charm'. Its discovery also proved the existence of this previously hypothetical physical property.

Evidence for a fifth quark, the 'bottom' or 'beauty', quark, emerged in 1977. By the year 2000, experimental physicists hope and expect to discover a sixth quark, which will provide a partner for the bottom quark. In the 1980s, it was provisionally labelled the 'top' (or 'truth') quark. To find a particle containing a top quark requires even more energetic collisions and particle beams than were used to discover the ψ meson. The energy level needed to create particles containing top or bottom quarks is many times greater than the mass of a single proton. (At the nuclear level, mass and energy are effectively the same. Einstein's famous equation, $E=mc^2$, demonstrated the equivalence of matter and energy.)

Gravity, in many ways the simplest and most familiar of physical forces – and the first to be comprehensively analysed, by Einstein – will nevertheless be the last force to be incorporated in unified theories of physics – if it ever is. In the 1980s and 1990s, a painstaking search will continue, using deep underground detectors, for gravity waves crossing the universe. Physicists are also still searching for evidence of the graviton – the quantum particle that is believed to communicate gravitational attraction, just as an electromagnetic photon carries light radiation. If these effects can be measured, theoreticians can test quantum theories of gravity, similar to the QCD theory of 'colour' forces between quarks.

By the end of the century, physicists should know whether or not there is likely to be yet another layer of matter concealed behind the quarks and leptons. After the discovery of the periodic table of elements, which decorates every school classroom wall, nineteenth-century scientists realized that their success at predicting initially 'missing' (at the time undiscovered) elements pointed to an underlying common structure for all atoms. Will the pattern of quarks soon point in the same direction – to some new and more fundamental type of particle buried inside?

In the 1980s, particle physics is at the forefront of 'big science', and

One of the world's largest accelerators: an aerial view of the CERN plant near Geneva. The white outline marks the position of the underground Super Proton Synchrotron.

research projects remain ambitious and costly. The world's largest accelerators are at CERN (the European Organization for Nuclear Research) in Geneva, at Stanford University, California and at Fermilab National Accelerator Laboratory, near Chicago. By the late 1990s, further high-energy colliding beam accelerators will be in operation at the German DESY laboratory near Hamburg, the Serpukhov and Novosibirsk Institutes in the USSR, and in Tokyo. In 1983, United States scientists announced a proposal to build a vast particle accelerator which would cover an area bigger than Belgium – more than 200 km (120 miles) in diameter. It would cost more than $2 billion. The giant size of such rings is dictated by the energy and speed of the charged particles in the beam – in this case, protons. The faster they go, the larger the required diameter of the accelerator. Meanwhile CERN researchers at Geneva are constructing a Large Electron–Proton Collider in the hope of unearthing new particles that would confirm the 'unified' theory of forces.

By the twenty-first century, these fundamental frontiers of physics will not have shifted significantly. In pure science there will still be massive investment in systems and experiments designed to further knowledge of the universe, and ever more massive accelerators, storage rings and systems for higher energy nuclear studies. Increasingly, research in astronomy and cosmology is overlapping with nuclear physics. The new insights enable the critical and ever earlier moments of the 'big bang' at the start of the universe to be understood. For example, after the first thousand-millionth of a second, the fundamental forces separated. After one-hundredth of a second, protons and neutrons were created.

Space: the new frontier

The bright prospects for significant new steps in understanding the nature of the universe are complemented by the expanding new frontier at the opposite end of the size scale, in space. Astronomers can increasingly reach beyond the limitations of having to peer through the earth's atmosphere. Because of absorption in the atmosphere, many important types of radiation emitted by stellar objects, galaxies or other sources – such as X-rays, gamma rays, and infrared and ultraviolet light – cannot be properly observed or monitored on earth.

The frontiers of research in astronomy had, by 1984, shifted to space. A wide range of astronomical satellites were launched during the 1970s, dominating that decade's progress in astronomy. The most successful of these was probably the Einstein Observatory, one of the three huge High Energy Astrophysical Laboratories sent into orbit by the United States. The first HEAO discovered evidence of a vast amount of intergalactic hot gas – which could have a total mass greater than that of the galaxies, with considerable implications for the understanding of the development and future of the universe. Most of the new astronomical satellites had, unfortunately, relatively short lives, so continuing research requires the participating nations to launch new generations of observatories. Since the 1970s astronomical satellites have produced so much exciting new knowledge about the universe that national space and scientific agencies have remained willing to launch further satellites, despite rapidly mounting costs.

By 1984, a new generation of international observatory satellites was operating in space. The International Ultraviolet Explorer charted the location and appearance of ultraviolet sources whose light would otherwise be heavily filtered before it reaches the surface of the earth. Exosat, a European satellite, and two Japanese satellites, Hakucho and Tenma, measured and plotted X-ray sources. The first infrared satellite intended to study infrared (heat-type) radiation was launched in January 1983. The European Spacelab, which will be launched in the mid-1980s, will be taken into orbit for seven days at a time on board the US Space Shuttle. By the late 1990s, an infrared space observatory will have taken over the task of infrared observation.

The Exosat satellite – an engineering model under construction by the X-ray Astronomy Group, Leicester University, UK.

The longest-lasting space astronomy project of the century will be the Space Telescope, to be jointly constructed and launched by the United States and the European Space Agency in 1986. To keep it operating reliably during its planned 15-year life, it will be visited and serviced by astronauts from the US Space Shuttle. The USSR is lauching a series of satellites which specialize in background radio measurements and has collaborated with the French government to launch a combined radio astronomy and visible ultraviolet satellite in the mid-1980s. In the 1990s, there are plans to launch two ultraviolet telescopes, a Japanese cosmic

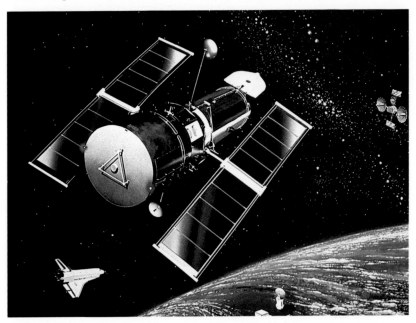

Artist's impression of a space telescope in orbit, showing the space shuttle in the bottom left-hand corner.

X-ray and gamma-ray telescope, and a European Infrared Space Observatory. New research on X-rays may enable astronomers to find and analyse such exotic cosmic objects as black holes and quasars (quasi-stellar objects).

Space exploration will not fare as well as astronomy in the future. In the United States, cuts in the space exploration budget in the early 1980s resulted in the cancellation of several major projects. But funds have remained for several long-range exploration missions before the end of the century, including a new series of probes to Jupiter and Venus. A sun exploration trip – the Solar Polar mission – was cancelled, but European, Japanese and American scientists may jointly work on a new set of exotic projects for the turn of the century, including probes to Saturn and its moon Titan, and to the asteroid belt. These projects, and the continuing development of the space shuttle, mean that the frontiers both of space and of the universe will continue peacefully to be pushed back between now and 2000.

Civil and commercial applications of space technology will continue to blossom. The first communications relay satellites of the 1960s provided a handful of communications channels, available only when the satellite was visible above the horizon in each communicating country. By the 1980s, almost every country on the globe was linked by a national satellite communications station, connected to one or more 'geostationary' orbit satellites, which maintain an apparently fixed position over the equator. The fifth generation of Intelsat communications satellites, launched in the early 1980s by the International Telecommunications Satellite organization, carry over 12 000 telephone conversations each, as well as many TV relay channels.

Specialized regional and even national communications satellites have proliferated during the 1980s, with nations such as India, Indonesia and Canada overcoming specialized national communications problems – for instance, long distances or wide areas of undeveloped land – by satellite. Maritime communications satellites, such as Marisat, have provided uniquely reliable links to ocean shipping. By the year 2000, specialized telecommunications systems will proliferate even more rapidly as many new applications are devised. Already, by the 1980s, there was a shortage both of radio frequency 'bandwidth' for linking satellites to earth, and of orbital positions in which satellites could operate without mutual interference. Research is focusing on using new, shorter wavelengths and higher frequencies, but these frequencies suffer from increasing disturbance by water vapour in the atmosphere. A major new application of the late 1980s and early 1990s is direct broadcasting from satellites. In the late 1970s, the first tentative experiments in satellite broadcasting were completed under the sponsorship of UNESCO.

Space meteorology is another field of important and continuing progress. By the early 1980s, the production of space weather pictures from Europe's Meteosat or the American GEOS satellites had become routine and quite familiar to television viewers in most Western countries. These satellites monitor the earth's surface using visual microwave sensors. New satellites to be launched in the 1980s and 1990s will provide

ESA METEOSAT 1.   EUROPE'S FIRST EARTH OBSERVATION SATELLITE
9 DEC 1977 * FIRST RAW IMAGE * VISIBLE

Meteosat 1, the first European meteorological satellite, produced this, its first picture of the earth in December 1977.

Below: Two commercial communications satellites being made ready for loading and transporting to the launch pad at the John F. Kennedy Space Center, Florida, in October 1982.

more detailed insights into the origins of weather systems and climatic changes by monitoring ocean conditions such as sea state (which includes information such as direction and frequency of the waves) and sea temperature. The first satellite planned to do this, Seasat, was launched in 1978, but failed after operating for only three months. New radar measuring probes will be carried by satellites to be launched in the late 1980s, such as the American Topex satellite and the European Space Agency's ERS-1 satellite. Their probes will measures features of the ocean surface to within a few centimetres, and make it possible to identify with unprecedented accuracy such features as currents and eddies. Although the broad structure of currents is well understood, much more detailed work has to be done on how these currents and eddies move heat from tropics to the polar regions, as these factors have a strong influence on weather conditions.

Space wars

A much more disturbing development in space technology is the proposal that new weapons and military battle stations should be placed into orbit. Although both superpowers have been developing and testing such space weapons as anti-satellite missiles since the start of the space race, the United States took a new lead in the 1980s with a campaign to turn high-powered lasers or particle beam accelerators into space beam

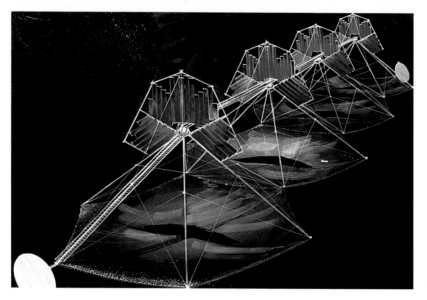

Artist's impression of a solar satellite.

weapons. Under the presidency of Ronald Reagan in the early 1980s, US military scientists were urged to invent and develop ways of using particle beams and powerful lasers as rays to be used from space to attack and destroy hostile satellites and missiles. The most optimistic groups urging these developments in the United States in the early 1980s believed that it would be possible, by the start of the twenty-first century, to achieve what they called a 'space-based defence system'. Space would become a new 'high frontier' for the United States.

Ironically, the phrase 'high frontier' had been in use much earlier, not to describe the possibilities of making war in space but to identify outer space as a new zone of peaceful exploration and possible colonization. International space idealism of this kind ended in the early 1970s, however, a few years after Neil Armstrong's first, epoch-making walk on the moon. Armstrong and his successors walked on the moon because the United States had made the success of his mission a political goal. After the goal had been achieved, the attraction of manned space exploration faded considerably. Unmanned probes, although not cheap, still cost less and operate longer. Now, the idea of giant space stations or moon colonies is no part of any serious vision of the immediate future of humankind. Collaboration will continue in new space experiments; the initially limited experiments aboard the orbiting European–American Spacelab, and the Soviet space stations, will become increasingly elaborate during the 1990s. But none of the dramatic space industry schemes of the 1960s and early 1970s now seem likely. One of the few elaborate large-scale applications of space technology that may still progress, at least on the drawing board, is a design for huge solar collectors to draw energy from the sun and beam it to collecting stations on earth by means of a radio microwave beam. But it is unlikely that the gargantuan cost of such a perpetual solar energy source would be competitive in comparison to either renewable or fossil fuel sources on earth.

Early in 1984, the first new space weapon of the decade was successfully tested by the United States Air Force. This is a missile launched from a high-flying plane, which enters the path of an oncoming satellite in low orbit, and destroys it. By 1989, the United States will have two squadrons of F-15 aircraft able to attack satellites in this way. Negotiations towards an international treaty banning anti-satellite (ASAT) weapons began in 1978, but the negotiations broke down. At the same time as the first ASAT missile was tested, President Reagan ordered United States scientists to begin a massive research programme to develop a ballistic missile defence system, using laser beams, X-ray lasers or similar 'directed energy' weapons. The most feasible beam weapon (if any) is likely to be an X-ray laser system which derives its initial energy from the explosion of an atom bomb at its core.

The development of either offensive or defensive space weapons has serious implications for both past and future attempts to control the militarization of space. After the first satellites were launched in the late 1950s, the United States and other countries agreed that space should be the common property of all nations. No country now threatens to shoot down other countries' satellites, which may orbit over their heads at altitudes as low as 145 km (90 miles). Treaties signed by the US and the USSR decree that nuclear weapons will not be orbited in space, and prohibit the development of anti-ballistic missiles, in order to avoid triggering an anti-missile race as an expensive new feature of the arms race.

Sceptics are certain that the 'high frontier' ideas will not work. Not only are there serious problems in providing renewable energy sources in space, but there would be exceptional difficulty in ensuring that the destructive beams deployed at space 'battle stations' were pointed at their fast-moving warhead or missile targets long enough to destroy them. The destruction system would only be as good as the system for finding targets. Like any other radar systems, it could readily be attacked electronically and jammed.

Nuclear power: the broken promise

In the glamorous areas of high technology, the application of science has fulfilled many technological dreams. The world has shrunk and international collaboration become closer through progress in transport and communications. Cheap computing power and machine intelligence have become available, as anticipated. But cheap energy has not been provided, despite the expectations of atomic engineers during the 1950s. At the high point of atomic optimism, it was claimed that nuclear-generated electricity might flow like water; it would be 'too cheap to meter'.

Technological progress is about making the world work, and nuclear power is one of the dreams that did not come true. Instead of expanding almost limitlessly – as was foreseen in the 1950s and 1960s – nuclear power developments in many countries almost came to a standstill by the 1980s. In the United States, by the late 1970s, there were no new orders to be had for nuclear power stations. Some nuclear reactors had by then operated successfully for over 25 years. But no large reactors had ever produced as much power, or been as reliable as their designers had hoped. Public criticism and alarm became so strong, and government regulation so tight, that nuclear reactors seemed impossible to operate both safely and economically. Nor had there been rapid progress on two future keystones of nuclear technology, on both of which great research effort has been expended. These aspects, which will still be under development in 2000, are fusion research and fast breeder reactors.

Fusion reactors may be distinguished from fission reactors by the nuclear reaction which produces energy in each case. In fission reactors, energy is released when the nuclei of certain isotopes (atomic species) of the heavy elements uranium and plutonium absorb extra neutrons, and split. Some of the mass of the nuclei is released instead as energy. Fusion reactors work on the same principle as the hydrogen bomb, as light nuclei at high temperatures join, again releasing energy. The problem of fusion power is that fusion energy can only be generated in a plasma, composed of high-temperature gas, is difficult to generate and impossible to contain at continuous high temperature. Early experiments in fusion power were confounded by the difficulty of containing the plasma in a magnetic field 'bottle'; the plasma proved too unstable to stay confined, and quickly cooled below fusion temperatures. Although scientists had easily achieved thermonuclear fusion inside a hydrogen bomb, confinement was not then a problem. The purpose of the bomb, after all, is to produce an

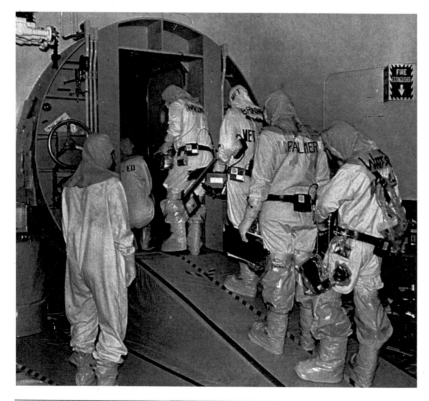

At the controversial Three Mile Island nuclear power plant in Middleton, Pennsylvania, technicians enter the outer airlock to the damaged reactor Unit 2 (1980).

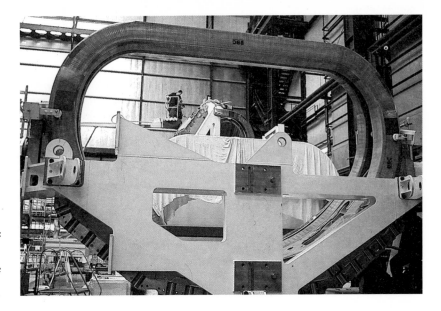

Joint European Torus (JET): the toroidal coil, a device used in experiments in nuclear fusion to confine the plasma (high-temperature gas) within a magnetic field.

uncontrolled and unconfined release of energy. Leading industrial countries are nevertheless continuing fusion research, although a working reactor is not conceivable until well into the twenty-first century.

Fast breeder reactors

Fast breeder reactors are part of the fission reactor system, but are planned to provide an almost 'everlasting' fuel cycle that does not require fresh uranium fuel to be continuously mined and extracted in order to keep the reactor going. Inside a fast breeder, high-energy neutron radiation turns a blanket of non-fissile uranium into plutonium, which can then be used to fuel the reactor's core. The early history of fast breeder reactors was unhappy, with major accidents in both the United States and the Soviet Union. The first US 'commercial' fast breeder reactor, the Enrico Fermi I, near Detroit, partially melted down in October 1966. A year then passed before engineers could properly examine the reactor's core; it was written off and abandoned. An experimental Soviet reactor, at Shevchenko on the Caspian Sea, caught fire some years later but was not permanently damaged.

By the mid-1980s, however, fast breeder reactors were once again under development for the end of the century – but slowly! Five European states – West Germany, France, the UK, Belgium and Italy – agreed in 1984 to collaborate on a plan to develop 'commercial demonstration' fast reactors. The three reactors, to be ordered from 1993 onwards, are proposed to be built in France, West Germany, and the United Kingdom. Although extensive delay in construction is now usual in the nuclear industry, the collaborating nations hoped to have the three 'demonstration' reactors operating by 2000. By 1984, the French were the leading nation in fast-reactor design, having constructed a 1200-Megawatt reactor – the Super-Phénix – at Créys-Malville in central France during the early 1980s. In the United States, work on a fast breeder programme which had been placed in abeyance in the late 1970s restarted in the 1980s. But one of the problems facing the US government, apart from the growing controversy about nuclear power, has been the shortage of plutonium to fuel the reactor. Most of the United States' plutonium reserves had been allocated to building extra nuclear weapons in the early 1980s, and the US therefore explored plans to purchase the necessary plutonium abroad, including from the British government.

Nuclear power has also created the spectre of nuclear terrorism. Many threats have been too convincing to ignore. Between 1975 and 1983 a special Nuclear Emergency Search Team operated by the US government Department of Energy decided that 20 threats were sufficiently credible to require emergency action. One threat was found to be real: a former nuclear employee had obtained spent reactor fuel rods, which he threatened to disperse. The most severe danger of civil nuclear power is if a nuclear weapon were to be fabricated from diverted or stolen fissile material. A terrorist threat to disperse nuclear waste by conventional means would be only slightly less terrifying.

Where is science taking us?

Among other important technological developments by the turn of the century will be the widespread availability of computer intelligence at home with powers of remote enquiry, purchasing, ordering, interrogating databases and linking to many other main computers or other terminals. Advanced personal recognition technology, including fingerprint recognition, voice-printing, and automatic facial feature recognition, will be another product of cheap computer power. As nuclear physics advances, the spread of nuclear weapons to over 10 nations is expected by the year 2000. (By the early 1980s, the USA, UK, USSR, France, China and India had tested nuclear weapons; Israel and South Africa were also believed to possess nuclear weapons, while Pakistan, Argentina and Brazil were believed to be well on the way.) Major undersea mineral exploitation will have begun, including both nodules and undersea mining. In the absence of successful treaty negotiations on the sharing of seabed resources, the exploitation of the sea-bed will probably be led by the advanced nations. Major advances in genetic engineering will have taken place, including the factory production of insulin and other complex biochemicals by genetic engineering techniques. But there will be more, rather than less, extensive use of 'old-fashioned' fossil fuel sources.

Scientific and technological progress is customarily represented, particularly in the press, as a series of automatic advances in which more and more of the universe is objectively unravelled. But science is not objective in this sense: the perceptions of a researcher affect the way that even fundamental physical laws are discovered. The progress of technology is even less straightforward. Particular forms of biology and chemistry, for example, whether genetic engineering or the development of nerve gases, have manifestly emerged because they have been explicitly *sought* as usable technology with a social (or anti-social) purpose.

Genetic engineering: removing an ampoule of cells stored in liquid nitrogen during the manufacture of interferon. Interferon, one of the body's natural anti-viral agents, was discovered in 1957 and subsequently hailed as a miracle cancer cure. Its mode of action on the body is still not fully understood.

Science and war: US Air Force planes spraying a jungle in Vietnam with defoliant in 1964.

Historical surveys of past scientific progress also show that the scientific world proceeds not in a smooth manner, but by means of establishing, and if need be subsequently overthrowing, certain ways of looking at the universe. These 'ways of seeing' are called paradigms. What are the implications for the future of this understanding of how science progresses?

The public character of science and technology will have changed dramatically by the close of the last quarter of the twentieth century. The clichéed image of the scientist – benevolent and wise, omniscient and far-sighted, independent and inventive – has gone. Science is tainted by its own life-threatening achievements, such as nuclear and chemical weaponry. The scientist, too, has been converted from an individualist theoretician to a member of a research industry. Individual genius remains, but most of the increasingly copious flow of scientific research reports are inevitably credited to team effort. That team effort, as we have examined, is socially directed. Applied science and technology move where intellectual interest, public good or private wealth are thought to lie. As a public good, pure science may now be thought independent of culture; in the year 2000, it will be seen more as a part of culture.

Transport

MICK HAMER

Developments in transport have wrought enormous changes in society. Before the railways the speed of travel was limited to the fleetest horse. In 1836 the Royal Mail's coach from London to Brighton took eight hours to cover a distance of 52 miles (88 km). It left Blossoms Inn, in the City of London, at 7.30 p.m., and arrived in Brighton at the ungodly hour of 3.20 in the morning.

Seventy years later a railway train had already broken the 100 mile-per-hour (160 km/h) barrier. And on a more practical level you could catch the 7.15 p.m. train from London's Victoria Station and arrive in Brighton at 8.45 p.m., just an hour-and-a-half later.

Before the railways each provincial town had its own time. But the railways operated to timetables in which minutes counted, instead of hours, and so a standard time, Greenwich Mean Time, was adopted in 1847/8. The railways became the conveyor belts of the industrial revolution. They carried coal to the factories, cattle to market and people to the new seaside holiday resorts.

The railways enabled our cities to grow. In 1782 Horace Walpole could write: 'An east wind has half starved London, as a fleet of colliers cannot get in.' London grew from a town with less than half a million inhabitants in the first years of the eighteenth century to around eight million by 1920, when it was claimed to be the largest city in the world. In 1830, the year that the world's first passenger railway opened (from Liverpool to Manchester), three-quarters of Britain's population lived in rural areas. But such was the growth of the railways that by the 1920s three-quarters of the population lived in urban areas.

All over the world the cities exploded. New York, which barely existed at the turn of the nineteenth century, had 3.4 million people by 1900. It now has nearly 10 million. San Francisco had a population of 340 000 six years before the great earthquake. By 1970 three million people lived there. And Los Angeles in 1900 was still largely orange groves, with a population of just 100 000. Now, seven million people inhabit that concrete jungle.

With the introduction in 1908 of the first mass-produced car, the Ford Model T, which sold for $850, Henry Ford revolutionized the car industry

Model T Fords lined up in
front of the Ford Motor Car
Sales office and garage in
Topeka, Kansas, in the early
1900s.

Traffic on the Champs
Elysées, Paris, 1931.

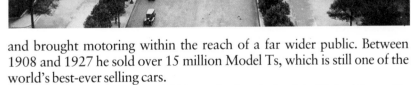

and brought motoring within the reach of a far wider public. Between
1908 and 1927 he sold over 15 million Model Ts, which is still one of the
world's best-ever selling cars.

In 1900 there were about 8000 cars in the whole of the United States. By
1931 there were 23 million, one car for every five people. Fifty years later
in 1981 there were 123 million, one car for every two people. Most of the
growth in the number of cars in Europe happened after the Second World
War. Britain, France and West Germany now all have about one car for
every three people. In 1931 France had one car for every 37 people, Britain
one for every 11 and depressed Germany one for every 127.

This vast increase in motoring has been accompanied by social change.
As fewer people have used local buses and trains, so rural services have
been cut. This produces the paradox that although there has been a vast

increase in travel, the people who enjoy this new mobility are car owners. People who do not own cars are far less mobile than they were, because there is less public transport.

It has been largely a process of the rich getting richer and the poor getting poorer. In Britain, which is a typical Western European country, nine out of ten of the 10 per cent richest households have a car. Only one in ten of the poorest households has a car.

The rate of technological change has now slowed up. The fastest trains from London to Brighton are barely 20 minutes quicker than they were in 1910, over 70 years ago, despite the replacement of steam locomotives by electric trains. In 70 years the change from horse- to steam-power raised the average speed of the London to Brighton journey from 11 km/h (7 m.p.h.) to 64km/h (40 m.p.h.). It has now increased to 80 km/h (50 m.p.h.).

For most forms of transport the great change came in the nineteenth century. To use a motoring metaphor, in the nineteenth century transport changed into a new gear. The twentieth century has only seen a modest acceleration.

The most significant exception to this generalization is the development of air transport. The first aeroplane did not fly until 1905. And it was not until after the Second World War, with the impetus it provided for aeroplane development, that aircraft replaced the luxury liners that used to ply the transatlantic and other sea routes.

Concorde is the fastest commercial aeroplane, with a speed of 1.8 times the speed of sound. On Concorde it is now possible to fly to New York and back in a day, provided you can afford the £2400 ($3400) fare. But although it cuts the flying time from Europe to North America from eight hours to just four, Concorde has not been a commercial success, and no supersonic aircraft are apparently being developed to succeed it.

How computers are changing the face of transport

The major change that is happening in transport, as in other spheres of our lives, is the increase in the use of new technology. There is one school of thought which sees the computer as eliminating the need for transport. Business conferences can be held by computer, without the need to travel. And people can work at home, at the end of a computer terminal, instead of having to commute into the office. However, most experts do not believe that the computer terminal can replace the need to travel, although it might reduce the market for some types of travel, such as the business trip. After all, telecommunications, in the form of the telephone, have been around for 70 years, without having any noticeable effect on the need for people to move.

New technologies are also unlikely to influence greatly the type of vehicles we travel in. Computers and microprocessors are likely to be found more frequently in cars, for example, but they will be substitutes for conventional control systems. The West German electronics company Bosch produces a computer-controlled car ignition system. In a conventional car a fuel and air mixture is fed into the combustion chamber of one of the cylinders. A sparking plug ignites this mixture, and the spark is geared to the rotation of the engine.

This system works, but it is crude. The fuel and air mixture can vary. The spark can be too early or too late. The ignition timing is adjusted only when the car has warmed up. This is fine on a long journey, but cars are mostly used on short journeys. It can take up to 16 km (10 miles) for a car to warm up and during the first 5 km (3 miles) it can consume 50 per cent more fuel than it would do when warm.

In the computerized system sensors gauge engine speed and temperature and monitor the performance of the engine. All this information is fed into a central processing unit which controls the spark and composition of the fuel and air mixture to produce optimum performance at all temperatures and speeds. This saves fuel and reduces pollution (a lot of which is simply the by-product of inefficient engines). On the exterior the computer-controlled car will look much the same as any other car. It will feel much the same to drive and will perform the same task.

Computerized traffic signals

The nerve centre of a computerized vehicular traffic control system set up in Tokyo in 1973 for an initial 5-year period. Computer technology was used to monitor and control traffic over a total of 100 km (60 miles), collecting data about traffic flows and estimating future problems.

The main effect that new technologies will have on transport will concern the information that passengers receive and the way we control our transport networks.

The world's first traffic signals were installed outside London's Houses of Parliament in 1868. They controlled the carriages and carts that thronged Parliament Square. But they didn't last long. They were worked by gas – and before many days of operation they blew up. Since that uncertain start, traffic signals have changed almost as much as the traffic they control.

Conventional traffic signals are controlled by detectors buried in the road on the approaches to the junction. After a set number of vehicles has passed over the detectors on the approaches where the lights are red, the signals change. When traffic is light, the signals work on a fixed time cycle, so that no driver has to wait too long.

This system works quite well for an isolated intersection. But in the heavily congested streets of our city centres the traffic using one intersection will affect others nearby. The desire of drivers to travel in different directions sets up conflicts at intersections. The unseen revolution in traffic control is that these signals can now be controlled by a central computer. The computer synchronizes traffic light changes so as to minimize the number of times a driver is stopped by red lights, thereby smoothing the traffic flow.

The first experiments with computer control took place in the UK, in Glasgow, in the late 1960s and were so successful that many cities have since introduced it, including Bangkok, Hong Kong and Manila.

Computer control depends on the pattern of traffic flow being repeatable – one morning rush hour is much like another morning rush hour. The computers have three different basic programmes, one for the morning rush hour, when traffic is flowing into the city centres, one for the evening, when traffic is flowing out, and a third programme for use outside rush hours.

An even more sophisticated computer-controlled system called SCOOT (the improbable acronym for Split Cycle and Offset Optimization Technique) is being installed in London. And similar futuristic systems are being tested in Sydney, Australia, Toronto and Washington DC. In the new system detectors buried in the roads will automatically feed back to the central computers details of how many vehicles are using each road and the length of queues at lights. The computer will then vary the timing of the lights to take account of varying volumes of traffic.

The difference between these two systems is that in the earlier version the timings of the signals were fixed by a predetermined plan. A change in the number of vehicles passing through a junction could cause a tail-back. However, the new system is much more flexible: the computer is told almost instantly of a build-up in traffic (for instance from a lorry turning over) and reacts swiftly to alter the timings of the signals.

Computerized passenger information

On public transport new technology will provide passengers with a better idea of how long they have to wait. In San Francisco, BART, the Bay Area Rapid Transit railway, has indicators that tell passengers how long the next train will be. And in England, London Transport has installed a similar computer-controlled information system. The indicators give the destinations of the next three trains, the sequence in which they will arrive at the platform (all of which information old-fashioned indicators give) but also how long they will take to arrive.

As a train passes a pre-set point, this information is fed back to a computer. From the timetable stored in its memory the computer can calculate how long the train should take to arrive. This information is updated as the train passes other timing points. If the train is delayed, the computer adjusts its forecast arrival time.

The bus company in the French city of Nice has a similar system at its bus-stops. The display is rather like a lift indicator: lights are illuminated as buses pass fixed points on the route. Similar schemes operate in Tokyo and in a suburb of Toronto. And London Transport is investigating an even more advanced system which will update the forecast times more frequently.

Electronics replace staff

In the year 2000 most vehicles will be similar to the vehicles of today. Cars will look much the same as they do now, as will buses and trains. Aircraft will be wider and able to carry more passengers, although they are unlikely to be any faster. But one trend that is already evident is the use of electronics to replace staff. Railways are well placed to take advantage of automation because of the 'closed' system and the high degree of automation which they have already. Trains, unlike buses, do not need to be steered – the rails automatically take the train on a set route.

London Transport introduced the first driverless trains on its Victoria Line in 1967, although these trains do have a guard whose job is to open and close the doors. The first train to carry passengers without any staff on board ran on the Victoria Line in the early 1970s – unintentionally. After closing the doors and the staff window, the guard has to press two buttons to start the train. The windows, doors and starting mechanism interlock so that the train cannot leave the station with the doors open. On this occasion the train failed to start. So the guard got out to report the problem and slammed the window shut. To the guard's horror, the train moved off for the next station, where it stopped – safely – but without anyone to open the doors and let the passengers off.

Arguably the most advanced metro system in the world opened in Lille, in Northern France, in 1983. It is a radical departure from conventional technology. The train runs on rubber wheels, but unlike the trains on the Paris metro it does not have a back-up set of steel wheels. The trains are

In 1984, 'arguably the most advanced metro system in the world', at Lille in northern France.

entirely automatic. The only staff on the 13-km (8-mile) long line are four ticket inspectors, whose job is to catch passengers who have not paid their fare. The trains have no drivers and no guards. In rush hours there is a train every minute. Yet the line is controlled by just 12 people (including the ticket inspectors). At one end of the line half a dozen controllers sit in a darkened room in front of computer terminals. On the walls of the room are banks of closed-circuit television screens which enable them to home in quickly on any problem. Passengers are in radio contact with the control room.

Despite all this sophisticated equipment, when trains are operating normally the only task of the operators is to change the computer programme from rush hour to the basic programme. The computer even sends the surplus trains into sidings. Only if a train breaks down do controllers intervene. The next train then slowly eases up to the broken-down vehicle and pushes it to its destination.

The attraction of driverless trains is that they economize on staff costs, which form a high proportion of the running costs of any public transport system. However, this gain has to be set against the cost of the automation, which even with micro-electronics is still extremely expensive, and the greater risk of vandalism.

A number of other novel city-transport systems are being built around the world. Adelaide, in South Australia, is constructing a guided busway system, developed by the German firm Mercedes Benz. This has electric trolley buses running along a concrete track. West Germany is also developing an 'H-Bahn' system, in which carriages hang from an overhead track.

Maglev, the hovering train

The most futuristic of these new forms of transport is the magnetic levitation train, or maglev for short. The trains 'hover' above the track on their magnetic suspension and are propelled by a linear induction motor, which draws the train magnetically along the track.

Two high-speed maglev trains are being developed: one in West Germany and another in Japan. Both trains have a maximum speed of 400km/h (250 m.p.h.), considerably faster than the fastest conventional train. The French TGV (train à grande vitesse) has a top speed of 270 km/h (168 m.p.h.). (A special lightweight version of the train holds the world speed record of 383 km/h (238 m.p.h.).)

The German maglev train, which is expected to be ready ahead of the Japanese version, started running on its 21-km (13-mile) test track in Emsland, in north-west Germany, in 1984. The Germans hope that the train will carry its first passengers in the 1990s. And in the United States plans are already being made to open a high-speed maglev line (with German technology) between Los Angeles and Las Vegas in 1991. The trains would cover the 370-km (230-mile) journey in 70 minutes.

The attraction of faster trains is that they may help the railways to win back some of the traffic they lost to the aeroplane. But conventional high-speed trains create a lot of maintenance problems. Maintenance

Maglev (magnetic levitation) high-speed 'hovering' trains are being developed by Japanese National Railways *(above)* and in West Germany.

The French high-speed train (TGV) uses 20 per cent less energy than average express trains and reaches speeds of up to 270 km/h (168 mph).

costs soar with speeds above 160km/h (100 m.p.h.), and the gain in traffic has to be considerable to offset these higher costs.

Maglev offers the prospects of extremely high speeds with low maintenance costs. Because the trains are not in contact with the track – they ride about 10 millimetres (0.4 inches) above it – there is little track wear. And the linear induction motor means that there are few moving parts, such as wheels, to undergo wear.

However, so far the only maglev trains to carry passengers at high speed were at a technology exhibition in Hamburg. There is already a maglev train in operation in Britain, linking Birmingham airport with the city's exhibition centre 800 metres (half a mile) away. The train, the first in the world to be used in public service, was developed by British Rail and started shuttling passengers to and fro in 1984. But this is no high-speed technology: it operates at maximum speeds of only 50 km/h (30 m.p.h.).

Rediscovered vehicles

Perhaps the most remarkable trend in transport over the past decade, and one which can safely be forecast to continue, is the rediscovery of old and discarded forms of transport.

One such example is the airship. The first regular air services across the Atlantic were flown by airships. German Zeppelins began carrying passengers in 1910, when heavier-than-air machines were – in many cases literally – struggling to take off.

British airship development stopped in 1930, when the R101 crashed into a hillside near Beauvais, in France. Among the passengers who died was the Air Minister. But the *Graf Zeppelin,* and from 1936 the *Hindenberg,* ran regularly to the United States and to Rio de Janeiro until May 1937, when the *Hindenberg* burst into flames at Lakenhurst, New Jersey. Thirty-three people died, and transatlantic airship services stopped before commercial aeroplane services had begun. Although the Goodyear Company in the United States built a number of airships for advertising, airship development ceased.

The Hindenburg disaster, Lakenhurst, New Jersey, May 1937.

Below: A Goodyear airship flying over St Peter's, Rome.

But in the 1980s, a British company, Airship Industries, started work on a new range of airships. The prototype, the Skyship 500, gained its airworthiness certificate from the government in 1983, the first airship to have one since the Second World War. Unlike the Zeppelin, which ran on highly inflammable hydrogen and had a rigid skeleton over which fabric was stretched, the Skyship is a pressure airship the shape of which is maintained by the pressure of gas inside the envelope, and its lifting gas is the inert helium.

The new airships will be used mainly to patrol territorial waters and will be tested out by Olympic Airways on passenger services to Greek islands. Airships have natural advantages for this type of service. They are quite fast, with cruising speeds of up to 160 km/h (100 m.p.h.), and do not need expensive airports. Airship Industries is designing a passenger-carrying airship with ten times the volume of the prototype and able to carry 100 passengers.

One of the more curious aspects of the evolution of transport in this century has been the eclipse of electricity. An electric car was the first car to break the 100-km/h (62-m.p.h.) barrier when it set the world speed record in 1898 of 104 km/h (65 m.p.h.).

Electric vehicles have a lot of advantages. They are quiet, pollution-free, cheap to maintain and very efficient at turning power into movement. These advantages, however, are offset by the need to pick up power from conductors, the inefficiency of power stations, and the difficulty of storing electricity. Electric cars could become viable if researchers succeed in producing a high-density battery, various alternatives for which are now being investigated. Meanwhile, trams and trolleybuses are set to stage a comeback.

The French city of Nantes opened a new tramway system in 1985. San Diego, in California, chose for its new rail system, opened in 1981, a tram-like vehicle which runs along city streets. And a similar choice may be made for the light railway that will ply London's docklands.

Trolleybuses often used to replace trams in British cities because the electric distribution system was still in good condition, but in time they followed trams to the scrapyard. Many cities in other European countries,

Birmingham, UK, March 1923. A new 'trackless tram' passes workmen pulling up the rails on which the old trams ran.

however, kept and modernized their trolleybuses. In 1982 the European Economic Community set up a special committee to aid the technical development of trolleybuses, and a year later the first trolleybus to run in Britain for more than a decade ran up a short trial section of wires in a backstreet in Blackpool. It was French, from the new French system in Nancy, which opened in 1982.

A commercial trolleybus operating in Nancy, northern France.

The French trolleybuses have two power sources. Like conventional trolleybuses, they can draw power from two overhead conductor wires. However, they also have a back-up diesel motor, which means that the operator can run the trolleybus under wires on the main sections of the route and run it on its diesel engine to serve less important 'feeder' routes on which it would be too costly to construct overhead wires.

Another relic which could make a re-appearance is the propeller aeroplane. Jet aircraft, such as the Boeing 727, replaced the old turbo-prop planes like the Vickers Viscount in the 1950s and 1960s because they had higher cruising speeds. (A wide-bodied jet such as the Boeing 747 can cruise at speeds of about 1000 km/h (600 m.p.h.), which is roughly one-and-a-half times faster than a Viscount).

When the 1973/4 oil crisis hit, however, the National Aeronautics and Space Administration (NASA) in the United States started looking at ways of saving fuel. Its research showed that one of the best ways was to return to propeller aeroplanes. It came up with a new design for a propeller, with curved wing tips. At speeds of over 650 km/h (400 m.p.h.), conventional propellers create too much drag. But planes with the new design can cruise comfortably up to 890 km/h (550 m.p.h.), at which speed fuel consumption would be cut by 20 per cent. Plans are to test-fly an aeroplane with the new propellers in 1985. If these tests are successful, the plane could be in production by the 1990s.

Pollution, an unacceptable by-product

The rediscovery of old forms of transport is very largely a response to the oil crisis. Transport is the major consumer of oil in the United States and in most Western nations. In 1955 just under a third of all oil was used for transport. By the end of the 1970s this proportion had risen to over a half. And the largest single user of oil is road transport. Ninety per cent of the oil consumed by transport in the United States is used by lorries, buses, and especially cars.

An unwanted by-product of burning oil is pollution. Petrol engines produce three main pollutants: carbon monoxide and various hydrocarbons from the incomplete combustion of petrol; nitric oxide, from the combination of the elements in the air; and lead, which is added to petrol as a cheap way of increasing the octane rating to give better performance. Diesel engines produce no lead pollution, and a lot less carbon monoxide, but more hydrocarbons and nitric oxide, than petrol engines.

Pollution is not only unpleasant (Los Angeles was notorious in the 1970s for its photochemical smogs), it is also unhealthy and may even be fatal. Carbon monoxide is a lethal poison. Running car engines in enclosed spaces, such as garages, often causes death; in tunnels carbon monoxide can build up to dangerous levels. Lead is also lethal. It builds up in the body and can cause brain damage in children even at low doses. Yet it is not an essential additive to petrol. In the United States lead-free petrol has been available for several years, and European countries are at last acting to curb the level of lead in petrol. The hydrocarbons cause cancer. And nitric oxide adds to 'acid rain', although power stations are the main culprits.

All of these pollutants are dangerous. Consequently people are concerned to find ways of coping with the oil crisis which also curb pollution.

Pollution of the air: smog over Mexico City.

The car – number one oil-consumer

The average car uses a lot of fuel. It carries a maximum of four people, comfortably seated, and does between 10 and 11 kilometres per litre (about 25 miles per US gallon). A double-decker London bus is far more economical. Although it only does about 3 kilometres per litre (7 m.p.g.) it can carry up to 70 people. Given that the car is the biggest single problem for the people planning our transport systems, there are three possible approaches.

The first is to cut the amount of fuel that cars use. Motor manufacturers are producing much more fuel-efficient cars than they were a decade ago.

Cars are better shaped aerodynamically and use less fuel to overcome the drag of air as it passes. Modern materials such as plastic can help to cut the weight and therefore fuel consumption of cars. However, there is a limit to the fuel economies that can be achieved. And while it is valuable to use fuel as efficiently as possible this does not solve the problem of oil dependence. It just defers the crisis.

The second approach is to find a new fuel to power our cars. The most commonly suggested substitutes for petrol are methanol or ethanol; a new liquid fuel being derived from coal; and high-output batteries for electric cars.

All these alternatives have their problems. Methanol and ethanol are made from the fermentation or decay of vegetable material. Brazil is currently using ethanol to mix with petrol, so as to reduce its oil imports. However, there is not enough living material around for these fuels to have more than a minor impact. And most of the countries with enough land to grow suitable crops (such as sugar to ferment into alcohol) have much more pressing problems in trying to feed their populations.

Possibly the best bet among the petrol substitutes is a new fuel made from coal. Before the Second World War, some fuels, such as National Benzole, were made from coal. These coal liquefaction processes were discontinued as the price of oil fell, but as it rises once more, they and their modern equivalents become more attractive again. There are large reserves of coal left in the world, so there is no immediate prospect of coal running out, and fuel from coal can be used in vehicles of the same design as those on the road today. However, liquid coal would be expensive: experts talk of prices two or three times the cost of petrol today.

There would be no danger of a shortage of fuel for battery cars either, given a large-scale nuclear power programme. The major technological problem with battery cars is the need to develop a lightweight high-density battery. Conventional batteries, like those used to start cars, are made of lead. They are very heavy and do not produce enough power to make battery cars practicable. Researchers are working on a number of alternatives, including a battery made of sodium and sulphur which would have seven or eight times the output for the same weight as a lead battery. Another disadvantage to battery vehicles is that a national network of recharging centres, or battery swap shops, would have to be created from scratch to replace petrol stations.

The radical approach: redesigning cities

The third approach is to rethink the way we plan our towns and cities. The increase in the number of cars since the Second World War has been coupled with the closure of local shops, post offices, banks and cinemas. These closures have forced longer journeys on us and have therefore increased our own fuel use. Another factor has been the development of suburbs so sprawling that almost every journey, from visiting friends to going to work, requires a car.

The premise of this latest approach is that walking is the easiest alternative to driving. It is a remarkably flexible form of transport, and

The cult of the car has produced drive-in restaurants, cinemas and banks, and now the drive-in church.

does not call for a tank of petrol. Its limitation is that only short distances can be covered. Yet in Britain, one of the few countries to have conducted any census of how much walking is done, one third of all journeys are less than a mile long (1.6 km), and half are under two miles long. Four out of ten journeys are already made entirely on foot, as many as are made by car.

If our cities can be re-arranged so that many of our most frequent journeys can be made on foot, people will have the option of leaving the car at home. If an oil crisis then comes upon us suddenly, people will have an alternative to driving. This approach has been British government policy since 1977, although little practical has been done to implement it. It is also an approach recommended by international bodies, such as the Economic Council for Europe, a United Nations study group.

One drawback to the approach is that many people equate this type of town plan with back-to-back housing, or the tower blocks of the 1960s, rather than the canal-side houses of Amsterdam, the boulevards of Paris, or the leafy communal gardens of London's Kensington. There is also the practical problem that it takes a long time for a town to be redesigned. A house lasts at least a hundred years, usually a lot longer. And it is recent housing developments that are least conducive to walking. In the United States, for instance, there are modern cities which are entirely designed around the car. It is so rare for people to walk in places such as Los Angeles that police often treat pedestrians with suspicion. There have been a number of recent newspaper reports of people being arrested in Los Angeles simply for walking, including one English tourist who had gone out to post a letter. These are the cities that most urgently need redesigning.

Dependence on the car has led to massive changes in town and country. Here, the landscape has been transformed by a motorway interchange around a city.

None of these approaches is exclusive; they can all help to save fuel. The most radical, and arguably far-sighted approach, is the last one, that of giving people the option of leaving their cars at home. If we do it once, then – who knows? – we might even begin to enjoy it.

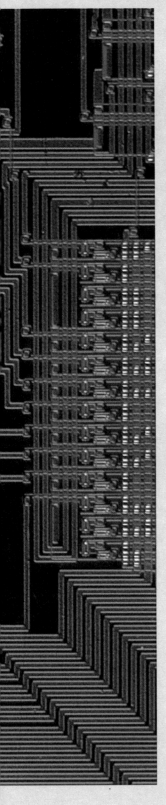

Chapter Seven

THE INFORMATION REVOLUTION

Recent developments in high-speed information transmission and processing – the so-called Information Revolution – have, quite simply, touched the lives of everyone. The spread of cheap computing power has been so rapid that we have hardly caught up with the implications it has for the present, much less the future.

Ian Graham looks at the pros and cons of the Information Revolution and considers future technological developments, including artificial intelligence.

But what will be the future of the press as we know it? Martin Walker is optimistic about the survival of 'quality' newspapers as providers of much-needed perspectives and background to up-to-the-minute television and radio news coverage; Michael Elkins is concerned that so much emphasis on sensation in news coverage will make us too impatient to bother with the all-important What?, When? and Why? of news stories.

The circuitry of the tiny 'silicon chip' – which forms the heart of the modern computer – is so complex that computers are used to help to design it. It is shown here, greatly magnified.

Communications present and future

Ian Graham

It is a popular notion, encouraged by gee-whizz technologists and trend-spotters, that we are at the beginning of the Information Revolution. Central to this notion is the assumption that information is now synonymous with power. Information has achieved its influential status, because it can be processed and transmitted faster than ever before; and capturing the right information first in the business world means getting the edge on your rivals. As we shall see, it also imparts power of a sort to the private individual.

The 'revolution' has come upon us because of an explosion in the development of two previously separate and incompatible technologies: the imposing information-processing power of the computer is being linked with high-speed telecommunications to form a data network spreading like a spider's web across the face of the earth.

Computers have been around since the Second World War and telephones have been in increasing use since the end of the nineteenth century. So, what has changed? Until recently, the telephone system was

A question of scale: *(left)* ENIAC (Electronic Number Integrator and Calculator), one of the earliest computers, was built by the Americans in 1945 to perform ballistics calculations. Today's computers are much smaller and much more powerful, thanks to the development of the silicon chip *(above)*.

too inefficient to carry high-speed computer data, but this was not a problem because, until the 1970s, the only people who could afford computers were governments and big businesses.

Served by teams of specialists, these computers were awesome machines occupying several rooms, their owners having complete control over the information they contained. However, by replacing large, fragile and power-hungry vacuum valves or 'tubes' with smaller transistors and then integrated circuits (or chips) each containing thousands of transistors, the computing power of these early mammoth computers was squeezed into a case the size of an average office typewriter. Eventually, the control centre of the computer itself, its central processing unit (CPU) containing thousands of separate devices, was successfully crammed onto a single chip, called a microprocessor, now known popularly as the silicon chip.

Microprocessor-based desk-top computers could be used by a single operator instead of a large team of specialists and, by the end of the 1970s, they were sufficiently compact and inexpensive to be offered for sale to the general public. The technology is now so cheap that children play games with computerized toys that sit in the palm of your hand. Millions of computers are sold in department stores every year and a computer sub-culture has sprung up, served by its own books, magazines, clubs and radio and television programmes. To use a well-known analogy – if the car industry had progressed at the same rate as the computer industry, a family saloon would now cost less than £5 ($7), run for life on a pint of fuel and generate enough power to shift the *QE2* along at a respectable speed. It is partly the very cheapness of the technology that permits it to infiltrate our everyday lives.

Meanwhile, in the office, word processors and electronic typewriters with computer memories are rapidly taking over from conventional typewriters. A word processor allows the operator to correct and edit correspondence, records, orders and so on, on the computer screen before printing them out, saving the typist from having to make several drafts before the final version is agreed. Larger office complexes may use a number of word processing terminals linked to a central computer, a system called networking, which allows several operators to share expensive facilities which would otherwise not be fully used by a single operator. Data in the shape of documents, correspondence, statistics, etc., can also be passed from one terminal to another in different offices in the same building or in different cities or continents. The data passing round the network need never be committed to paper. This is, in effect, electronic mail.

But the Information Revolution is more, much more, than simply an upsurge of new technology for pushing office paperwork around or for playing Space Invaders. The availability of small, cheap computers means that vast amounts of information can be stored in computer databases and retrieved extremely quickly. Different files can be compared and correlated, enabling operators to spot trends or anomalies that might otherwise be missed. The tiniest computers can be used to control

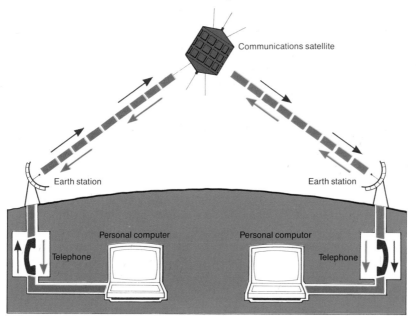

Computer communication using the telephone lines. Computer to computer links by telephone may include a satellite relay.

anything from office and industrial machinery to home heating systems or even robots, and the hunt is now on for ways of producing ever more intelligent and independent computers, capable of what can reasonably be described as 'artificial intelligence'. The problem with predicting how this technology will affect us in the future is that we tend to underestimate the pace of technological innovation and fail to interpret accurately how future social, political and commercial factors will influence the 'take-up' of technology by society at large.

Data communication

Communication is now easier than ever before. You can pick up a telephone and talk to someone almost anywhere in the world. An increasing number of countries are changing to computer-compatible digital systems which offer a much better quality of voice reproduction.

The medium of communication today – into tomorrow: hair-thin optical fibres. Optical fibres consist of an inner core which carries the information, coded into pulses of light, and an outer cladding which surrounds it. They will replace the bulkier and less efficient coaxial telephone cables (below).

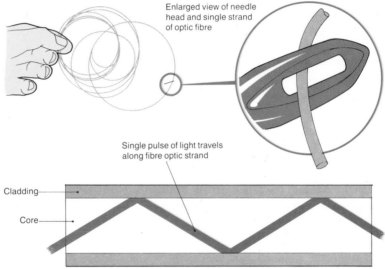

Enlarged view of needle head and single strand of optic fibre

Single pulse of light travels along fibre optic strand

Cladding

Core

The older 'analogue' system is subject to electrical interference on the line. Using digital coding, the voice is transformed into a series of pulses resembling the morse code. As long as a pulse is present at the call's destination, regardless of whether it has suffered any interference, it is read as a pulse. The receiver detects the pattern of incoming pulses and reconstitutes the voice from them, ignoring the intereference. Well, that's the theory at least.

The older copper telephone cables are, in many places, reaching their maximum call capacity. They are gradually being replaced by optical fibres, in which voice and data signals are carried by a very fine laser beam travelling along a hair-like strand of glass. These glass fibres are capable of carrying television and computer data signals in addition to voice telephone calls and they can carry many more calls than a copper cable of the same diameter. Optical fibre telephone lines are also claimed to be impossible to tap – something of interest to computer operators who distribute data by telephone.

Communications satellites are certain to play a more prominent role in the future. The current trend is for satellites to become larger and more powerful, with a corresponding reduction in the size and complexity of ground equipment. According to predictions from Lockheed and British Aerospace, by the year 2000 we should be able to communicate with one another using wristwatch radios and powerful satellite radio-links. Perhaps they will be the twenty-first century equivalents of the mobile radios now used by the emergency services and others to keep in contact with base.

Security

It used to be the case that large, unwieldy computers were needed to store, process and interpret information, but the availability of powerful microcomputers means that anyone can process and interpret data to their own ends. Thus, in future, computer data itself must be protected more effectively. Information once held in card files and in filing cabinets is now much more portable. It exists in computer memories, and it also travels along telephone lines and through the atmosphere as high-frequency radio waves. It may be stored on magnetic tapes and disks compact enough to be hidden in a small case. Computer security is becoming a major headache.

How do you stop someone dialling your company computer and reading all your confidential files? The programs that manipulate sensitive data in a computer have built-in safeguards. Before you can read the files, the computer must be satisfied that you are authorized to do so: it may ask you for a password, but clever computer snoops have been able to bypass password security.

It is even more difficult to stop someone from intercepting data transmissions from a satellite. The security risk is not simply that someone might read the data. If the electronic intruder manages to link his personal computer to, say, a bank computer (no mean feat in itself), he could not only read the contents of its memory, he may also be able to put bogus data into the computer – perhaps creating a healthy balance for his non-existent account – or he could erase important files. The miscreant need not even risk a traceable telephone call to his computer victim. In some parts of the world, the United States for example, small inexpensive radio transmitters can quite easily be bought and used. The transmitter can tap the existing phone lines allocated to the computer (which may not be as secure as the computer itself) and the data it picks up can be received on an ordinary domestic FM radio, recorded on tape for later use or fed directly into another computer.

Public data

It is relatively easy to acquire the hardware and software (computer programs) necessary to use a public 'Viewdata' service. A central computer holds constantly updated information on the national and international news, weather, travel problems, finance and television and radio programmes. You simply call it up on the phone and, once your home computer is linked up to the central database, select the information you want from a 'menu' or directory which appears on your computer's screen. As your computer is physically connected to the database by a telephone cable (or optical fibre), two-way communication is possible. When an index page (or frame) appears on your screen, the database computer waits for you to tell it which option you want, by pressing a key on your computer or touching the screen. Some systems, like Prestel in the UK and The Source in the United States, offer an electronic mail service. You type messages into your computer and send them by telephone to the database, where they are stored and await collection.

In many businesses all work is now handled through computer systems. This is the London dealing room of a large international bank.

In an alternative videotex system (the generic term for a system that distributes computer-generated information which is viewed on computer screen or adapted television sets), pages of data are broadcast on the unused lines of the television picture signal. The service is broadcast free with programmes, so it is not (yet) capable of supporting two-way communication as in the case of cable-distributed Viewdata.

Of course, not every kind of information is freely available. Airlines store their passenger booking information in computers. If you visit a travel agent, he or she will probably book your flight by communicating directly with the airline's computer via a telephone link. Why can't you do that yourself from home? In theory you can, but the travel agents are, not surprisingly, jealously guarding their private computer links. Other computers hold confidential information on stocks, shares, insurance, exchange rates and so on, and if the general public had access to and understanding of it all, a well-heeled layer of our society – professional financial consultants – would virtually disappear. Thus, there are areas of very useful data, which are at present exclusively available to specialists in those areas, and which are unlikely to be offered to the public for reasons of commercial or political protectionism.

More information should not be confused with better information. Information stored in a computer must have been put there by someone. So, when faced with a television screen full of information or advice from a database, ask yourself where it has come from and what interest the 'information provider' has in it. If possible consult alternative sources.

Artificial intelligence

The Nippon Electric Corporation has announced a translator device capable of 'listening' to spoken English and translating it into Japanese. NEC claims that by the year 2000 simultaneous translation between any two languages should be possible. Imagine how such a device could transform international relations. It's yet another example of a development in technology that breaks down barriers between nations. Of course, it also means that an indiscreet pronouncement from any government, translated and distributed in the wink of any eye, might provoke an extreme and ultimately undesirable response which today would be avoided by the delayed release of diplomatically sanitized statements.

It is much easier to make a computer speak than to make it understand spoken language. The problem with voice recognition is that we all speak at different rates, with different accents and with different degrees of clarity, using colloquialisms and idiosyncrasies. A device that could cope with all that still could not assume that we all use our respective languages perfectly, leaving no room for confusion. NEC's DP200 Connected Speech Analyser seems to be on the way to solving those problems.

There are basically two methods of making a computer talk. It can store a given vocabulary spoken by a human 'teacher'. The stored words can then be put together in different ways to make the required sentences. This method limits the computer to the vocabulary it was given, but the voice is very lifelike.

The vocabulary limitation can be overcome by the second method. A selection of vowel and consonant sounds can be stored instead of complete words. All the words we use are composed of around 50 sounds, called phonemes. Each phoneme may be pronounced in one of several ways – called allophones – depending on how it is used. If a computer is programmed with these allophones together with the rules of the language to be spoken, it has an unlimited vocabulary. The disadvantage is that the voice is not yet very lifelike because it is not modelled on a real voice.

Voice synthesizers are already much in evidence. In the UK, Leyland's Maestro car tells you how it is 'feeling' – engine too hot, low fuel and so on. Children's toys give spelling tests. Some recorded telephone messages, so-called because they were once recorded on magnetic tape, are now generated by computer voice synthesizers. Voice boxes are often available for home computers.

Just because a computer can hear and speak does not mean that it is an intelligent machine. It will recognize and produce only those words it has been programmed to. Research, principally in the United States and Japan, is aimed at developing new computer programming languages and techniques to enable the next generation of computers to make assumptions and to jump to conclusions in the same way as we do. It is by no means certain that the research will bear fruit – research in artificial intelligence (AI) has been going on for more than 20 years and has made very little progress. Even so, there is so much at stake commercially and militarily if the research pays off that an international AI race is gradually picking up momentum and governments are releasing more funds for the work.

Robotics

The contrasting functions of robots. *Top:* The 'Salisbury Hand' holding a glass of wine. This is a 4-degree articulated gripper robot under research at the University of Massachusetts. *Bottom:* A bomb detection and disposal machine on duty in the streets of Belfast.

Robotics researchers have a difficult time. Whatever marvels they achieve in the laboratory, these pale against the walking, talking, reasoning metal men that populate science fiction sagas. Most of the devices that we call robots are merely computer-controlled industrial mechanical arms. Today's programming methods are simply not up to building a robot capable of reasoning. Computers do precisely what they are told to do. The next generation of computers should do rather better, using thought processes similar to our own. They may use heuristics (rules of thumb) to gain a knowledge of the world. That is the problem. Computers today operate in a vacuum: they store facts as a rag-bag of unconnected items which are called into a program as required. We need a method of treating information as a network of interconnected and cross-referenced items, not only subject to the rules of the language but also related to an understanding of the real world – a microelectronic model of the human brain, in fact.

Interestingly, developments in computer hardware may take computer design closer to that of the brain itself by using protein molecules instead of silicon crystals to store information. This is the much-heralded 'biochip'. Today, computer chips, each carrying hundreds of thousands of components, are produced by etching microscopic circuits onto a sliver of silicon by means of ultraviolet light projected through a photographic mask onto the chip. Using this method, transistors one-tenth of the diameter of a human hair can be made, and lines can be drawn on the chip's surface only one-thousandth of a millimetre apart!

The race is on to develop ways of writing finer lines on the silicon substrate to produce more and more densely populated chips. The more devices that can be packed onto a chip, the faster it will operate, because the electrons (the electrical charge carriers) have shorter distances to travel. It also means cheaper chips. The cost of making a chip has stayed roughly the same for the past 20 years, but the number of devices contained on that chip has increased by hundreds of thousands. Design has become such a complex operation that Computer Aided Design (CAD) equipment is now essential in the production of ever more complicated chips. If you like, the present generation of computers is being used as an aid to designing the next generation.

The increased complexity of computer chips makes it more difficult to ensure their reliability. It is one thing to guarantee reliable operation of a chip containing, say, 50 000 devices. It is quite another to provide adequate quality control for chips containing perhaps a million elements, each of which has to be exactly right. And these are chips whose behaviour is, or should be, perfectly predictable and repeatable. How does the industry go about quality controlling a biochip computer whose major attribute is that it can make assumptions and jump to conclusions in a creative manner? How do you know if it is working properly if no two problem situations need necessarily result in the same action or solution?

The future – social and political effects

What does the future hold for us? More information? More computers? More communication?

In the leisure field, computers games are sure to progress, possibly in conjunction with video disk technology, offering us more-demanding games to test our hand–eye coordination. Some commentators have expressed concern over the increasing popularity of games in which you track the enemy fighter or spacecraft and once your fire control system has locked on to it, you blast it out of the 'sky'. The players are distanced from the killing, desensitizing them to the effect of their actions.

In the real world of military defence, computers already play a vital role and we have seen what can happen when defence computers interpret events wrongly. The problem is that in response to the ever-watchful computer network, weapons systems are necessarily becoming more adept at evading detection until the last possible moment in order to give themselves the best chance of getting through to their targets. Delivery systems, too, are getting faster in trying to strike home before the enemy has time to respond. That, in turn, calls for even faster missile detection, identification and response. Ultimately, it reaches the insane stage where, if one power is to retaliate to a nuclear attack, it must do so as soon as the other's pre-emptive strike is detected. But what do we do, if, after the missiles are on their way, we discover that the computers have made a mistake? For that reason, I think that total computer command of strategic weapons systems is extremely unlikely to come about.

We shall certainly have greater access to information of all sorts in the future, and communication between individuals throughout the world should be easier, barring political interference. The computers used in our homes are sure to be more 'user-friendly' than they are today: they will be almost as easy to operate as the average hi-fi. If voice recognition research pays off, what could be more user-friendly than a computer that understands verbal commands. There is no reason why this facility could not be extended to other consumer products, but it might have disadvantages – watch what you say, the microwave might overhear and take offence!

Of course, the worry in many people's minds is, will computers replace them at work, fuelling unemployment? Political and commercial pressures, however, are as much factors in the equation as the technology. Computers will still continue to disrupt current work patterns, but not always for the worse. Someone has to design, build, sell, install, maintain, repair and provide supplies for computers, and the people who fulfil those functions need to be clothed, fed and supplied with all the materials necessary for their work, thus creating jobs elsewhere. Computers have also made possible a new breed of home worker. People who work mainly with information (journalists, accountants, clerical workers, and so on) need not waste time and money commuting to and from a central work-place. They can do all their work on a home computer terminal and send it to a central collection point by telephone. Indeed, some people already work in this way.

Where once the ownership of computers was severely limited because of high costs, they are now produced so cheaply that they are regularly used in education from the primary level onwards *(below)* and in the home for both work *(right:* a journalist's word processor) and pleasure.

But are we ever going to create the world envisaged by E. M. Forster in *The Machine Stops*, a world in which people live like battery hens in individual cells, never meeting, communicating through their video phones, their micro-environment regulated for maximum comfort and cleanliness? It is extremely unlikely that we will turn ourselves into battery hens, unless of course we really want to. By and large, we get the society we want, and human beings are social animals. The technology is more likely to enable us to be better informed, and that can't be a bad thing. However, the existence of more and more computer files charting the leisure, expenditure, employment, health and private paths of our lives is a matter of concern for us all. Linking the computers that hold all this information could form the basis of a powerful surveillance and social control network, which we surely ought to resist.

Computers, communication and artificial intelligence undoubtedly bring benefits undreamed of even a few years ago, but like any tool they can be used wrongly, to the detriment of the individual. It is in our interests, therefore, that technological progress should be accompanied by measures designed to safeguard the liberty and privacy of the individual. If computer files are to assume more importance in our lives, then we ought to be able to examine and if necessary challenge the information held in those files. In some countries this is already possible. In a word, technology should be our servant, never our master.

The future of the press

MARTIN WALKER

At any time up to the 1970s, Gutenberg or Caxton could have walked into the press room of any newspaper in the world and been familiar with the printing technology that produced it. Newspapers were still dependent on a system of movable type that had endured for five centuries, bringing daily newspapers, magazines, mass literacy and cheap books in its wake. The development of Gutenberg-style printing involved a cultural and social revolution. The new technology of the 1970s and beyond, of printing by computer and laser beams and satellite, will bring another kind of social change. The problem is that nobody knows what kind of change that will be.

Some firm predictions can be made. By the end of the century, grass will be growing in London's Fleet Street, as the rumbling, inky heart of the business, the great rotary press machines which can print a hundred million pages a night, are finally retired. Newspapers will still be written and edited in Fleet Street, but they will be written onto computer tapes, and printed at dozens of small print-shops around the country. This will save time and money and will allow national newspapers to insert pages of local news and advertising for each area in which they are printed. In Britain, this involves a revolutionary change in the finance of the press. For a century, national newspapers have been printed in London and distributed around the country by rail. This meant that only advertisers with national products to sell wanted to buy space in their pages. They will now be joined by advertisers buying space on the pages inserted for the local market.

In the United States and Australia, where sheer distance has inhibited the development of a nationwide newspaper service, changes will be rather different. The *Washington Post* is now planning the newspaper of the 1990s; 24 pages costing a dollar at today's prices, in contrast to the current 100-page paper costing 25 cents. The difference is that the massed pages of classified advertisements selling homes and cars and offering jobs will almost certainly be surrendered to the databanks. This began to happen in Britain in the 1970s, when houses, cars and even potential spouses went on to the Teledata computer, available via a local telephone call.

The Gutenburg Bible, 1457. Early printing was designed to look like the writing of scribes – Gutenburg called his invention 'artificial writing' and wanted to limit printing to small numbers of fine books.

Until the 1970s, basic type-setting methods *(right)* had changed remarkably little over several years.

A modern printing works, the Goss Community Press, Sweden.

The *Washington Post* will be selling to its readers not the daily local marketplace of the last hundred years, but a high-quality assessment of the news and information being generated in the government centres of the Western world. The US federal government is on the *Post's* doorstep. Indeed, the paper is the city's second biggest employer after the federal government. But whereas traditionally the *Washington Post* has taken 75 per cent of its income from advertising and only 25 per cent from sales, that revenue—sales ratio is likely to be reversed. In 1980, the *Washington Post* could have given away the 600 000 copies it sold each day, and still have made a profit from advertising alone. By the year 2000, if it is to be financially self-sufficient, the sales income will be vital.

Enter the multinationals

This change in the pattern of funding accompanies a change in the nature of newspaper ownership around the world. The classic newspaper proprietor until the 1960s was the press baron, someone who owned newspapers and nothing else, and loved the sensuality of power that went with it. But, increasingly, the newspapers are becoming only one part of huge, corporate empires. The *Washington Post* owns television stations, warehousing companies, timber and pulping businesses and *Newsweek* magazine; and the *Washington Post* and the *New York Times* are now both big enough corporations in their own right to qualify for the list of the 500 biggest US businesses. This pattern of corporate growth is international. In the UK, the giant Trafalgar House property company owns the *Daily* and *Sunday Express* and the London *Standard*. Lonrho, the mining multinational, owns the *Observer*. The *Times, Sun* and *News of the World* are owned by publisher Rupert Murdoch, who owns papers, television companies and an airline in Australia, and papers, radio stations and magazines in the United States. Murdoch and the Canada-based Thomson newspaper empire (which sold London's *The Times* and

Sunday Times to the Australian) are the first of a new breed, the multinational publisher.

The process is still in its infancy. So far, there have been only hesitant attempts to merge the news-gathering functions of the globally-owned papers. But given the high expense of covering international news, it is inevitable that large corporations will reduce their costs by using their global news staffs to give each of the papers within the empire a common service. Already they can offer advertisers a global market, selling space in papers across three continents in one convenient transaction. The process is made the more lucrative by the trend towards newspaper monopoly markets. Only 20 American cities still have more than one paper to offer their citizens, which means higher profits for the corporate owners, but less choice for the readers.

And the profits of newspaper publishing, thanks to the new labour-saving technology, can be immense. In the course of the 1970s, the profits of the *Washington Post*, for example, leaped from $4000 per employee to $17 000. But because of the databanks' threat to the old monopoly of classified advertising, the *Post* is aware that such profits may be a temporary phenomenon, generating the cash to finance further investment in the satellite technologies of the future.

Newspapers vs television

It is unlikely that the newspapers will see much challenge to their role from the other beneficiaries of satellite technology, the television and radio news systems. Experience suggests the reverse. The increasing saturation of the US market by television has been paralleled by an increase in the profits – and the power – of the papers that learned to live with the new media. It was the *Washington Post*, not a television station, which exposed Watergate and toppled an American president. In Japan, it was the papers and magazines, not television, which hammered away at the Lockheed bribery scandal until Prime Minister Tanaka was driven from office.

A 60-minute television news programme contains about 6000 spoken words – or about the same as one-and-a-half pages of the *New York Times* or *Washington Post*. The papers not only give more news, but they put it into a fuller and more coherent context. Papers have long since abandoned the idea of trying to compete with television and radio for immediacy of news. But the raw data of a news event is only of limited value, without the kind of background information, the cross-referencing and assessment that papers have the space, and the incentive of an increasingly informed and literate audience, to give.

And if newspapers fear the competition of television, there is nothing to stop them competing directly. The *Washington Post* and *New York Times* and the Murdoch group already own television stations. In Japan, experiments have been under way for some years into the electronic newspapers, in which readers can 'buy' individual pages of *Asahi Shimbun* through their television screens. Up till now, the results of the experiments suggest that readers still tend to buy the whole newspaper package.

The headquarters of Times Newspapers, Gray's Inn Road, London.

During the Falklands crisis of 1982, the British *Sun* was guilty of the worst kind of chauvinism. *The Guardian*, politically to the left of the *Sun*, was more restrained in its tone.

Television screens simply cannot match the portability and the convenience of the newspaper, although it is cheap to 'view-buy' the paper by scanning its pages on the screen. But, so far, to have those pages printed out by a printer connected to the television set is about seven times more costly than it is to buy the paper at a news kiosk or on subscription.

But if the future of the quality papers, which survive on their high standard of news assessment and review, seems assured, the popular press has already found its own method of living with television competition. Britain's *Sun*, with a daily circulation of over four million, has become an entertainment rather than a news package, running about one-third of the number of pages devoted to public affairs that its predecessor, the *Daily Herald* did in the 1930s. It devotes a minimum of four pages a day to television previews and features, and has become a daily guide to the leisure industry, finding popularity and prosperity in the process.

All newspapers, 'quality' and 'popular', have a political influence and power, a capacity to set the agenda for public debate, to impose the editor's own perspectives and priorities upon the reader's attention. This power of the press is likely to increase, rather than diminish, although the new corporate owners of the papers may deploy this power in the corporate, rather than the public interest. The Trafalgar House group in Britain, which also owns the Cunard shipping line, directly used its *Daily* and *Sunday Express* newspapers to demand public subsidies to build ships in Britain, rather than buy them more cheaply abroad.

And the power of the press is becoming international. The *Wall Street Journal* now publishes, through satellite technology, in Asia and Europe as well as across the United States. The *New York Times* has outgrown the city which bred it, with satellite printing in Chicago, and eventually in California. London's *Financial Times* now publishes in West Germany too, and the *Toronto Globe and Mail* now publishes across Canada. The press is using the new technology to move beyond national constraints, and a potentially alarming international influence will follow. The fundamental question now is whether journalists' and editors' responsibility and integrity will grow to match that frontier-crossing power, and to restrain its temptations.

Television 'news'

MICHAEL ELKINS

On 27 March in New York City at 8.37 in the evening, a man named Arnold Barnes unlocked the door of his flat in Concord Towers on Madison Avenue. He walked into his bedroom and began beating his wife to death. However, Mr Barnes, who was apparently under some emotional stress at the time, forgot to switch off the alarm system within the required eight seconds of the entrance to his flat. And the following resulted.

The infrared sound cameras were activated, recording the action on videotape and instantaneously transmitting image and sound to the monitoring screens at the Manhattan headquarters of the Argus Security Company. At the same time the camera's code number automatically flashed on the screen. The duty supervisor typed the number on the monitoring keyboard which called up from the memory bank all the relevant information concerning the Barnes family. He then pressed the red button, and all this – picture, sound, information – was immediately conveyed to the alarm centre at Manhattan's 18th Precinct police headquarters. There the night-shift commander flashed the details to the car consoles of the three police patrols closest to Concord Towers. The first officers to the scene rushed into the building, took the express elevator to the 18th floor, shot the lock off the door to the Barnes's flat and burst in – just in time to grab at and to miss Mr Arnold Barnes as he hurtled out of the window and crashed to his death on the pavement 144 feet (44 metres) below.

Inside the flat, Mrs Barnes was already dead. The entire incident, from the time Mr Barnes entered his flat to the time he left it, took five minutes and three seconds. It was witnessed in exact detail and as it was happening by 310 272 residents of New York City and its environs. This, as the subsequent audience poll showed, was the number of fortunate people who were awake and in their homes at the time, and were subscribers to TNCN – the Time News Cable Network which has the exclusive on the line rights to the Argus Security Company's system in the New York area.

On that same 27 March and at almost the same time – New York time – 118 000 New Yorkers were watching a National Cable News transmission, via the Cosmos Communication satellite, of the voting in the European Parliament which would eventually bring about the first government of the United States of Europe. And also at the same time, 1.5 million subscribers to the cable sports features in the Greater New York area, were watching the world heavyweight championship fight being staged in the Central African Republic. And about five million New Yorkers were tuned in to one or the other major networks; among their choices was a rerun of one of the old Johnny Carson shows, and the latest episode of *Sons of the Ewings*.

And in Cincinnatti, in Chicago, in Miami Beach and in Los Angeles the sons and daughters, the grandchildren, the nieces and the nephews of Marcus Eliason's extended family were watching over closed-circuit television the Bar Mitzvah of the patriarch's first great-grandson taking place in New York City.

Visual news can be transmitted quickly by wire to be used in newspapers or stored in agency files.

All that on 27 March in the year 2000. I present these fancies in the spirit of a 'docu-drama', which is itself a lusty, awkward and difficult offspring of our contemporary first age of television, and, as in the docu-drama, my scenario has more than fancy in it.

We have at this moment the technical knowledge, and will very soon have all the technical equipment, to bring about everything I have suggested, and to extend the horizons of communication to a reality as yet unimagined.

Right now, in my own city of Jerusalem, anyone with a couple of thousand dollars or a credit card can buy what is called a ground receiver. Plug it into a variable-direction antenna, and you can receive any television programme, live or videotaped, being transmitted anywhere in Europe. With the new American Mid-East commercial satellite in operation, such a ground receiver will enable you to pick up any programme being transmitted at any time anywhere in the United States of America.

We can already transmit visual material, including film and videotape images, over an ordinary telephone line, across the United States into home receivers which reconvert the electronic impulses back into picture and sound. Potentially we can do this from anywhere in the world, to anywhere in the world. Pocket-sized video cameras using infrared and light-intensification devices are already in production. Linked to orbiting satellites through hand-carried consoles the size of an attaché case, these cameras will render meaningless time, distance, light, dark.

What are the probable ramifications of all this? Closed societies, closed countries, will be wrenched open like oysters being raped of their pearls, by men and women and, for all I know, ultimately by robots and *doppelgängers* equipped with miniature video cameras and *boutonnière* microphones. To such societies and such countries every reporter, every tourist, will be a spy – uncontrollable, except by being locked out or locked up. And then what? By then the great media conglomerates will have hooked on to the spies-in-the-skies satellites, or sent up satellites of their own.

In time, such media use of satellites will have to come under some form of national or international control – spying, after all, has to be reserved to governments. And then what? By then, and in accordance with well-established practice on less stratospheric levels, government sources will leak satellite information to the print media, and pictures and sound to the electronic media, for political purposes, just as now.

The amount of information available and the speed with which it comes to the communication centres will in turn dictate an ever-increasing speed with which it must all be transmitted to the reader, to the listener, to the viewer. The stuff must get to the consumer. It must be eaten quickly, otherwise it spoils. Minutes can turn news into history, and who is interested in history?

News and the media

In general television, and to some extent in general radio – what might be called the massive mass media – the pressure of the information available will leave no air time for anything other than its transmission. This transmission, so quickly done, will be an undigested, indigestible lump. Information without context is no more than sensation, a BBC colleague once told me. Never mind, sensation is saleable. News analysis, however, like truth, is the daughter of time, and there will *be* no time. So, in the massive mass media there will be no analysis, particularly not in television news. There is little enough now. The commentator, that guy who stands in front of the camera even now is known contemptuously in the trade as the talking head. Who listens? It is the pictures that count.

Television news bulletins – a 'talking head' presents information without background, context or analysis, but his audience is more interested in the pictures than in what he is saying.

It used to be that the indispensable ingredients of a news story consisted of answers to the questions Who? What? When? Where? and also, Why?

Not any more. Not in general television, little in general radio. You cannot see a 'Why?' or hear a 'Why?' – that takes too long. The 'quality' print media at least, for want of an easier word – a few newspapers, fewer news magazines – will continue for a time to analyse the news and put information into a meaningful context. But if they do too much of that, too few will read it, and if they do too little of it – well, television can do a lot more of too little, and do it a lot better.

I have a great deal of love, but not much hope, for the good newspapers. Back to television then. Perhaps there is a smidgen of hope there. I suggested at the beginning that cable television will proliferate, and will begin to specialize – seeking to sell a special product to identifiable groups of consumers: Crime News Cable Network, Cable Sports Features, and so on. Perhaps we will get the thinking man's cable television, CNAN –

Right: Pressmen outside the Prime Minister's London Residence, 10 Downing Street, during the Falklands conflict in 1982. Access to information about the crisis was strictly controlled by the government. The debate about national security and freedom of information in Britain remains unresolved.

New technology has produced smaller, more portable film equipment, giving the camera operator and the viewer access to more and more places, people and situations.

Cable News Analysis Network, but I doubt it, and anyway, not for long.

I have concentrated on television because it is already the dominant news medium, and the technical marvels that will emerge within the next two decades will, I think, make that dominance absolute. It is a prospect that gives me little joy. Perhaps I am wrong. Prophecy is an uncertain art. I hope I am wrong, but I am reasonably certain of one thing: the problems of the media and the public weal which people have been discussing for decades past will still be unresolved when the year 2000 rolls around.

The symbiotic relationship between government and the media, the right of the people to know, the need of the government for confidentiality, issues of freedom of the press, and public accountability, the right to publish, and the right to privacy, investigative journalism, campaigning journalism, and what is now emerging from the Third World, what might be termed developmental journalism – all these media-related issues, which bedevil us now, will continue to haunt us well into the year 2000 and beyond.

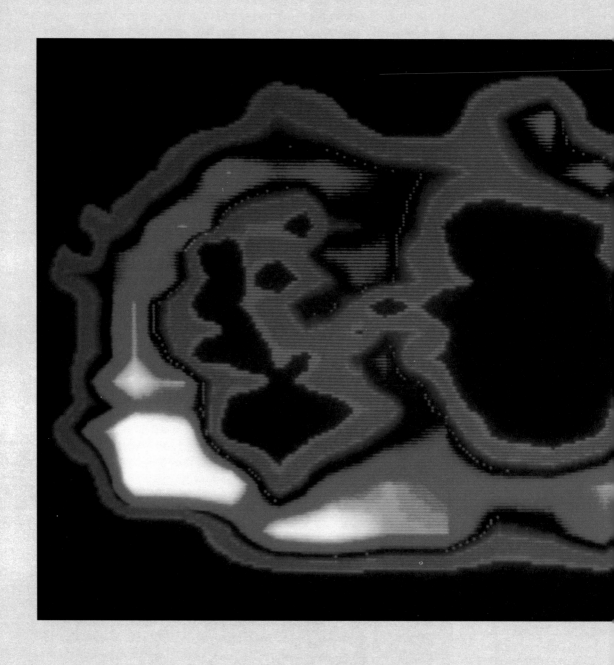

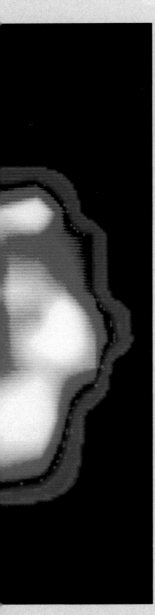

Chapter Eight

NEW DIRECTIONS IN MEDICINE

Richard Hawkins presents a critical overview of some of the more
startling technological innovations in medicine – their successes and
failures – while hinting at a paradoxical call from our society to change
the course of medical practice. Ironically, this comes at a time when
China – one of the main practitioners of alternative medicine – is
reassessing its own medical philosophy and looking more towards
Western technology. Christiaan Barnard takes up the dilemma
concerning the place of medicine in the world today and its way forward
in the future.

Photograph of a cancer cell, taken with a Nuclear Magnetic Resonance Scanner.

High-technology medicine

RICHARD HAWKINS

'Shulubin dragged himself from one outpatient clinic to another complaining about frequent calls of nature, rectal blood and the pains. They did every imaginable test on him except the simplest one of all, feeling with the finger. He read, understood, and with his own finger he felt his own tumour.' With these simple words from his novel, *Cancer Ward*, Alexander Solzhenitsyn scorns the crass stupidity of technological medicine thoughtlessly applied. It is an oft-repeated theme. Even Aldous Huxley admitted that George Orwell in *Nineteen-Eighty-Four* had presented a more plausible picture of the future than his own image, in *Brave New World*, of a world made stable and happy by scientific discoveries and chemical conditioning.

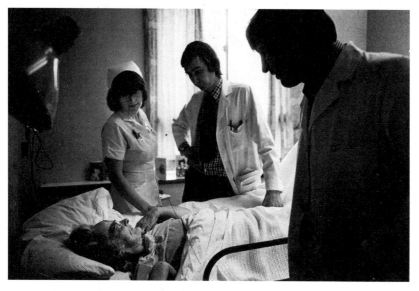

In an age of high-technology medicine, a rapport between doctor and patient is still important. Doctors, nurse and patient at Bromley General Hospital, UK.

In the UK there has been a swing of the pendulum away from 'hi-tec' medicine, as the ideology of optimism that once drove Aneurin Bevan to create the National Health Service has now given way to disillusion. Bevan passionately believed that by massive, initial expenditure on health he could create a nation so healthy that it would hardly need any further medicine. He was sadly mistaken.

New emphasis is being put on 'person-centred' medicine, in which the patient him- or herself is primarily important, and not the technology surrounding the patient. Many doctors and patients would seem to welcome the move. At the same time it would be absurd to abandon or ignore the astonishing technological advances that have been made in recent years. Let us consider some of these successes and some of the failures.

Birth control

No medical fields have seen more exciting developments in recent years than the fields of contraception and fertility. These developments have made real the future possibility of safe contraception, and a child for every couple who wants one, even if they have brought with them certain moral problems that cannot simply be ignored.

The 'pill' remains a technological triumph. It has been in use for over 20 years now and despite strenuous efforts to link it with cancer of the breast and cervix (neck of the womb), no major complications have so far emerged. Gradually formulations of the pill are being marketed with lower and lower doses of the female sex hormones, estrogen and progesterone, that control conception. These lower-dose pills are believed to be safer to use that the original higher-dose ones.

Manufacturing the contraceptive pill, men wear protective clothing.

However a number of problems still persist. To be effective the pill has to be remembered every day (the hormone levels are so low); and therefore it is ineffective if vomited up, or when the patient becomes seriously ill. (Occasionally women have discovered that they have conceived after a severe illness or bad accident, despite continued use of the pill.) Moreover it still makes some women suffer from depression, some put on weight and others feel unwell. For these reasons a number of alternatives have been considered.

One of these is the 'morning-after' or 'post-coital' pill which is only taken after intercourse. It is hoped that, wisely used, this pill will further reduce the total amount of hormones that a woman has to absorb, and therefore minimize the side-effects. A further variant is an intramuscular sex hormone injection which gives protection for long periods. The nearest to receiving widespread recognition so far is a preparation called Depomedrone which needs to be injected monthly, but it is expected that longer time-spans will be achieved.

The idea of a male contraceptive pill was popular at one time, but its realistic use remains some years off. The main trouble is that most pharmaceutical companies have lost interest in developing it. For one thing, research has proved expensive, but also it is now thought that it would be unacceptable to either men or women. Men might be afraid that taking hormones continuously would have a lasting effect on their fertility; women might be unhappy at leaving all the responsibility to their partner. In addition, it would prove particularly costly: it has been estimated that 5000 kg (11 000 lb) of male hormone would be needed annually compared with the 14 kg (31 lb) of female hormone used at present. Furthermore men would need to take hormones much longer than women because they remain fertile well into old age.

By contrast there is considerable enthusiasm for developing a contraceptive vaccine. Such a technique would be particularly suitable for developing countries where sophisticated, expensive contraceptives are not appropriate; and where an infrastructure for the administration of vaccines already exists. Unforunately, major technological problems are being encountered, so that this option will not be available for many years to come.

Coping with infertility

The most exciting developments in recent years in the Western world have been new methods of conceiving and screening babies. This might seem a harsh irony for the Third World, awash with healthy, unwanted babies but, of course, for the individual couple it represents a most marvellous advance.

The oldest form of artificial reproduction, artificial insemination, has been used since the English surgeon John Hunter helped a childless couple conceive a child using a warmed syringe filled with the husband's sperm. This technique has recently been improved so that it is now possible to enrich and concentrate the man's sperm if it tends to be weak, and thus increase the chances of a conception. If the man's sperm is completely infertile, the couple can now be offered artificial insemination by donor (AID) – the donors often being medical students. This is possible because of the recent development of sperm banks, where sperm can be successfully frozen for as long as 15 years. Up to 10 000 babies a year are born in the United States using AID, and it is becoming ever more popular because it raises the possibility of a child not only for childless heterosexual couples but also for single women and lesbian couples.

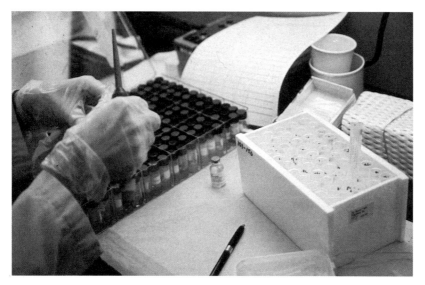

The existence of sperm banks, where sperm can be frozen for up to 15 years, raises many controversial issues. On the one hand they spell hope for childless women, but on the other they open up the possibility of undesirable social controls.

The major cause of female infertility is blockage of the Fallopian tubes. This prevents the sperm from reaching the female egg (ovum) to fertilize it. All sorts of methods have been tried to unblock these tubes including, most recently, microsurgery. Some success has been achieved, but new hope was given to those who remained persistently infertile by in vitro fertilization, a new technique developed by Robert Edwards and Patrick Steptoe, in 1978. For the first time ever an ovum taken from a previously infertile woman was fertilized outside her body, and then replaced in her womb where it grew into a normal baby. These techniques have been considerably modified, so that successful pregnancy rates of up to 50 per cent are now being recorded.

Today, it is even possible for an ovum taken from one woman and fertilized in the laboratory to be put into another woman's womb. A perfectly normal baby will grow although the mother has no genetic link with it.

There is another technique that also works along rent-a-womb lines. A woman is artificially inseminated with semen taken from the husband of an infertile wife. The resulting embryo forms in her womb but, before it can become firmly attached to the walls, it is flushed out and transferred to the womb of the wife, who carries and gives birth to the child – although, again, she has no genetic link with it.

The different combinations and possible ramifications are complicated. The important point is that a woman can now carry and give birth to a child with whom neither she nor her husband or partner has any genetic link. At the moment the focus is on the thrilled couples and the superb technology. But the future sociological, psychological and even genetic implications are quite unknown.

Producing the 'perfect' baby

For some couples conception is easy; the problems start when they have an 'imperfect' or handicapped child. 'Hi-tec' medicine is beginning to go some way towards preventing this.

Considerable publicity has been given in the media recently to the concept of 'cloning' humans, or the manipulation of genetic material within cells so that unwanted features are eradicated, desirable features introduced and a 'perfect' baby produced. However, the reality is quite different: the most that has been achieved so far is that substances such as insulin, growth hormone and interferon have been produced by these genetic engineering techniques. Even if society were prepared to condone it, the day when super-humans can be 'cloned' is still a long way off.

More immediately relevant to preventing handicapped children being born are the recent developments in ante-natal screening. Much the most important of these is the use of ultrasound scanning which has become so common on both sides of the Atlantic that a copy is regularly included in the family picture album. It seems entirely safe and can pick up congenital abnormalities (e.g. spina bifida) between seven and eight weeks of pregnancy.

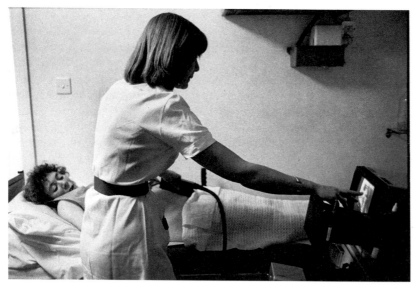

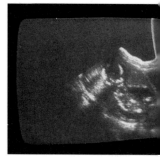

An image of the fetus appears on the screen during ultrasound scanning. The woman is 14 weeks pregnant.

A 15½-week-old fetus as seen on an ultrasound scan screen. Ultrasound is used to detect fetal abnormalities in women thought to be at risk. In some countries it is now used as a matter of 'routine'.

The other major development is called trophoblastic sampling. By this technique a sample of the webby filaments that surround the fetus can be safely taken at seven to eight weeks via the neck of the womb, and examined for congenital abnormalities. This so-called trophoblastic tissue has exactly the same genetic composition as the baby because it has developed from cells from the mother's egg, after fertilization with the father's sperm.

The main advantage of these techniques is that a diagnosis can be made at seven to eight weeks of pregnancy so that an early abortion can be arranged if desired.

These 'hi-tec' medical sampling techniques have significant implications for the future. As many as one in ten people are affected by a disease with an appreciable genetic component, such as Down's syndrome, congenital heart disease, spina bifida, thalassaemia, haemophilia, cystic fibrosis, epilepsy or diabetes. If genetic mapping techniques also advance to the point where the chromosomes that carry the genetic 'mistakes' causing these and other diseases can be accurately described, then this knowledge could be combined with the sampling techniques to screen for the unwanted diseases. The ethical issues attached to this procedure, however, are likely to stimulate a great deal of public debate.

Heart disease

In the 1960s the 'epidemic' of coronary heart disease (CHD) in the Western world was widely compared to those of plague or smallpox. In England and Wales alone, mortality among men had risen by 41 per cent in the decade between 1950 and 1960. CHD had become easily the commonest cause of death before age 60 – causing three times as many deaths as road traffic accidents, lung cancer and breast cancer combined.

Yet, since the 1960s, the epidemic has slowed considerably. In some countries there has even been a dramatic reversal. In the United States, for instance, mortality from CHD declined by 29 per cent in the years 1968–78. In other countries such as Australia, Japan, Israel, Canada, New Zealand, Norway and Belgium there have been lesser but still substantial declines. Another triumph for 'hi-tec' medicine, perhaps?

Unfortunately not. The astonishing fact is that the outlook for a patient having a heart attack is little better today than it was 20 years ago – despite the huge sums spent on research, special coronary care units, drugs and specially trained staff. Recent trials have shown that, on average, a patient having an uncomplicated heart attack is just as well off at home in bed, as in the middle of the best-equipped coronary care unit. It is a damning indictment of 'hi-tec' medicine in the curative field.

Since patients are not being cured of CHD fewer must be developing it. No one is certain why this should be; it is probably due to a combination of many things. Certainly there are fewer people walking about today with very high blood cholesterol levels (often believed to be associated with heart disease); and generally, consumption of high-cholesterol foodstuffs such as butter and cream has declined. In the United States it fell by about 25 per cent between 1963 and 1980. There are also fewer people with dangerously high blood pressure, and smoking too is on the decline.

Surgeons performing open heart surgery on a one-month-old baby, London 1983.

The major influences on the decline of CHD are thus the so-called primary preventive factors. 'Hi-tec' medicine, however, is also beginning to make a small but significant contribution in helping to prevent CHD. Most important of all is coronary artery bypass surgery, which in the US is now a more common operation than appendicectomy. This is a remarkable achievement considering that sophisticated equipment like artificial heart pumps has to be used every time the operation is done. The purpose of the operation is to replace the patient's narrowed or blocked coronary arteries with veins taken from the legs. At first the operation only helped patients to enjoy life more; but now, with improved techniques, they live longer as well.

Early diagnosis is a vital ingredient of a successful preventive programme. The heart trace electrocardiogram (ECG) has been making diagnosis easier for some years, but even more helpful results are now being achieved by a miniature heart recorder, which is strapped to the patient and records the patient's heartbeat continuously. Most usefully, it can record changes that occur when the patient has chest pain or suddenly feels unusually breathless. Before long it will be possible for this heart trace to be transmitted onto a screen in the doctor's surgery so that he can make an instant diagnosis, and start treatment if necessary.

It is often assumed that this sort of high technology must be prohibitively expensive, but it need not be so – particularly as the techniques become widely available. For example, in the United States a coronary bypass operation is more expensive than a hernia repair but less than a major bowel operation for cancer. Set against the costs of a patient with heart failure repeatedly having to see doctors and be admitted to hospital, the operation costs do not seem so high.

The artificial heart and other techniques

The logical extension to replacement of damaged coronary arteries is replacement of the whole heart. Both heart transplants using donors, and, more recently, a total artificial heart implant have been attempted. In December 1982 Dr Barney Clark, a retired dentist suffering from severe heart disease became the first patient to receive an artificial heart. He lived for 112 days after the operation. The heart itself functioned well, but Dr Clark suffered recurrent lung and kidney failure and one prolonged fit. Throughout he bravely asserted that it was all worthwhile, but there seems little doubt that the technique is still experimental.

Some surgeons believe that the technology involved in the total artificial heart is still too complex for the immediate future, and that a more realistic

The major blood vessels of Jarvik 7, the artificial heart used in the first human total artificial heart implant on Dr Barney Clark in 1982.

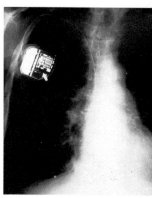

Left: Pacemaker monitoring equipment linked to the patient; *(above)* X-ray photograph showing the implanted pacemaker in position.

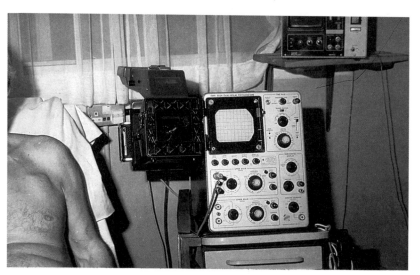

approach is to insert electrical assist pumps which help a diseased heart to pump blood round the body. So far, only diseased calves' hearts have been helped by the pumps, but the technology should not present major problems. The pumps are expected to be widely used by the late 1980s.

Much simpler but already well tested is the artificial heart pacemaker. Over one-third of a million people have already benefited from them since the first one was inserted in 1958. The latest-designed ones have the capacity to give a little shock to the heart should it develop a dangerous rhythm that might bring on a heart attack.

The most futuristic, but perhaps most hopeful, development would be the use of laser beams to 'core-out' blocked coronary arteries. First produced in 1960, the laser is now used for delicate brain, eye and skin surgery, and for destroying lung, throat and bladder cancers. Its use would be a great step forward for heart surgery since no traditional operation would be needed. The scalpel would be bloodless.

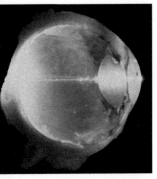

How a laser beam is used in eye surgery. The beam passes through the eyeball (right to left) to weld a detached retina.

Stroke

Just as the heart may fail if its blood supply is cut off, so the same thing may happen to the brain. This condition is known as 'stroke'. About three-quarters of stroke cases are caused by blockage of the arteries to a particular part of the brain; the remainder are due to a haemorrhage through a weakness in the walls of an artery. It is a major cause of death and long-term ill-health. In Britain about 50 000 people die each year from stroke. In the US it is the third commonest cause of death: at least 200 000 Americans die annually, or one in ten of the population. Almost as important are the same number of people who survive a stroke but are permanently handicapped by it. Fifteen per cent are so disabled they have to stay in a nursing home permanently; only a half recover enough to be able to look after themselves.

Clearly, strokes present a major challenge to modern medicine. Yet the sad fact is that, like a heart attack, the outlook for a person having a stroke today is little better than it was 20 or 30 years ago. It is true that brain scans conducted after a stroke can now differentiate between the major types, but this is as yet an almost worthless advance since so few of the stroke types can be treated. In just a minority of patients who have survived a haemorrhage, skilled neurosurgery may help to reduce the chances of a recurrence or alleviate the symptoms, but the numbers are very small. In the vast majority of cases the best that 'hi-tec' medicine can do is to make the lives of the patients a little more comfortable. There can be no question of a cure.

The key to the eradication of this disease must therefore be prevention. The risk factors are similar to those for heart disease except that a person with raised blood pressure is at much greater risk: seven times more likely to have a stroke than someone with normal blood pressure. The 38 per cent fall in death due to stroke in the US since the introduction of the National High Blood Pressure Education Program in 1972 is proof that a preventive programme can work, and, if the estimated remaining 23 million Americans with high blood pressure were also screened and treated, it is predicted that the overall stroke death-rate would fall a further 20 per cent.

Cancer

Cancer is a condition in which some cells of the body get out of control and multiply out of proportion to their site and function. This uncontrolled growth may cause solid tumours (lumps) as in lung and breast cancer, or be widespread cancers like leukaemia. With a few notable exceptions – Hodgkin's Disease, leukaemia, cancer of the ovary and testis, for example – 'hi-tec' medicine has so far made pitifully little difference to how many people get cancer and how long they survive once they have it.

Many scientists feel that the major advances in the fight against cancer have been made by the sort of important studies of the distribution and incidence of disease (epidemiology) which have linked lung cancer with smoking, X-rays with marrow cancers, and low roughage diets with bowel cancer. They believe that we should be spending our resources on preventive studies rather than on expensive 'curative' high technology. The problem is that there are already many patients with cancer and they cannot simply be abandoned while we await the results of studies which often take years to produce reliable, meaningful conclusions. As Sir George Godber, Chief Medical Officer at the Department of Health and Social Security (1960-73), wrote in the *British Medical Journal*:

get away from this silly emphasis on prevention which is said to be better than cure. Prevention is better than curing only if you have not got something that needs curing, or more commonly, needs support. Prevention is needed for its own sake, and is not an alternative to someone else's cure – or even an economy now in most cases.

Other scientists feel that since so little is as yet known about preventing cancer, the answer is to screen populations at risk continuously so that it can be detected early, and removed before it spreads to other parts of the

Someone's protest in the continuing controversy in Britain about the ethics of cigarette companies' advertising and sponsorship.

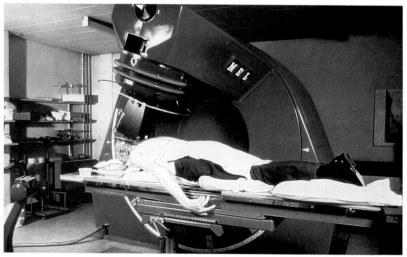

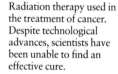

Radiation therapy used in the treatment of cancer. Despite technological advances, scientists have been unable to find an effective cure.

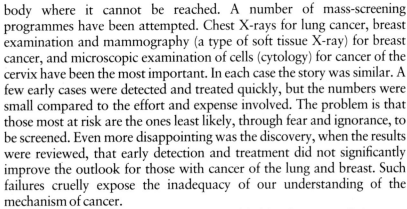

body where it cannot be reached. A number of mass-screening programmes have been attempted. Chest X-rays for lung cancer, breast examination and mammography (a type of soft tissue X-ray) for breast cancer, and microscopic examination of cells (cytology) for cancer of the cervix have been the most important. In each case the story was similar. A few early cases were detected and treated quickly, but the numbers were small compared to the effort and expense involved. The problem is that those most at risk are the ones least likely, through fear and ignorance, to be screened. Even more disappointing was the discovery, when the results were reviewed, that early detection and treatment did not significantly improve the outlook for those with cancer of the lung and breast. Such failures cruelly expose the inadequacy of our understanding of the mechanism of cancer.

The anti-cancer armamentarium assembled by 'hi-tec' medicine now includes surgery, radiotheraphy (X-rays), chemotherapy (drugs), hormone therapy, immunotherapy (strengthening the body's own defence systems), nutrition and psychotherapy. It might seem a formidable array but cancer remains the third biggest killer in middle and old age. The major limitation has always been that the treatments themselves so often cause unacceptable side-effects. What has been noticeable in recent years, however, is a move away from blunderbuss surgery towards more discriminating forms of treatment. Most interesting of all has been the discovery of monoclonal antibodies. These are antibodies that can distinguish between healthy cells and cancerous cells wherever they are in the body. It is hoped that one day they will be linked with cell-killing drugs to produce a lethal combination which will spare healthy tissues, but destroy all cancerous cells.

The pros and cons of transplantation

For hundreds of years man has fantasized about the possibility of prolonging life by exchanging old, diseased organs for new. Only in the last couple of decades has this dream become reality. The ethics and desirability of each transplantation remain the subject of intense argument. On the one hand it seems both absurd and immoral for the Western world to be spending millions of pounds on procedures which only benefit a few, while elsewhere in the world millions of people are dying for the want of a few pence. On the other hand, as Professor Roy Calne of Cambridge University has argued so forcibly, pain and suffering are not confined to undernourished, underdeveloped people alone. They occur in every country and it is the duty of every country to do its best for its citizens. If, by organ transplantation, men and women can be returned to full lives, then all the research, resources and effort are justified.

Transplanting organs is, in any case, nothing new. As long ago as the turn of the century successful attempts were made at transplanting goats' and sheeps' kidneys to human beings. But it was the discovery in the early 1960s of drugs that suppress the body's rejection of donor organs that set the transplantation programme alight. Now in the UK, for example, nearly 1500 transplants are performed each year. Using the latest anti-rejection drug, Cyclosporin A, a one-year survival of the transplanted kidney is expected in 75 per cent of patients – which makes it a very cost-effective operation.

On the other hand, heart transplantation has remained controversial since the first operation was performed by Professor Christiaan Barnard in South Africa in 1967. The latest results from his Cape Town Medical School show that there has been an average one-year survival rate of 58 per cent in the 64 transplants performed between then and 1983. Since the introduction of the drug Cyclosporin A the one-year survival rate has risen to 80 per cent. Admittedly, the average life-expectancy of these patients without the operation was one month, but there must be very real doubts as to the contribution of heart transplantation to the huge population of heart disease sufferers. Many scientists feel that it is a scientific cul-de-sac because there will always be a limited supply of donor hearts available. They believe that resources should be spent on artificial hearts, assist pumps, better drugs and even animal organs.

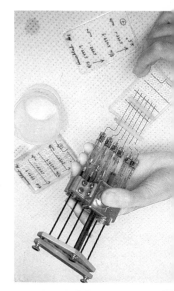

Transplantation – successes, failures and alternatives

Lung transplantation is not technically difficult but success so far has been limited. The delicate, newly transplanted air-sacs are particularly vulnerable to a rejection reaction and to infection from the air. So far over forty patients have received grafts of whom only a handful have survived longer than six months. The logical extension to heart and lung transplantation is to combine the two operations into one – the heart-lung transplant. Surprisingly, the operation is not much more difficult technically, but it is bedevilled by the problems of infection and rejection. In recent years there has been an improvement in techniques to suppress the body's rejection reaction, so that occasionally a patient survives for a year or longer. One American woman, for example, who was operated on in California in March 1981, has long since returned to her busy editorial office job.

The first pancreatic transplant was performed at the University of Minnesota, in 1967, on a patient suffering from diabetes. Diabetes is a condition in which the pancreas cannot produce the insulin needed to maintain the proper workings of the body's internal organs. Normally, the patient is given injections of insulin, but the transplant operation offered the hope of a more permanent solution. Unfortunately, it was not successful. Many more have been performed since, but all the results have been disappointing. The major problems have been technical, not least the tendency of the transplanted pancreas's own enzymes to digest the pancreas!

The major advances in the treatment of diabetes are likely to be elsewhere. In 1980, seventeen volunteer diabetics at Guy's Hospital, London, received insulin made by genetic engineering – the first time humans had ever received a substance made by genetic engineering. The trial was a success, and in 1982 both the UK and the United States licensed genetically engineered insulin as safe for humans.

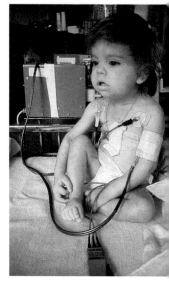

Top: Analysing tissue compatibility for an organ transplant.

Above: A little girl on a dialysis machine waits for a suitable kidney donor for a transplant.

Producing insulin at the Wellcome Production Centre, UK. The production of artificial insulin makes available purer, cheaper insulin for the estimated world population of 60 million diabetics.

This development has great implications for the estimated world population of 60 million diabetics, more than half of whom live in the developing world and are rarely diagnosed or treated. The world's stocks of insulin are now expected to increase markedly; the cost may be reduced by up to one-half and it is anticipated that the insulin will be much purer that that produced at present from cattle and pigs.

Better methods of delivering the insulin are also being actively developed. The most recent advance has been a specially adapted portable electro-mechanical syringe pump, which is implanted into the superficial tissues of the abdominal wall and slowly infuses insulin into the body. It is hoped it may even prove possible to fine-tune the syringe to respond directly to the body's need for insulin. This remarkable system, however, would itself be superseded by the development of oral insulin – a goal that has been pursued by scientists for many years and which may now be realized within the foreseeable future.

The first attempts at bone marrow transplantation were not made until the early 1980s and ended in almost universal failure. More recently, however, techniques have become much more sophisticated, especially since it was discovered that leukaemia, thalassaemia and aplastic anaemia can be successfully treated in this way. The sad irony is that whereas, for example, in the United States, as many as 12 to 15 patients a week receive marrow transplants, those countries round the Mediterranean where thalassaemia is widespread, and where the need for transplantation is therefore greatest, are among those which can least afford it.

Looking ahead, it may even be possible to transplant the brain. Up till now, it has been assumed that the brain can never be transplanted. However, a recent experiment reported in the scientific journal *Nature* showed that memory in adult males could be restored using fetal brain tissue transplants. Clearly this is only a start, but it does suggest that, sometime in the far future, brain transplantation might be a frightening possibility.

Transplantation is very much part of the ethos of 'hi-tec' medicine but, as a technique, it is seriously limited by its dependence on harvesting donor organs – something doctors, patients and relatives find distressing. The UK and the United States rely on citizens 'opting in' by carrying donor cards or by relatives giving permission for organ donation. Some European countries, like France, have decided that this scheme does not produce enough organs. They have instead adopted a system of 'opting out', in which organs can automatically be taken from a dead patient provided there is no specific prohibition to the contrary. This will undoubtedly increase the number of available organs, but many people also feel it involves the loss of a fundamental right to do with one's body what one wills.

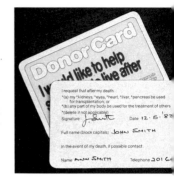

Advances in diagnostics and surgery

One of the most dramatic growth areas in medical technology has been that of diagnostics – in particular that of non-invasive diagnostics, in which the necessity to 'open the patient up' to make a diagnosis no longer exists. Today, imaging and scanning techniques, electronic and optical devices, and computer and microprocessor-aided monitoring units are beginning to replace the old surgical techniques.

Public imagination has been particularly caught by the total body (Computerized Axial Tomograph) scanner which has replaced kidney dialysis units as the favourite gift of hospital charities. The CAT scanner is able to detect structures a little over one centimetre (about half an inch) across by combining scanning X-rays and computer display facilities to produce a three-dimensional picture. Although a very expensive instrument, many countries rushed to buy it when it was first developed, quite neglecting the fact that its annual running cost amounts to nearly 15 per cent of the purchase price. Now many lie idle or only partially used. Japan, for example, invested heavily in CAT scanners and now owns over one-third of the world's supply. New Zealand, by contrast, has refused to spend any money on them until they are better evaluated.

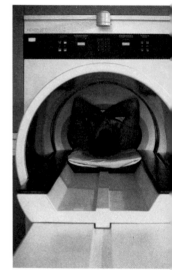

The New Zealanders may have made a wise decision. A very new form of imaging called Nuclear Magnetic Resonance (NMR) tomography is already widely expected to replace CAT scanning. NMR has two major advantages. First, it does not use the potentially dangerous X-rays to produce its image, but rather a magnetic field and a radio frequency pulse which produce a response from the positive atoms within living tissues. Secondly, it seems able to make distinctions between different body tissues, including the important difference between healthy and diseased tissues.

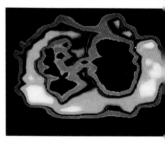

The total body scanner: the NMR (Nuclear Magnetic Resonance) scanner and, beneath it, NMR photograph of a cancer cell.

In surgery, as well as diagnostics, materials and instruments are far better than they used to be, and certain technological advances have kept surgery to the forefront of medicine. One very important new instrument is the operating microscope. This can achieve magnification of up to 100 times the normal, and makes surgery on the brain, eye, ear, Fallopian tubes or amputated limbs much easier.

Another important field is the use of telescopic instruments which can be introduced into the body cavities safely to examine and treat internal organs. The throat, stomach, bowel, gall-bladder, lungs, bladder, ovaries and joints can now be visualized. This is mainly due to the Japanese development of fibre-optics which were first researched in the UK. Other technological advances, like laser and ultrasound screening, can be added to the telescopic instrument to make diagnosis and treatment easier. A good example of the application of these developments can be seen in the treatment of patients with dangerously bleeding peptic ulcers. Previously a difficult abdominal operation fraught with complications was necessary; now it is hoped that laser beams introduced into the body via the telescope will stop the bleeding from inside, making a formal, open operation unnecessary.

For their part orthopedic surgeons are becoming increasingly enthusiastic about the use of electromagnetism to speed up bone healing.

Brain surgery in progress. The operation is conducted through a covered microscope.

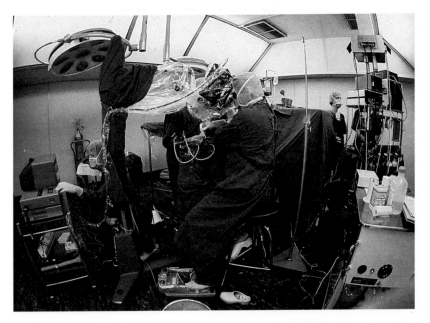

Ever since Galvani in the eighteenth century suggested the idea of a 'vital force', there has been research into the effects of electricity and magnetism on body functions, but only recently has there been a breakthrough. It has been found that bone (even if infected) can be stimulated to heal much quicker than normal if an electromagnetic current is put across it. This discovery could considerably affect the length of time patients need to spend in bed or in plaster.

Helping the old and infirm

As many as a fifth of the population in the Western world may either be old or infirm. Only recently has the magnitude of the problem begun to force high technology to consider how best it can help this vulnerable population.

The old and crippled spend a lot of time in bed but it is only lately that any imagination has been applied to designing beds. Water beds have been available for some time but they are heavy and expensive. Much better are the new 'rippling' beds with alternating air-cell pressure systems to minimize the chances of causing bedsores, or the 'beds' produced by millions of air-fluidized glass beads being agitated by warm air to provide a moving cushion.

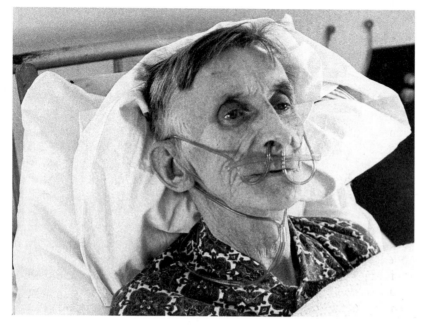

Industrial illness: an ex-miner suffering from pneumoconiosis.

Wheelchair technology is improving all the time, but sophisticated machinery is still very expensive.

All sorts of other sophisticated aids are now on the market. Powered wheelchairs have been developed which will mount shallow stairs or pavements, and in Sweden there is a model entirely controlled by microcomputer. For those too crippled to write there is a light-sensitive typewriter which can easily be operated by the patient. For the deaf there are now elegant hearing-aids which have almost eliminated the past problems with interference. There is even a new instrument which responds to words spoken by displaying them on a television screen.

In many of these developments, and in modern Western medicine generally, computers play a central role. Their impact on society as a whole would seem to be akin to that produced by the change from stone age to bronze age, to the introduction of writing, the discovery of printing or electricity. Certainly, their value to medicine is unquestionable: not only for providing displays for sophisticated tools like CAT scanners, but also in the routine, humdrum work of medicine – filing, checking prescriptions for accuracy, ensuring immunization programmes are up to date and so on – which is such an important part of good quality medicine. They are an ally, not a replacement for the doctor. There is an old joke that after the computer is introduced into medicine, the only place you will see your doctor is in the golf club. If this happens it will not be the computer's fault.

Alternative medicines

When Prince Charles in his opening address as President of the British Medical Association in July 1982 said, 'Medicine today tends to be more and more chemistry, and less and less healing in the classical sense. I do not for one moment decry the chemistry because we owe it too much, but I do not want to do it the disservice of pretending that is is the whole answer', it seemed that he was putting into words the thoughts of many people in the Western world. They have become disillusioned with the seemingly costly, inhumane, unequal face presented by 'hi-tec' medicine. Instead, the so-called alternative fields of medicine such as acupuncture, homoeopathy, chiropractice and osteopathy are attracting increasing interest. In particular, people have turned for inspiration to the East and the great country of China.

Ironically, China for her part is now turning to the West and high technology for her inspiration. In 1964 Chairman Mao had already criticized what he believed to be a new concentration on high-level technological research. By 1978 the Minister of Health, Jiane Yizhen, accepted there had been a major shift in China's health policies. There was to be a new emphasis on the importance of science and technology and a rehabilitation of many of the medical scientists disgraced during the Cultural Revolution. In the same year his deputy, Gian Xinzhong, said at a National Science Conference, 'Great progress must be made in modernizing China's medical, pharmaceutical and public health work and in raising the country's science to advanced levels by the end of the century.'

The last five years in China have seen great advances in heart and kidney transplants, microsurgery for limb re-attachments, plastic surgery, the treatment of burns, computer diagnosis, and in new drugs and equipment. There has also been a swing towards training scientists and doctors, and away from the famous 'barefoot doctors', who have declined in numbers from 1.8 million in 1976 to 1.4 million in 1982.

Even the prestigious *Chinese Medical Journal* now devotes its pages to scientific articles by highly trained doctors, many of whom teach in Western-style medical schools. Significantly, there have been no political editorials since 1978, and very few articles on preventive or industrial medicine.

The argument about the value of 'hi-tec' medicine, as opposed to other forms, thus remains unresolved. If there is a solution it probably lies between the two, between the medicine of the West, with its emphasis on advanced technology, and the more holistic approach of the East.

Medicine negated

Christiaan Barnard

Today, more than 400 million people in the world are suffering from malnutrition. If population trends continue as expected, rising to over six billion by the turn of the century, this figure will also increase dramatically. United Nations projections paint a frightening world situation of economic, political and social disorder in which the figures for hunger, disease and death from starvation continue to rise.

In the meantime, health budgets world-wide continue to climb as the cost of medical training, hospitals and high technology medicine rises beyond the pocket of ordinary people. World health projects on the scale envisaged to cope with even basic Third World problems are stalled for lack of funds.

The solutions that have so far been attempted including the so-called Green Revolution – 'agribusiness' in the form of larger and more economic farming projects with high technology inputs – mammoth birth control schemes and the marshalling of medical help on a global scale have not only failed. They have often made the situation far worse.

Limits imposed by lifestyle

Health is largely a matter of lifestyle, but the lifestyle of an individual is largely determined by the ruling ideology. Choice operates, but only within certain limits. This was dramatically demonstrated for me on a recent visit to a developing country.

I sat in the aeroplane, ready for departure, my briefcase bulging with copies of research papers which had been delivered at a conference held in that country. They detailed among other things the differences in illnesses suffered by the affluent, the poor, industrial workers and peasants, the wealthy white Westerner and the black tribesman.

As we took off I could see from the plane window large areas of burnt bush. Down there a multinational company with an interest in agriculture was clearing thousands of hectares of land for a monoculture of peanuts. The locals didn't eat peanuts but somebody had figured out on paper that the money earned in the export of peanuts would pay for food imports.

Nobody had figured out how the peasants would earn the money to pay for the food once it arrived.

On the horizon was the city, capital of a potentially wealthy country, yet its slums were swamped by the tide of peasant farmers who had been dispossessed in the bush-clearing operation. They had been thrown off the land in their thousands and had flooded into the city, squatting in family groups along the river-bank while their shacks and shanties crawled up the hillside like a cancer. These were the new urban poor. Previously they had been well off, earning a living as subsistence farmers while surrounded by their wives, children and the warm relationships of the extended family. Richly endowed with space and air, they had been socially and psychologically secure, from the cradle to the grave, security which needed no expensive imports.

Now, their future was the factory floor and the assembly line, industrial diseases, slum living and an early death. The scenario would certainly include broken family ties, neurotic concern for material things, rising levels of crime and violence, a lowered standard of living and a lonely old age.

From the aircraft I caught a glimpse of a skeletal structure. It was the new hospital, rising on the edge of the slums. Costing millions in foreign aid, it would be desparetely needed to combat the illness brought upon the peasants by life in an industrial slum.

Rich and poor

The neo-natal unit at the Hammersmith Hospital, London. The survival of premature babies in Britain depends largely upon the facilities available in the area in which they are born.

Among other outcomes of an inequitable society, disease, injuries and malnutrition among infants and children bring crippling costs. These are not reflected directly in most budgets, though to give an indication of the consequences I could point at the incredibly expensive intensive care required to nurse a single child back to a healthy condition.

Possibly of more importance in the long term are the cultural deprivation and latent brain damage suffered as a direct result of the disease processes. Once psychically and physically maimed, the cost of maintaining these damaged personalities throughout adulthood is an ongoing charge on the nation.

In contrast, the cost of attacking malnutrition and childhood diseases at source is minimal. Medicine is negated each time we fail to drive that point home to the administrators and the budget-makers.

What of birth control as a means of improving the quality of human life on our planet? Birth control schemes have come and gone, the late and unlamented mass-sterilization promoted by the former Gandhi government in India being the most notable failure. They failed mainly because they were propagated by the socially elite for the socially deprived and as such were seen as an imposition.

It is unlikely that any family planning scheme aimed at the poor and the underprivileged will ever succeed without some minimal guarantees. Essentially this means job creation, housing, improved income, social security and a crash literacy programme. In short, giving the poor more control over their own lives. For many countries, this will entail reconstruction of the entire social order.

Misdirected effort

Medicine, alas, has followed the pattern of bigger is better, its real function being obscured under its fixation on the space-age technology of the twentieth century. The antibiotics, product of high technology and massive capital input and once hailed as a universal panacea, have not realized a brave new world but rather a more disease-resistant old one in which it costs a lot more to be ill. The infant mortality rates of some Third World countries are on the increase, and even those of many so-called developed countries have shown no real positive change for some time.

Factors relating to stress: (*left*) inadequate housing; (*right*) poor working conditions. Boring, repetitive work in a noisy environment is a major stress-inducing factor.

Russian poster warning against the abuse of alcohol and the damage it can do to the digestive system and the liver.

ЗЛОУПОТРЕБЛЕНИЕ АЛКОГОЛЕМ

ТАК РАЗВИВАЮТСЯ

ГАСТРИТЫ, КОЛИТЫ, ЯЗВЕННАЯ БОЛЕЗ ЗАБОЛЕВАНИЯ ПЕЧЕ

Figures show that stress diseases in Western society are on the increase, with alarming trends in associated pathologies such as alcoholism and mental breakdown. It isn't difficult to point to some of the main factors which cause the rise in stress, such as the increase in population pressure leading to competition for less and less goods, housing and space; faster pace of living, deteriorating environment and general alienation. But it is less easy to find a form of treatment that is really effective.

More and more tranquilizers, stimulants and other 'happy' pills are handed out every year, but they serve only to hide the cause of the problem. We have to find and remove or reduce the stress. And to do that, we have first to confront the problem and then to work out a solution.

The patient who is doped to the eyebrows and vaguely happy about the whole world has little chance of doing this. All he or she is doing is putting off the evil day when all the chickens will come home to roost. The trouble is that, in time, such a patient loses the ability even to recognize the chickens when they do arrive.

A sick society

Apart from our pat solutions to clinical problems – a form of automated medicine – we have also lost our medical souls in terms of specialization. For that we have to thank the modern industrial model where each man has specialized to the point of lunacy.

We have division of labour so far that while one mechanic fixes your car another fixes your ulcers, a third your heart, a fourth your head and so on. Your mind is the province of another expert who will de-coke and retune your mental life so that he can send you back to the automated office or production line. And while the experts are doing all this the figures for stress diseases, divorce, suicide, crime and all the other indicators of a very sick society are climbing.

'Technology is neutral, it's what you do with it that causes the problem,' a very learned social psychologist once told me. A nice idea, if it were true. But look at any theory of economics, politics or sociology. If you expect to find some theory of work as the basis of all human activity you'll be disappointed. You'll find all kinds of theorizing about profit and loss, scarcity and value of land and goods, but nothing at all about what the work does to the worker.

Technology continues to add more and more complications, more and more divisions of labour, more and more calls for growth and consumption, more and more soulless ways of earning a living.

Take a look at modern Western legislation covering factories. It goes into minute detail about how many people can share a washbasin or how long and how often they can have a cup of tea during working hours. It even worries about the air they breathe, the level of noise they hear, the amount of light they have, the temperature of the workplace and the composition of the floors they stand on. But nowhere is there a rule about mental stimulation or the spiritual quality of life. Nowhere is official concern expressed about what repetitive drudgery does to the worker's mind. That, according to theories of administration, is someone else's domain.

Which is where we of the medical profession come in. But our place in it all is a bit like cleaning the Augean stables. We keep on wiping the floor without turning off the tap. Ideologies and social systems and economic theories – all of which we consider to be beyond our legitimate ken – are responsible for producing the disease processes we are fighting.

Prevention or cure?

In my own country, South Africa, it is only very recently that doctors took note of their responsibility for the diseases of the body politic and joined in an affirmation of the need to guide social forces in positive directions. The trend in medicine in the past decade has been towards preventive rather than curative work. Doctors hope to move away from the era of gigantic disease palaces staffed by thousands and stuffed with millions of dollars worth of expensive diagnostic equipment, to a society which follows basic health rules.

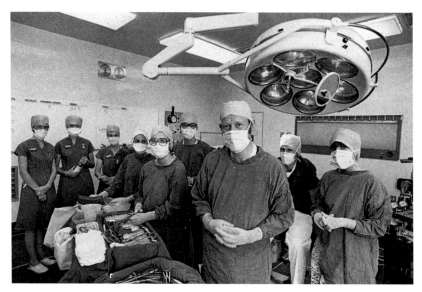

Courtiers of the 'disease palace': a highly equipped surgical team ready to perform an operation.

It's not a new idea. The Old Testament prophets harangued the Israelites on the dangers of living in low-lying hollows and the eating of suspect forms of food. Nearer our own time a man called Thomas Crapper took what was probably the biggest step in preventive health measures in London in the last century when he developed the flush toilet. Possibly one of the few persons who really appreciated his gift to mankind was Queen Victoria who knighted him. Sir Thomas Crapper, whose name still lives on evocatively in the English language, was not a doctor – he was a plumber.

Prolonging the agony

I have mentioned specialization and a preoccupation with technology. Hand in hand with this view is the tendency towards heroic intervention – a striving officiously to keep alive patients who have hope of little more than mere existence.

A televised report recently showed a home for congenitally disabled and retarded children. Many had been 'stabilized' surgically. That is, through surgical intervention they had survived infancy and were now a charge on the nation. They had no hope of anything beyond a meaningless existence chained to a hopelessly physically and mentally deficient body. A generation ago such children died at birth as a matter of course.

Today's doctors – blinded to reality by technological gimmicks – sew, stitch, repair, intubate, pump, drip feed and intensively nurse these mindless cabbages in a travesty of medicine that is aimed as much at assuaging parental guilt and massaging professional pride as it is at human considerations. Machines cannot give love. Life is more than air, and iron lungs can only give air. No sentient being can relate to intravenous feeding. Hell is any place without love and there can be no real love in a machine-supported life.

The report showed the children lying in babbling rows, mindlessly moving arms and legs, some incapable even of normal continence. They are awakened, cleaned, fed, dressed, exercised, lulled to sleep and wakened again to begin another day of frustration and boredom.

Perhaps there is a case for caging adults in life-support systems which keep them lingering between life and death, but medical practitioners should think hard before being a party to such situations. For example, there was strong 'political necessity' for the teams of doctors who worked day and night shifts to keep General Franco 'alive' until his successor was assured. In doing so they linked him to a respirator and kidney machine, dripped blood and sustenance into his veins, carried out three major abdominal operations and successfully foiled several heart attacks. Mercifully, the old man, already in mental limbo, could have known little of the assaults on his body.

The profit motive

Sophisticated modern medicine has lost touch with the real needs of humankind. Where once we sought to improve the quality of living for all, much effort is spent on increasing the quantity of life for a few.

The profit motive is not far absent in these efforts. Hillary P. Ojiambo, a Kenyan professor of medicine, told the *Kenyan Standard* in 1981 that drug dumping in the Third World was a major problem. A sizeable proportion of the drug budget was spent on expensive drugs for use mainly in large prestigious hospitals at the expense of health care in rural areas. Because there were few, if any, pharmaceutical companies owned by developing countries, most of the drug budget was spent on buying the manufactured article elsewhere.

In the Third World, most drug companies have a monopoly of information as medical journals are few and far between. This has meant that doctors have had to rely on the drug company to keep up with the latest drug advances, which in itself is an undesirable situation.

At a World Health Organization conference in Stockholm in 1976 the influence of medical technology was referred to as 'psychic and cultural' pollution. One delegate complained that our medical systems were not very well adapted to the healthy, let alone the needs of the ill.

Evidence was offered to show that medical technology in the form of resuscitators and other paraphernalia may actually hinder recovery through the imposition of mental stress.

The decrease in breast-feeding, particularly in the Third World, was attributed to glossy advertising of artificial baby foods. Impoverished mothers diluted feeds, creating malnutrition in previously well-nourished infants and denying them the immunizing effect of breast milk. Loss of lactation, known as a natural (if unreliable) contraceptive, also led to increased birth rate and failure of natural child spacing in the family.

The Western habit of garlanding doctors with mystique had affected Third World medical practice. Patients accepted medical advice as law, placing all responsibility for their own well-being on the shoulders of the doctors and ignoring the traditional concept of self-care.

Setting the record straight

In general, the technology of medicine has not been effective in coping with the major killers of mankind such as malnutrition, heart disease, cancer and so on. For example, the reduction of TB rates in the developed world took place long before the drug advances of the 1940s, and even then it is doubtful that medical intervention was the decisive factor. More likely it was improved nutrition, housing, sewerage and piped water that did the job.

The efficacy of medical treatment has been doubted in many quarters. A commission of inquiry in the United States found that only 10 to 20 per cent of treatment had been validated by the acid test of a controlled trial.

For some countries the problem with medicine is not technological but economic. Health costs are accelerating faster than incomes. For others the crisis is the maldistribution of health resources, with the bulk of these being devoted to curative treatment. According to one report, about 50 per cent of health care expenditure is being spent on people who will die within the next 12 months. Moreover, medical resources are concentrated in areas where health needs are lowest, and conversely most sparse where death and disease are greatest. Politics, it is often said, is far too serious a matter to be left solely in the hands of the professionals. So too is medicine.

Doctors world-wide are providing a disease service rather than a health service. Instead of promoting health, they are trying to displace disease. Yet, in spite of the training and treasure poured out in the pursuit of this very laudable object, results have largely negated the practice of medicine as we in the West know it. It wasn't the doctor who wiped out typhoid, it was the plumber. It wasn't the drug researcher who halted the advance of TB, it was the social planner who attacked poverty and overcrowding. Nor was it the paediatrician who cut the infant mortality rate, but more likely the school teacher and the district nurse.

Western advertising has had a profound effect on other countries. This billboard was photographed in Lagos, Nigeria.

Few medical schools emphasize public health or social science subjects in their curricula. Most are heavily drug-oriented. What they do is to produce competent technicians who can recognize and treat a disease in isolation from its social context. But it is often the system that produces the disease, which the doctor then has to make better – all at tremendous cost and with little alteration to the annual health figures.

What is to be done?

The medical practitioner is on a merry-go-round. Today – nearly four decades since the end of World War II – we continue on our cycle of international interference, reading research papers, occasional breakthroughs in odd, obscure specialities, much trumpeting of scientific know-how and mutual back-slapping. Yet while this is going on, hundreds of millions in the real world are dying of starvation and many more are suffering from a range of horrifying ills. In the crisis areas one child in five will never see a second birthday.

We do not need more research to tell us what to do. The answer is staring us in the face: it is time for a rethink, a spiritual and moral regeneration and a realization that in the practice of twentieth-century medicine we have negated its primary aim – a sociologically and physically healthy family of nations in which quality rather than quantity of life is the prime concern.

Chapter Nine

ADULTS AND CHILDREN: IS THE FAMILY OBSOLETE?

The future depends on the next generation. But what future can our children look forward to now that the family is weakening as the central unit of society? Humphrey Evans looks at the issue of children's rights, James Coleman examines the changing role of the family in socialization and outlines possible strategies for the future, and Betty Friedan puts the case for a new set of values that transcend sex roles and allow fathers a greater say in child-rearing.

Scenes like this are familiar enough. But is the family unit as we know it under threat?

Children's rights

Humphrey Evans

Children link us with the future. They will grow up into it, they will help to change it and in turn will raise further generations. Some of the children I know – Sarah, who is nine, Steven, who is seven, Anna aged six, and Alex, four – could themselves become the mothers and fathers of people who will live to see the end of the twenty-first century. On a wider scale, half the people living in Brazil are under 18 years of age.

Adults-in-waiting

Parents and all who have anything to do with the care of children are constantly aware of this human continuity, and with it the notion that children are adults-in-waiting. Perhaps a better way of putting this is to say that people treat children in ways that gradually bring them into the adult community, and that the children respond. As Steven once said to me, 'I will be able to do that when I am bigger.'

Becoming bigger is the simplest of aspirations, although I can't remember it in myself. Looking back, I seemed to be the right size at the time, but that, I suspect, reflects that fact that we adults forget our childhood experience, overlaying it with later concerns. I still live, at the age of 40, with the anguish of having accidentally smashed a girl's front tooth against a climbing frame at the age of ten. I don't remember, although I am told this happened, taking my younger brother on a long expedition, at the age of five, across a main road to reach a park where we had played. Some things stick and some things go.

Size is worth thinking about just because growth itself is continuous. Children are small, adults in general are large. Adults all know that they were once small, yet in the public environment of industrialized societies little allowance is made for the small. Self-closing doors in supermarkets or hotels often require a hefty shove to open them. Restaurant chairs and tables cater for one standard size of customer. Control buttons in the elevators of apartment blocks are set so high that short people cannot reach them. Children have no apparent existence.

Shifting now from size to age, adults know that they were once young, but again this knowledge somehow disappears. The voting age in Britain, the United States and the Soviet Union is a common 18 years. People above that age can take part in the political process, however nominally, by voting. Those below have no apparent presence.

Or move from size and age, both at least measurable, to a more tenuous concept such as self-development. Adults in industrialized societies pursue their plans in more or less individual ways. But children confront a standardized system, school exams, tests, university entry, that forces them all into one mould. Again, the child as an individual with aims of its own seems to disappear from view.

The rights of children

One of the changes that will probably come about in the future is the realization that children can and should play some part in organizing their own lives. This realization of children's rights is analogous to the consciousness that women, ethnic minorities, the old, all wish to command their proper respect within society, defining the contribution that they might make in ways that affect the whole.

London children at a play centre for the under-fives.

Children's rights, like those of many other groups, conflate needs, desires, demands and aspirations. To some extent children can rely on human responses: a small child, alone and crying in an urban setting, will quite probably attract the attention of adults who will try to find out what is wrong. However, children are also part of the culture into which they are born: a child raised in central Africa will have different tastes in food and different expectations of adult life from one raised on the island of Bali or in the mid-western United States. Yet this still leaves an immense area of negotiation over how children may hope to be treated, as human beings, as young creatures not yet fully able to fend for themselves, and as rational people on their way to adulthood.

In 1959, the United Nations listed a series of children's rights that are eminently humane: the right to equality, regardless of race, colour or religion, sex or nationality; the right to healthy mental and physical development; to a name and nationality; to sufficient food, housing and medical care; to special care if handicapped; to love and understanding; to free education, play and recreation; to immediate aid in the event of disasters and emergencies; to protection from cruelty, neglect and exploitation; to protection from persecution and to an upbringing in the spirit of worldwide brotherhood and peace.

Children's rights as human beings merge with those of people in general. The right to sufficient food, housing and medical care depends on society as a whole. Where adults are starving, poorly housed and cut-off from health care, children are unlikely to do better. In Britain, for example, the Child Poverty Action Group continually confronts the fact that the best way of minimizing the potential effects of poverty on children is to ensure that no one ever falls into destitution. Resources can be guided towards children within a social setting, by giving benefit payments direct to mothers who are taking responsibility for child care, for example, but children cannot be wholly insulated from that setting.

On a more dramatic scale, famine provides another example. Is it the case that the world produces too little food to feed its teeming millions, as some believe, and that specific supplies should therefore be allocated to feeding children? Or does famine come about because of a political and economic system that depends on people paying for their food, no matter how poor they are? If the latter is true, then surely some changes should be made to that system.

Inequalities in the lives of children. *Left:* Victims in Ethiopia. In one sense these children are lucky – they have received supplementary relief in the form of gruel. *Top:* Children in Soweto, victims of South African apartheid. *Above:* White children in New Zealand growing up in a society where problems such as those suffered by children in rural Ethiopia and black South Africa are completely unknown.

Health care provides further examples. In developed countries, the revolution in health care for children was more dependent on the availability of clean water and sewage disposal systems than on the efforts of individual doctors, heroic though these may have been. In developing countries today, opinion is split on the merits of providing hospital-based medical care and vaccination programmes for the young, methods which rely on technological backing, or the use of simple remedies such as sugar-in-water feed that can prevent diarrhoea in infants from becoming fatal. Some four million children under the age of five die each year from diarrhoea in Asia, Africa and Latin America. Even such a simple remedy, however, requires that knowledge be allied to common sense. A look back to the nineteenth century in Britain and the United States shows how easily child-carers convinced themselves that to keep children quiet they could reasonably dose them with opium, in the form of laudanum or Godfrey's cordial. This could, and sometimes did, kill the child who took it.

Child care practices

Care for those who can't yet fend for themselves recognizes that children are not yet fully competent human beings. They need food and shelter to be provided for them, they need protection, and they need something more. The technical term is stimulation, but what this comes down to is the company of other people, both old and young.

One of the most interesting aspects of the future is that all of us, whatever countries we live in and whatever our cultural backgrounds, are becoming more aware of the presence of other peoples, of the existence of different practices even in something that seems as basic as child-rearing. This enables us to examine and even question some of the things that seem obligatory, and therefore natural, within our own communities.

Over the past 50 years, in countries such as Britain and the United States, for example, we have seen childbirth itself become a managed event within the hospital. We have seen shifts in fashion from breast-feeding to swift weaning followed by bottle-feeding, then back to breast-feeding. We have seen fixed-regimen feeding come and go, we have discovered that children in other cultures may not be weaned until the age of two or even three, and so on.

Present ideas about child care in the West have been influenced by the work of researchers such as Myrtle McGraw, who organized a major project at New York's Columbia University in the 1930s, observing the progress of about a hundred children week by week and month by month. 'I started in the delivery room,' she said, 'sitting and watching for hours and hours. Then they let me scrub up and handle the baby to get some of the first reactions to birth.'

From there she moved on to look at what happens as the child grows, although her aims were slightly different from those of other researchers. 'They felt the thing to do was to get a scale of development against chronological age. I wanted to know how this development comes about.' One of the babies that came under scrutiny was her own daughter.

Child care starts with the notion that children's abilities, both physical and mental, develop through the interplay of growth and experience. We know that children who miss out on adult help and encouragement, children in understaffed orphanages, for example, will be long delayed in acquiring basic abilities such as sitting up and walking. We know, too,

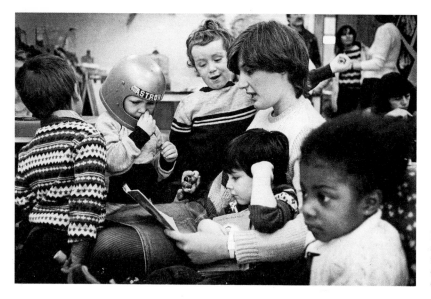

Pre-school education is available to most children in the UK. Here, a group of children is being read to at a day nursery in London.

that very young children who spend time with each other in established groups develop a cooperative awareness far in advance of children raised in the relative isolation of an adult-dominated household. Young children who are used to taking meals together will help each other to food and drink, a reciprocity that does not occur when children are fed by adults.

We might imagine an ideal environment as giving a child contact with both adults and other children and stimulating physical and mental activity while providing protection from domestic danger – easily accessible power points or unguarded fires, for instance. Yet other cultures have developed child care practices that might imply different ideals. Margaret Mead noted in her essay 'Children and Ritual in Bali' that Balinese children are involved in every activity, from house to field to temple, and that they are teased and ignored in a cycle that teaches them to accept provocation without response. In India, village women prepare food on mats spread on the kitchen floor, and young children are therefore drawn in more easily than if the person who is cooking works at a high table. In Chinese schools, the teacher is likely to demonstrate what the child must know, while in American schools the teacher is seen as a guide for the child's own explorations. We know that some cultures cannot imagine striking a young child, while others make use of corporal punishment.

The practices of some cultures can upset or even horrify people from other backgrounds. Europeans are wary of the American emphasis on orthodontics, or height adjustment in adolescence through drugs or surgery. Both Europeans and Americana abhor the practice in some African countries of female circumcision, in which young girls have the clitoris and parts of their genitals cut away. But whatever the initial reaction, there is a need in future for differing groups to comprehend the basis of each other's practices; they will then be able to adopt them, view them with neutral interest, or seek to change them in a spirit of understanding.

In Zaire, small children are usually looked after by their mothers.

Influences, responsibilities and guidance

Margaret Mead's work addressed the interesting question of how children become members of the particular group within which they find themselves. The answer is that everything counts: the way they are treated as young babies; how they learn trust and suspicion; different expectations of boys and girls; the assumptions underlying the organization of schools and such like; society's 'hidden curriculum' (whether cooperation or competition is encouraged); and so on.

Children's stories are a case in point. A European tradition produced stories that frightened children, quite possibly because a frightened child was likely to keep quiet and do what it was told. Even today the stories printed in children's books are often more attractive to the adults who pay for them than to the children who are meant to read them. The versions of *Jack and the Beanstalk* told in Britain and America differ slightly in ways linked to differences in the two societies.

With the shift we have mentioned towards thinking of children as prospective adults comes the realization that aspects of adulthood should be prefigured in childhood. Children may be viewed as happy innocents but they are also capable of taking on responsibility. Children like work that gives them a useful role. Think of the early-morning newspaper round, or the effort that children in rural areas put into raising their own animals. They like testing their capabilities in new activities. They like dealing with money, and making plans for the future.

Children's relationships with animals also vary from country to country. *Right:* In Ayoru, Niger, children work herding livestock. *Above:* In the UK, urban children see animals only as pets, and even those in farming communities rarely work with animals themselves.

All these aspects of the young person's move towards adulthood require some sort of balance. The useful experience of making a contribution to the community should not slip into exploitation. Watchful care by adults should not become over-protective prohibition. Youthful liveliness must be guided away from forms of expression that threaten the child's future. Take money as just one example. Young people need to learn about the various transactions that make up the financial environment, but children and adults together need to set limits on spending and indebtedness.

Community care 1: volunteers helping mentally handicapped children in a residential home in the UK.

Young people can be rational, but they lack the gradually acquired knowledge of how things are that gives the adult some deliberate pace when taking decisions. Historian Barbara Tuchman, writing about the calamitous fourteenth century, points out that the sudden upheavals, the toings-and-froings, the almost random eruption of conflicts and battles become much more understandable once you realize that many of the key figures were still teenagers.

Children and young people need help, too, in learning to deal with emotions and moving through family and other social groupings. We can imagine how this might best be done. Children need care from adults, whether within some kind of family group or in another setting, but they also need some autonomy, a sense that they are not the chattels of the adults who have care of them. Children need guidance and information about friendship, sex, commitments of varying kinds. From friends, parents and other adults, they need to learn how to respond to others.

Children and the elderly: connections and conflicts

Philippe Ariès begins his book *Centuries of Childhood* with a chapter on the ages of life, noting that childhood, like other ages, is a relative matter. In the past, when lives were shorter, young adults were the privileged group; today we might see people in middle life as dominant. Children are marginal in terms of their social weight. So too, Ariès points out, are the doddering old. Shakespeare depicted old age as a second childhood, 'sans teeth, sans eyes, sans taste, sans everything'. But another phrase that Ariès quotes suggests a different connection: a person of worth who has reached the age of 60 years or more should then pass on to young people wisdom and charity to fill their minds and hearts.

Young and old connect – and any call for children's rights summons up the echo of equivalent provision for the old. We were all children once, and many of us will one day be old. The subject of rights for the old again produces tensions. In the more industrialized societies, birth rates and health care are interacting to produce a surge in the proportion of older people in the population which will require adjustments in the resources demanded by, and available to, various age groups and which may spell future conflict. The value of money gives some indication of what could happen. A powerful sector of younger people within a population might favour high inflation rates – borrow now, pay back later when money is cheaper. A large population of older people might favour anti-inflationary measures to protect their savings. Housing could become another area of contention, with communities needing to decide whether to build housing specially suited to the old.

Community care 2: the 'Grandparenting Center' of the Care Unit Hospital in Los Angeles, where grandparents volunteer to look after children whose parents work during the day.

Old people, of course, are perfectly capable of a good active life, and some exercise considerable power. The world is used to political leaders who are past the age of retirement. But old age is relevant in the present context because most old people, like children, have little influence. The future demands that we address the question of how to handle the needs of the old, the young and other groups with little power. How can all of us be equally involved in the society within which we live?

Child-rearing

James Coleman

An inquiry into the social processes by which infants are brought towards adulthood is an exceedingly important part of the issue of what kind of future we are preparing for humankind. At first glance, such an inquiry seems simple indeed: despite extensive variations in social organization throughout the world and over time, the family has been the primary institution of socialization throughout recorded history. Studies of primate behaviour suggest an even stronger conclusion: that the family as the central institution of socialization predates humankind itself by a long period of time. Yet it seems possible that child-rearing in the twenty-first century and beyond will make some sharp breaks with history.

To gain some idea of how these changes are coming about, it is necessary to go back some distance in history. Around the thirteenth century in England and Europe, a new kind of organization began to come into existence. Before the law it was a new kind of person, *persona ficta*, in contrast to ordinary persons, whom the law called 'natural persons'. The king of England in the thirteenth century began to issue charters to boroughs or towns, which meant that the town became a 'person' before the law, able to exact tariffs and tolls, able to rent lands, with a treasury, a seal and the legal right to sue and be sued. On the European continent, the churches began to have similar rights. The law came to regard the church or the town as a corporation, a *persona ficta*, as real in the eyes of the law as a natural person, with certain special ways of 'deciding' and 'acting'. This posed the problem, however, of who had the right to act in its name.

The church came to be classified in the same category as infants, with the cleric as the guardian of the church empowered to initiate actions in its name. Boroughs or towns in England came to take actions through a set of burgesses, leading citizens whose actions in their capacity as burgesses were actions of the town as a corporation, not of themselves individually.

As trade developed, these corporate bodies, which had their origins in the fixed social structure of the Middle Ages, came to serve as the model for a corporate body of a wholly new kind, best exemplified by the great trading companies of England. These trading companies were corporations formed by the combined resources of a few men, yet they came to have rights and obligations distinct from those of the men who had brought them into existence. The legal principle of limited liability extended this separation and created the legal setting for the Industrial Revolution.

The modern corporation

The characteristic of the modern corporation which grew out of the earlier kind of corporation is that it has an existence wholly independent of particular persons. Its component parts, its elements, are not persons but positions. Persons are merely *occupants* of the positions, moving in and out of the corporate body, or moving from one position to another within it. This corporate body, which had its great period of growth in the nineteenth century, is exemplified not only in what today we call corporations, but in government, in trade unions (which have extensive staffs of employees), in non-profit organizations, in every corner of society.

The character of these corporate bodies can be seen by contrasting them with the medieval university, a corporate body of the old form, which in some cases retained the old form into the nineteenth and even twentieth centuries. The master or the fellow did not merely exchange time for a wage; he was wholly encompassed by the college, which had authority over what we would regard as the personal aspects of his life. It was not until the second half of the nineteenth century that fellows at Cambridge and Oxford could marry. It was not until the early 1970s that the obligations of Queen's College, Cambridge, to house, feed and care for a fellow terminated before the fellow's death. The college was a community of fellows with extensive controls over and obligations towards its members.

The family was 'the building block of the social structure'. Haymaking in the East Riding of Yorkshire in 1892. The bearded patriarch is the Rev. Joseph Hutton, Rector of West Heslerton. Also in the picture are his sons aged 5 and 7 and a grown-up son (seated on the haystack) who was also his curate. On the ladder is his half-sister; standing on the hay cart are the Rector's second wife and his son's fiancée. Among the servants are the groom/ gardener and the village bootmaker. At that time most country parsons and their families farmed a small quantity of land.

Now, in the last quarter of the twentieth century, the majority of adults 'occupy positions' in corporate bodies of the new form, which have brought about a freedom and individuality never before known. The new corporate bodies have come to constitute the stable, relatively fixed components of social structure, as did the old form of corporate body. But unlike the old form, they themselves are not composed of persons, but of positions. Persons have a freedom to move in and out of positions without disrupting the functioning of the structure itself. If the director of the Social Security Administration in the United States – or its counterpart in other developed countries – resigns, another person comes to occupy the position, and no elderly person goes without a social security payment. Nor do the elderly go without a payment if any of the thousands of other employees of the agency leaves.

The family – a relic from the old social structure

But matters are not quite so simple. There is one corporate body of the old form remaining in society – the family. The family is a body composed of persons, not positions. An adult who leaves through divorce retains obligations to the children, and sometimes to one or more adults in the family. If an adult leaves the family through death, divorce or desertion, or a child leaves through death, that person is never really replaced. Even the language recognises this, with terms like stepfather, stepmother and stepchild. Children are raised not by impersonal corporate bodies whose positions are occupied by persons, but by persons who taken together constitute a family. No viable child-rearing substitute for this intense set of personal relations has emerged throughout the whole of human existence.

The Victorian family business in a more urban environment: Bishop and Son, Dairymen.

When society as a whole was composed of corporate bodies of the old form, made up of persons rather than positions, these other corporate bodies were extensions of the family. Most productive enterprise, in the more developed countries, even less than a century ago, was carried out in the family or as an extension of the family – whether on the farm, or in a skilled craft, or in the family store. There was a consistency between the family and the institutions that surrounded it. In a real sense, the family was the building block of the social structure – as it is today in many Third World countries. Muslim law, for example, does not recognize corporate bodies beyond the clan, or extended family.

Today, however, in modern societies, the corporate bodies outside the family are alien to it. They have a different structural basis, composed of positions rather than persons, using the time and services of persons, but not composed of them. This leads to disjunctions of a severe sort, which have both benefits and costs for adults, but mostly costs for children.

The four principal ways in which these foreign bodies surrounding the family impose special costs on children have to do with the locus of adult activities; responsibility and dependency; personality types and the genesis of social norms.

The locus of adult activities

When the productive activities of society moved outside the family, that took a large part of the *man's* life out of the family, behind the closed doors of a modern corporate body in which he 'occupied a position'. This had its most immediate and direct impact on women, for women were the central authority in family activities, and so long as the family was central to the functioning of society, women were either at the centre of that action, or not far from it. But when the family became an anachronism surrounded by foreign bodies into which husbands vanished for much of the day, women were left in a backwater which was increasingly irrelevant to the central activities of society. However oppressed they were in the social structures of the past, they held a certain power by their central position in the family, which itself was central to society's functioning. This power they lost in the new social structure; yet the change was so difficult to pin down that they found it hard even to identify the source of their malaise. It was that malaise, I believe, more than any other single thing, which has led to the extraordinary movement of women into the paid work force.

A strict hierarchy prevailed at all levels in the large households of Victorian England. This 1886 photograph shows a house-keeper and her five 'slaveys'.

The next impact of this alien social structure was on the persons whose lives remained confined to the family – that is, children. When the productive activities of society either were located within the family or grew directly out of it, adult men and women carried out their productive activities in close proximity to children. Even when the children were sent into 'service', as was the custom especially in England over a broad range of social classes, this was service within a household. This close proximity of children to adult activities had both benefits and costs.

The costs have been described in hundreds of tracts, pamphlets and books calling for the segregation of children from the sordid activities of adults, from the exploitative work relations and from sexual degradation. The benefits of the old social structures can be seen by noting what is left after men's and women's productive activities moved outside the household. This shift took away much of the social activity of the adults and much of their interest as well. Cocktail parties and baby-sitters replaced family social activities which had contained family members of all ages. The vacuum of social relations this left for the young has come to be filled by an intensified set of peer relations, and new forms of youth-specific social activities perhaps best exemplified by the rock concert.

Some of this vacuum has been filled by formal institutions, in particular the school. But one characteristic of schools (except when they constitute close communities, ordinarily in boarding schools) is that nearly all the personal and social relations are among the children themselves, not between the children and adults. It is only in the lowest grades of primary school that a personal relation to the teacher competes in a child's attention with the relations to other children. As the child moves from family to school, there is a shift from involvement with adults to involvement with others of the same age. But if by adolescence that movement has progressed to the point where the family is incidental, then relations with adults are not there to facilitate the transition to adulthood. Instead, the age cohort moves to adulthood as a kind of self-socializing unit with few strong personal ties to adults – a condition conducive to alienation of the type that is ordinarily attributed to economic classes. And it moves towards an adulthood that it knows only from afar, having had little direct contact with adults in their everyday activities – that is to say, activities other than child-rearing.

Responsibility and dependency

In the old social structure of which the family is a part, responsibility was for the whole person and dependency was absolute. In the new social structure in which adults exchange portions of their lives in return for a wage, responsibility is for a set of activities, not for a person. When the person no longer occupies a position in the corporate body, or when he is engaged in activities other than those he is performing for the corporate body, the corporate body's authority and responsibilities cease. We sometimes forget that it was not always this way. It was not only the colleges of Oxford and Cambridge that exercised authority over and took responsibility for their members; it was every part of society. So long as the productive activities of society were carried out within the household or as extensions of the household – and until the advent of the modern corporate body – the household or its extension was the principal locus of both authority over, and responsibility for, people.

For persons who are in the prime of life and with marketable skills, this new freedom from the hierarchy of the old social structure is beneficial, even invigorating. For the old, the young and the sick – for all those who must be dependent, which of course includes all of us at some points in our lives – there is a vacuum of responsibility. The vacuum has been partly filled by the new corporate bodies themselves – either by social services, such as old age insurance, unemployment insurance or health insurance, provided by the state (a pattern established in Europe by Bismarck, and followed less extensively in the United States) or by private corporations (a pattern more characteristic of Japan). Schools have partly come to fill the vacuum for the young, and schools everywhere are provided principally by the state.

Schools, of course, may be ineffective or inappropriate, and there is not much evidence that they exercise a powerful influence over and above that of the family. But this is not the most serious problem concerning responsibilities for the young.

Central responsibility for children still lies with parents. The principal costs of child-rearing are borne by parents, for whom children are an increasingly great impediment, both to their working and their social lives. And children are of decreasing value to parents. Adults live longer than before and child-rearing occupies a shorter span of time, so it loses its place as the central activity of adults and becomes instead a distraction from whatever the adult's central activity is.

Part of the reason is the loss of the family's productivity and responsibility functions. Children are no longer useful for the work they do, since the family is no longer the productive unit of society. Children are no longer useful in caring for their parents in old age, as the family has relinquished that function to the state. The question becomes, in a social structure in which the family is no longer responsible for its ageing members, and in which children's labour is no longer useful, why incur the costs of bearing and raising children? I have seen no satisfactory answer to this question. While the population problem in societies with the old social structure remains how to limit a family's interest in additional children, in the new social structure it is how to maintain or create that interest.

Patterns of education, employment and family life in the UK have changed radically since Victorian times. Children at school (*left*) now frequently become 'unemployed youth' (*below*) at the age of 16.

Personality types

The new form of corporate body encourages freedom, individualism and a certain lack of responsibility among those who occupy positions within it. Ambitions are unfettered, and the enticements of having no responsibilities for others, only for one's job, create personalities incompatible with the long-term obligations of the family. The continuity of the family is an anachronism unsuited to persons shaped by the freedoms offered in the social structure outside the family. Thus the family is not only besieged from without by the foreign elements of the social structure which surround it. It is destroyed from within, as its members fail to have the qualities necessary to give it continuity and stability. And this reduces its capacity to serve as the basic unit of socialization of the next generation.

Long ago the French sociologist Emile Durkheim showed a strong relation between the psychological state of social isolation and suicide, a relation which has been confirmed many times since. Between 1950 and 1975, the annual suicide rate for young white males in the United States increased by 27 per cent, a stark indicator of the increase in individualism carried to the extremes of isolation and self-destruction.

The genesis of norms

The fourth major change in child-rearing brought about by the new social structure is in the social norms to which children and youth are subject. In

Modern families on the whole are smaller than those of a century ago. But there are exceptions, like this Glasgow family.

the old social structure, social norms were extensions of the ideals and demands of the family. The family had at its disposal an extensive set of adjunct guardians over the actions of its children, whether in the form of the extended kinship group or of the community. Everyone who has grown up in a small town has experienced the constraints of those norms and the sense of freedom when they are left behind.

But these norms, which are oppressive to the adolescent and the young person, are important instruments of socialization. There is a phenomenon, which has always been regarded by sociologists as somewhat curious, that illustrates this. When lower-class families move from rural areas to the city, it is not the generation which has grown up in the rural areas – those who are adolescents or young men and young women at the time of migration – who suffer most from unemployment, delinquency and crime. It is the first generation raised in the city (and sometimes later generations as well). The explanation, though I have no direct evidence for it, is, I believe, a simple one. In rural areas, the family has an extensive set of social reinforcements in its child-rearing in the form of the rural community. In this setting, the family is an effective instrument of socialization. In the modern city, surrounded by corporate bodies of the new social structure, it is not.

The norms generated by these bodies are by-products of their commercial interests in gaining an audience or selling a product. The use of sex in advertisements and in commercial entertainment media illustrates this: sex is a major device to attract attention or gain an audience and is used to further the interests of the corporate body in selling its products. And norms which make high consumption an admirable trait are probably inimical to the long-range interests of youth. Generated by commercial interests, they replace the norms which in a rural area or small community made frugality admirable.

If norms are consistent and reinforce each other, then they establish within the child a sense of what is right and what is wrong. If they are inconsistent, and conflict with each other, that sense is less fully developed.

The consequence of these changes in norms is greatest for children. The reinforcement which the community once provided for the parent has been replaced by content which is disconnected from, and often subversive to, parental prescriptions and proscriptions.

The role of the school in socialization

I have focused so far on the family as the principal instrument through which new generations are brought into society, and have scarcely mentioned the school. The reason is straightforward: the school has, since its birth, been a supplement to the family, never a substitute for it. The single most powerful generalization that can be stated from research on achievement in school is that the effectiveness of schools depends very much on the family. Children from weak families do poorly in school; children from strong families do well. As a simple example of one way in which this occurs, doing well requires a child to do homework. In the United States, where the family is weakest, the amount of homework set has declined steadily along with achievement levels, and, if I am correct, the family's reduced capacity for taking responsibility for its young is the source of the decline.

Doing well at school means doing homework. But homework requires concentration in an atmosphere of domestic harmony.

Strategies of child-rearing

The question of the future must be: how can the environment of children and youth be restructured in this setting, so as to reconstitute the ability of the species to continue itself by raising new generations? There are two fundamentally different strategies:

1. to attempt to strengthen the family's capacity for child-rearing, by making the new social structure surrounding it less alien, or
2. to assume that the family as a corporate body of the old form, composed of strong and enduring personal relations between parents and children, will no longer exist for most children, and to devise an alternative form of child-rearing compatible with the new social structure.

In the old structure, relations develop between children and the parents of their peers. These relations both strengthen the basic parent–child relations and shoulder part of the socialization task of those relations. The new structure draws the parents away from the child, and provides no support for the establishment of relations with that child's peers.

One strategy is to attempt to reconstitute the school so that it will generate or reinforce relations between the parents of the children who attend it. In practical terms this means making the school smaller, more parochial, more controlled by parents and responsive to them, more an extension of the parents' religious or philosophical views. Over the past half-century, most educational change has been in the direction of larger schools, more professionalized and insulated from parents, with less contact between teachers and parents, and more responsive to government, though there have recently been some moves to reverse these trends in US schools. The benefits of such a direction included the partial re-creation of a portion of the old social structure, that is, a community of adults with shared values able to impose norms that reinforce the family's ideals, and more likely to contain adults with a personal interest in individual children and youth. The costs are a certain parochialism and a possible reduction in equality of educational opportunity, as the family's influence on school functioning increases.

Building upon the new structure

The second strategy – devising alternative forms of child-rearing compatible with the new structures – can take two forms, as I see it:

Planned construction of communities of children and youth, of the sort found in boarding schools and less often in day schools. These communities, of which the widest example is English boarding schools, are detached from and not dependent on the family. They tend to generate greater self-responsibility among the young because of their capacity to impose norms that shape desirable behaviour.

The benefits and costs of such self-socializing communities with artificial environments are much the same as those of any close community. They bring the additional benefit of freeing the child from the parochialism imposed by parents and the additional cost of increasing the insulation of children and youth from everyday adult activities, and thus possibly exacerbating the difficulties of transition to adulthood.

The development of age-balanced organizations with an age distribution approximating that in society as a whole. This strategy accepts the dominance of the new social structure composed of corporate bodies made up of positions, but it imposes additional goals on those organizations: nurturing the young and care for the aged. There is some slight movement in this direction with the introduction of day-care centres and nursery schools in some workplaces; but incentives to these corporate bodies (for example, in the form of reduced taxes commensurate with the services provided) would be needed if they were to be used on a large scale. Perhaps the closest current approximation is the paternalistic corporation found in Japan.

This approach is the most radical of any suggested here, for it accepts the new form of social structure and in effect argues that the principal defect of these new corporate bodies as the central institutions of society is that they have no place for dependents, and in particular do not constitute environments in which the next generation can grow. The virtues and faults are less clear than in the other forms discussed, because they constitute a sharper departure from any present practice.

The future of women

BETTY FRIEDAN

The women's movement has been the most massive, far-reaching movement of social change in modern times. It has changed our lives and the dimensions against which we measure them, and we are only beginning to glimpse its far-reaching implications. Yet the women's movement itself is only a stage. It is the first stage in a revolution in sex roles, and it is part of a broader evolutionary change. Civilization is at a critical juncture, and the women's movement is the one visible piece of evidence of evolutionary change that gives us the hope that we can surmount this juncture and that civilization can survive.

Women's movement towards equality was the first step, not of a war of woman against man, but of a massive sex-role revolution, of woman *and* man breaking through the stereotyped feminine and masculine roles that have kept both sexes from reaching full human potential. These roles were at one time probably necessary for human survival, but now, from evolutionary necessity, they must be transcended. What is needed is a new human definition of both man and woman, so that we can reach our full potential and redefine and restructure institutions built around these polarized sex roles. This change had to start with women moving to equality in primarily male terms.

A reversal of roles. This stereoscopic card of 1897 shows the 'new woman' with her bloomers and bicycle standing over her husband at the washing tub.

Anatomy is no longer destiny

Woman's life was defined in primitive society – and indeed in all societies until quite recently – primarily in terms of her child-bearing and child-rearing. When babies often failed to survive, when children were needed to till the earth, to fight wars, to carry out the tasks of their society, when sons were the only social security for old age, when women had little choice about child-bearing and few years to live after it was over, then anatomy was destiny, as Freud said. Maybe it was a necessity for evolution.

However, with the advent of the Industrial Revolution, the important tasks of society, the tasks that seemed to carry society forward, came to be more and more concentrated in the cities, more specialized and more dominated by men. The work that was left to women – looking after the

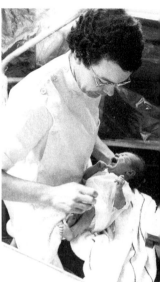

home, family and children – had no monetary value (money was now the coin) and was less valued by society. As industrial society advanced, the polarization became more extreme. Woman has had to break through the constraints of being defined solely in relation to others, as wife, mother, sex object, bearer of children, server of physical needs.

The first stage: fighting for equality on male terms

It is probably not a coincidence that the modern women's movement in the United States began with women who had already borne children. I began to write *The Feminine Mystique* when my youngest child, now a doctor, was born, and I finished the book, and helped start the women's movement, as she moved into school. I then had over half my life ahead of me. This was also the situation of increasing numbers of educated women in America. We had to break through what I called the feminine mystique because it was no longer a necessary definition of woman. A definition of woman solely in terms of the family – as wife, mother, housewife – was obsolete. It didn't fit reality any longer. It kept women from developing and using their other capacities and from facing the need to use their life energies, to have a function in society throughout life, and to be able to support themselves and their families financially.

The people who were afraid when the women's movement became conscious, as it had to do, were not men. They were women, because women had to risk themselves in new ways, and there really was no choice. We were unable to take our identity from previous generations. We had to be self-made in new ways.

We had to break through the barriers, visible and invisible that kept women from moving in society. The action, the power, the recognized values in society seemed to be concentrated in professions and occupations dominated by men. So the first stage of women's movement to equality was, almost perforce, defined in male terms. These were the

Some of the barriers between traditionally 'male' and 'female' jobs are being broken down in the West in the last quarter of the twentieth century. *Left:* Dr Sally Ride, an astronaut on the seventh US shuttle flight. *Centre:* A male midwife in training at a London hospital. *Right:* A few more women are now working in science and engineering.

The struggle for votes for women (indeed, for universal suffrage) in the UK was a long and bitter one. Miss Billington at Westminster in 1912.

only terms there were, in a certain sense. All the values and experiences of women were denigrated as female. Women's nurturing values and experiences were not seen in the same context as men's values and powers. They were not public and seemed to have little direct influence on society.

The women's movement took the values of US democracy – respect for the individual and for freedom and dignity and the right to a voice in decision-making – and for the first time applied them to women. But what was unique about it was that it couldn't be seen in male terms. Because this movement came from women's experience and was applied to women's experience, which is primarily defined by the 'dailiness' of life, it had a concrete immediacy that changed people's lives through the medium of home and family, though it seemed at first to be against the family and home. This change was effected with far greater speed than is the case with old-style male revolutions, which are usually based on abstract either/or blueprints devised by intellectuals to be applied to the situations of other people in future generations and therefore lack concrete immediacy. From the very beginning, the women's movement not only sought equality in the professions that had been defined by males, but also politicized experience that had never been treated as political before. The home, the family, child-rearing, housework were made political in new ways that sometimes seemed silly at first but were not silly at all.

Improved mental health

A remarkable change has occurred in the last 15 years, and it has taken epidemiologists and demographers by surprise. Fifteen or twenty years ago, the mental health of women was shown by large-scale American studies – the Mid-Town Manhattan Study, for example, and the study of the National Center of Health Statistics – to deteriorate with age, declining consistently after the age of 20, but especially after 40. Men's mental health, on the other hand, remained more constant. The sociologist Jeffrey Bernard used to say that marriage was very good for men, because married men live longer healthier lives than single men, but that it was driving women crazy. Now it seems that women are well off, or better off, than men in terms of mental health. New studies have shown that, on every index of mental health, women in their forties and fifties are just as healthy, if not more so, than they were in their twenties and thirties. Their new self-respect and sense of control over their lives have been good for women, whether they are housewives or work outside the home. Even women with the double burden of paid work and work in the home are showing this new vitality.

The vitality of older women – a group of over-60s cheerleaders in Arizona, USA.

Right: Dr Finola Poyntz, a Metropolitan Police forensic scientist. She has analysed a new protein in semen which is of significance in investigating cases of rape.

Women are healthier than men in their seventies and eighties, too. Massive studies of ageing show that they survive longer and better than men. And that, I believe, is because they have one great survival skill – the ability to create, sustain and re-create human bonds of loving, caring, mutual support in family or family-type networks. This ability keeps them alive in the most literal sense.

The second stage: bridging the gap between the sexes

The gains of the women's movement could never have been made without the mass media to carry its message to those women, who were legion, whose yearnings needed to be made conscious. Yet the media also distorted the movement, picking on extremist actions and rhetoric that made it for a while seem like a war of women against men – women, the oppressed class, against men, the class oppressors. Down with men, women seemed to be saying, then, by extrapolation, down with marriage, home, family, child-rearing and everything women had ever done to attract men, including make-up and shaving under the arms. There were germs of truth in this extremism, but to see the movement as a war of women against men, a revolution on the old model, where one class

Right: There were far fewer opportunities for further education and training for generations of women who grew up before and during the Second World War. A traditional 'woman's' job – washing up in the school canteen.

overthrows the other, takes power and switches positions, is to miss the essential paradigm change that is in fact taking place and to abort its evolutionary significance.

The notion that we are moving from the first stage of sexual revolution to the second, and my new book, *The Second Stage*, in which I put this notion forward, have been controversial in the United States because it is unsettling even to the makers of change to be told that any movement of change must itself keep evolving. This time, above all, the revolution must deal with the very situation it has created, by evolving, correcting, staying in tune with what is happening on the way.

New problems, pressures and paradoxes

The women's movement has affected lives, and on the whole enormously for the better. It has been a life-opening, life-changing movement. 'It changed my life. It changed my whole life,' women say about the women's movement, which is why I called my intermediate book just that: *It Changed My Life*. Few women would want to go back, and probably not many men either. But there are new problems and pressures.

Most women know that they will have to spend most of their lives working outside the home, from sheer economic necessity. Young women are able to prepare themselves for this and aspire to the more rewarding jobs and professions. Women are training in the professions in greatly increased numbers. Yet statistics show that, in the US, women overall now average only 59 cents for every dollar that men make, and the gap has widened in the 15 years since the women's movement began. Why is that? Partly because women mostly work still in sales, clerical and service jobs, which are underpaid because they have always been done by women, and partly because most of the women who have moved into the labour force in recent years have done so after years as housewives and mothers and they do not have the education or experience needed for better paid jobs.

The changes wrought by the women's movement have led to some interesting paradoxes. The first generation of women who refused to get caught up in the feminine mystique placed a lot of emphasis on career and professional security, while postponing marriage and postponing or rejecting motherhood, and they sought too much of their identity, perhaps, in the way that men traditionally do. So we have seen the paradox of women 'dressing for success', to use the American term, along male lines, while corporations were paying social psychologists to teach men the traditionally feminine skills of sensitivity and intuition.

The women's movement has been accused of destroying the family. Yet, paradoxically, research has shown that in families where both partners are earning, a greater value is placed on the family. According to polls, men are attaching greater importance to family and self-fulfilment, and less to success in the male rat-race, the old definition of masculinity.

The women's movement fought for medical access to abortion in the belief that the woman must be in control of her own reproductive process. It is an enormously liberating factor for motherhood to be a freely chosen act. Motherhood does not require the martyrdom of women. What we are seeing now, as we move into the second stage, is an explosion of child-bearing by women in their late thirties and even early forties who are successful in their careers. Even fiery feminists who fought for the right to abortion are opting for motherhood as their most freely chosen act.

Restructuring work and home

The rhetoric of the early women's movement was strident because women needed to break through as independent beings. But we can, and must, see it differently now. We cannot look just at the position of women. In the next stage of evolution we must look also at the role of men and at the need to restructure work and home.

What made me write *The Second Stage* was the clear sense of new, agonizing conflicts and problems. There are women in jobs and professions who cannot afford to leave them because the economic survival of their family depends on them. But those jobs and professions are structured in terms of the lives of men in the past who had wives to take care of all the details of life. So, at work such a woman competes on masculine terms, not yet being confident of her own, different, strength, then she comes home to meet standards set by women in the past who had to find the whole of their power and identity in a perfectly run home and perfectly controlled children because they had no control over their lives in a larger arena. Trying to be super-mum at home and would-be superman at the office is likely to produce the same signs of stress, heart attacks and ulcers that men suffer from.

Younger women may be shying away from this terrible burden and reverting to the either/or position. But women are losing out if they have to choose between their traditional role, which is also part of their biological potential – children and the satisfactions of love, nurturing and home – and having rewarding work and a voice in political decisions.

The concrete measures needed to restructure work and home so as to prevent the superwoman burden will not be taken, either politically or economically, by and for women alone. They must be taken for the benefit of men also, and for society as a whole.

Those qualities that are thought of as 'feminine' – the qualities that give life its sensitivity, its concreteness, its juiciness, its humanity, almost – have been suppressed in men and have remained the monopoly of women. Yet they are essential to men's survival. (Men are dying in the United States nearly ten years younger than women of the same age group.) Younger men are beginning to realize that these qualities can enhance their work and their lives. Even at a time when economic conditions are making great careerists of American men, these men are saying, 'I want a good relationship with my children.' The film *Kramer versus Kramer* was such a hit because the hero – not tall, stalwart John Wayne, but short, nervous, sensitive Dustin Hoffman – from being a hollow man in an advertising agency saying 'yes' to the boss and going to the bar with the boys afterwards, really becomes a man by taking care of his young son.

As women continue to share with men the task of earning, and as the new sense of values permeates society, men and women will share

Some men are now becoming involved in child care.

child-rearing in new ways. There will be a restructuring of work, with flexitime, parental leave, sabbaticals for parents. People will no longer be defined only by their chosen profession; they will continue to renew themselves, to grow, to change again, to go back to studying. And the change will not be just in patterns of child-rearing and work. We will become more concerned with the *quality* of work and life issues, and this movement will be given impetus by economic and political conditions. Even at times of great economic crisis, restructuring work is less inflationary than wage increases, and it does much for the quality of life.

The female influence in the world at large

Everywhere there will be a greater value placed on communality, and bridges will be built between 'male' and 'female' values. The professions – law, medicine, theology – will become more holistic and life-oriented, both in their theory and their practice, with less emphasis on disembodied abstractions. Freud thought women were deficient in a sense of justice, and this wisdom has been perpetuated by the Coberg scale, which measures moral, educational and psychological development. Women score lower than men on the Coberg scale, which takes the highest level of development to be an abstract sense of justice and morality. But recent research in Canada shows that men and women diverge in their moral and psychological development. Whereas the abstract principles that men value so highly are divorced from reality and can be misused, women at their highest stage of development so perfectly integrate an abstract sense of justice and morality with the concreteness of life experience that they cannot be measured on the Coberg scale.

As women become ministers, priests and rabbis, and as theology comes to be written by women as well as men, and by men with a new sensitivity, we will see less of the abstract morality that preaches the sermon on Sunday or on Friday night then fights the war or pollutes the environment the rest of the week.

In medicine, the move towards a holistic approach has gone hand in hand with women's demands that they should have some control over their own bodies as patients. Women are helping to set the terms themselves, whether as patients or as nurses, instead of treating the doctor like God. As we approach the year 2000, we are beginning to see a bridge developing between the traditionally undervalued and underpaid skills of the nurse and those of the doctor, and we will see a new kind of doctor.

In the field of the arts, too, we can expect to see important differences. It has often been said that if women are equal there should have been more great women artists and musicians. To be a good artist you must have self-confidence, you must take yourself very seriously as a person, you must be able to say 'no' to conventional or existing forms in favour of innovation. So it is not even a question of overcoming the explicit barriers of discrimination. Women's creativity in the arts will flower as they say 'yes' to themselves as women and people and stop trying to follow male models. Among men, too, creativity will flower as they free themselves from death-dealing machismo.

Chapter Ten

WHERE TO GO AND HOW TO GET THERE

Not so long ago, at the beginning of the 1960s' boom, it seemed that the West's desire for the future would be to have more and cheaper consumer goods. But Martin Walker has identified a later trend – beginning in the late 1960s and still growing – away from the mass-produced and towards what he defines as the New Luddism: real ale, real bread and clothes in natural as opposed to synthetic fibres. Allied to this, have been political ecology movements and trades unions whose members are being put out of work by new technology.

But technology, Raymond Williams argues, is only a part of the future and a part over which we have far more individual control than many governments would have us believe. His essay 'How We Make the Future' is a fitting finale for the book. 'We can describe the future as black or golden,' Williams concludes, 'lived in this way or that, but what matters much more is to regain the confidence and to find the means and institutions in which more and more of us can take active and informed responsibility for it.'

Greenpeace protesters at a nuclear site in Nevada, USA.

The anti-futurists

MARTIN WALKER

There is nothing inevitable about the future, except in the trivial sense. The old Chinese Empire established an institutional system which was designed to inhibit change and its disruptive effects, and which succeeded for two millennia. It took the navies and the merchants of the West, equipped with the gunpowder technology the Chinese had invented but chosen not to develop as weapons, to impose modernity upon China. And those Western invaders were heirs of an industrial revolution which had had its own resistance. As the new textile machinery came to English factories in the Midlands and the North after 1811, there was a 10-year wave of industrial sabotage, smashed machines and factories where the workers made jobless by change left their calling-card – a letter condemning the new machines and signed by 'King Lud'. The Luddites lost the battle, but the campaign goes on. As the twentieth century draws to a close, a new Luddism is emerging in the West, not only in industry, but

Engraving by Hablot Browne (1840). The Luddites who wrecked the new machinery which brought them unemployment, low wages and starvation. In the absence of a civilian police force, soldiers were used to repress the protesters and protect the machinery.

also among consumers concerned about their 'way of life'. And, ironically, the resisters of change are bringing a different, more subtle kind of change in their wake.

Food and clothing

Perhaps the most visible part of this process has been in the food and fashion industries. Blue jeans began as a cheap, workman's garment, more useful than elegant. By the 1980s, this mass-produced pair of labourer's trousers had become a desirable and high-priced fashion item, with that little touch hinting at hand-made care – the designer's label. Those great virtues of the factory assembly-line system, cheapness and availability, had been transformed into expensive 'chic' that was *not* mass-produced.

Blue jeans: from American working men's overalls to international high fashion. What was a practical garment worn by workers such as the Arkansas farmer *(above)* has been transformed into a high priced, designer-styled fashion item *(right)* as advertised in Mexico City.

The British brewing industry provides an even better example. By 1970, the process of industrial concentration had left five major producers of beer. Each of these five 'modernized' its plant to produce a single product that could be marketed across the nation. It therefore had to taste the same wherever it was bought, and thus had to be protected from unskilful barmen and innkeepers. The beer was therefore 'killed' (its innate organic content sterilized in the brewing process), and stored in mass-produced barrels whence it was decanted under the pressure of a gas.

A number of consumers who disapproved of this process founded, in 1971, a small club called CAMRA, the Campaign for Real Ale. They produced a newsletter, publicizing the small independent brewers who still survived and produced the traditional live beers, warm and flat and tasting of the yeast that had gone into the making. It became a kind of consumers' guerrilla campaign, and it had a phenomenal success in the teeth of initial opposition from the big brewers. CAMRA grew fast enough to buy its own inns, and the small brewers grew with it, until the big brewers surrendered, began once again to make and market the traditional ales, and were proud to post little notices in their pubs saying that they were listed in CAMRA's *Good Beer Guide*.

The Campaign for Real Ale spawned a number of similar groups, a campaign for real bread, for real cheese and so on. That basic logic of industrial modernization, the mass-production of a uniform product, had failed in the market place which preferred the good old ways. And the consumers wanted the old product enough to pay a premium to get it. Cheap factory cheese gave up some of its space on supermarket shelves to home-produced goat cheese; and consumer resistance to the cheap, mass-produced sliced white loaf led to a remarkable revival of the small bakery, producing 'traditional' bread on its premises.

Again, as the British textile industry began to wither away in the 1970s in the face of competition from cheap Third World imports, a boom developed in another sector of the market. The hand-knitted, individually-designed sweaters, and the old looms of the Scottish crofters who wove Harris tweed began to enjoy a successful revival. The old and natural materials, the wools and cottons and silks, ate into the market so quickly that the growth industry of the 1960s – man-made fibres and the petrochemical plants that produced them – had gone into dramatic decline by 1980. The Teesside factory that Britain's giant ICI combine had boasted in 1960 was big enough to produce a new nylon shirt a year for every British male, was closed in 1981. The market had collapsed.

Conservation

The same social and marketing phenomena were apparent in every economic sector across the rich, Western world. In housing, the cheap tower blocks that had been erected in the 1950s and 1960s through systems-building became a national embarrassment. The American city of St Louis was the first to start demolishing these white elephants of the industrial era of housing. But throughout the West, there was an uncanny similarity in the way that the values of the old, slum houses in the inner cities soared, while tenants could not be persuaded to move into 'modern' blocks of flats. Instead, on the Boston waterfront, on San Francisco's wharf, along the docks of London and in the historic wine warehouses of Bordeaux, the old buildings were renovated rather than knocked down, and sold off for high prices in a market that was suddenly prepared to put a very high value on conservation.

Indeed, conservation itself became a growth industry in the 1970s, offering at least a chance of fulfilling employment to the humanities graduates coming onto a gloomy jobs market. In London in 1981, a building by Mies van der Rohe, one of the undisputed masters of modern architecture, was stopped by a conservation campaign that preferred to retain several blocks of awkwardly-shaped and rather ordinary Victorian office buildings. The fashion for conservation was not restricted to the West. In 1982, Libya's controversial Colonel Gadafy personally vetoed a development scheme for his capital city which threatened the medieval fort of Tripoli, and the undistinguished blocks of shops and offices erected by the Italian colonizers in the years before 1914. In Saudi Arabia and in

Paddington, Sydney. Restoration of property has transformed a slum district into an expensive, exclusive neighbourhood.

Jordan, the royal families gave powerful patronage to their local conservation societies. In Sydney, Australia, the old slum and red-light district of Paddington was not demolished, but restored to become an expensive and desirable quarter.

And to get around their conserved cities, the inhabitants increasingly took to that veteran system of personal transport, the bicycle. Clearly, this was not just simple nostalgia at work. The rise in petrol costs after the OPEC oil price rise of 1973/4 played a part, as did the strangulation of city centres by the increasing number of cars that the new post- World War II prosperity made possible. But the cycling enthusiasts in Europe and the United States promoted their bikes in the style of a political, or even a consumer campaign; in Britain, they used the slogan 'Pedal Power'. In France after 1975, the cycle division of the giant Peugeot empire recorded the fastest growth and the highest profits.

Positive Luddism

There are a number of significant features about this wave of resistance to the 'modernization' of housing, goods, cities and urban transport. The first is the eventual enthusiasm with which the capitalist system was able to adapt to and cater for it. The second is that, in a number of ways, these trends were inherently desirable, contributing towards what people considered their 'quality of life': bicycles do not pollute the air, nor are they noisy; it makes economic sense to rehabilitate old buildings rather than replace them wholesale. There is an intelligence at work here, a highly rational calculation of benefits and costs in the way that a key sector of the public resisted change and modernization. We need a name for this phenomenon, and we could hardly do better than call it Positive Luddism.

There is another side to the coin. In some societies any hint of consumer resistance was stamped upon in the name of modernization. In the Soviet bloc, the ideology of modernized agriculture locked the system into visibly

'Positive Luddism' – cheap, practical two-wheeled transport.

inefficient collective farms which, in spite of massive investment in tractors and fertilizers, proved dismally incapable of feeding their own people. (In the years before 1914, tsarist Russia had been the biggest grain exporter in Europe.)

In this sense, cynicism about the vaunted benefits of modernization was a feature of the West, although the city centres of Tallin, Warsaw and Budapest suggest that the urge to conserve buildings certainly crossed the ideological frontier. And if we look for the roots of this trend in the West, we find a number of clues to the process. In the Consumers' Association (publishers of the *Which?* guides and the *Good Food Guide*) in Britain, in Ralph Nader's consumer campaigns in the US of the 1960s, in the Danish and Swiss consumer clubs we see the development of a discriminating and educated choice within an already pampered market. In the hippies of the 1960s, we see a generation (which is now at the peak of its purchasing power) turning its back, briefly at least, on the consumer society whose wealth underwrote and indeed made possible the hippy lifestyle. And if the hippies did not win, they at least secured an honourable draw.

The students of 1968 who went to the Paris barricades against 'the tranquillized society', or the hippies who went to San Francisco, have seen not the defeat of consumerism, but its speedy development into a consumerism of discrimination. Indeed, they helped to create it. Many of those hand-knitted sweaters which dominate the market stalls of London's Covent Garden were designed and made in the Welsh farmyard communes to which so many of Britain's hippies trekked. In the street markets of France's medieval towns in the Dordogne, it is the ex-hippies who make the goats' cheese, the *pâté de foie gras*, the specialized fat cakes of the Perigord.

Just as a generation of hippy tourists financed its travels by making and selling jewellery on every street corner on every Greek island, so the new flea markets of London's Camden Lock and Paris's Goutte d'Or and Amsterdam's Waterlooplein were first revived, then served, manned and patronized by what we can, with only a little licence, call the children of '68. And increasingly they are being joined by the children of the great depression of the 1970s, the punks, the kids who went straight from school to the dole queue and into their own generation's cultural rejection of a society that found no use for their labour – except in the black economy of the flea markets, buying and selling the junk of their elders. As the mass market fragments, the new speciality markets emerge – whether on street stalls, in the new channels of cable television or the booming trade in special-interest magazines.

Political Luddism

In the modern economy, consumers are also producers, as indeed they are planners, teachers and administrators. And if there was fragmented opposition to the industrial and modernizing process from consumers, there was very much more resistance from those institutions which were themselves industrial products. Trades unions throughout the West, with greater or lesser success, set themselves against change with the fury of the

Unemployment across Europe. Striking print workers from the London *Times (top)* and French steel workers *(above)* demonstrate and organize to fight job losses.

first Luddites, and the bland assurance of the old mandarins of imperial China. In the US, newspapers' efforts to modernize their printing technology became a minor war, with the print unions at the *Washington Post* in 1975 putting bullet holes in the windows of the production manager, attacking their printing presses with fire, acid and axes while the management hired helicopters to ferry out each day's papers over the heads of the besieging workers. In Paris, in Frankfurt, in New York and in London's Fleet Street, the new technology brought in its own labour unrest and resistance to redundancy and loss of skilled jobs. Ship-builders in Scotland occupied their shipyards on the Clyde rather than see them closed and modernized. French steelworkers in Lorraine fought pitched battles with riot police to keep their jobs from 'rationalization'.

But these forces of resistance were pulling in opposite directions. If consumers voted with their cash against mass-produced goods, then there was little hope of retaining the factory jobs that produced those goods and which the unions tried to defend. The fragmentation of the industrial process inolved a parallel fragmentation of the labour force, a strategic weakening of the trades unions, and of the political parties established to defend the interests of the working classes. It was one of the great ironies of the depression of the 1970s and 1980s that capitalists could see in robots and automated factories the dream of running capitalism without the need for a working class. But if people were not working and earning, who would have the money to buy the goods the robots dutifully produced?

For the rest of the century, the erosion of the traditional status and influence of the trades unions could only increase, at least in the exposed industries of engineering, steel, textiles and ship-building, those labour-intensive trades where Third World economies could most effectively compete. And one effect of this was to push trade-union activists deeper into the secure bunkers they had established in the 1970s, in strategically vital sectors such as mining, and in public service jobs less exposed to competition. The OPEC price rise itself almost overnight changed the prospect and the status of coal-mining unions throughout those Western economies lucky enough to have coal. And having used their economic muscle to push their way to the top of the wages league, the miners' next priority was to secure their monopoly by opposing pit closures and the development of nuclear power stations. Other unions, in the construction, engineering and electronic sectors, whose members' jobs depended on such power stations being commissioned, took the other side of the argument.

Those who opposed nuclear energy because it threatened their jobs found themselves alligned with the ecology movement – the political wing of Positive Luddism that had gained momentum throughout the West in the 1970s. The ecology movement first gained political weight in California, with the election of Governor Jerry Brown, a current which helped Jimmy Carter to the presidency in 1976. But it was in Germany in 1982 that the Green political party became decisive, undermining the Liberal–Socialist coalition of Helmut Schmidt, and ironically paving the way for the Conservative chancellorship of Kohl. The Greens had their counterpart in France, where their support helped President Mitterrand to

'Political Luddism' – West Germany's Green party at a press conference after the 1982 election in which they won 9 seats and 8 per cent of the vote. Standing: Petra Kelly. Left to right: Lukas Beckamann, Raphael Keppel, Jochen Hielhauer, Frank Schwalba-Hoth.

power in 1981, on a platform that included a commitment to review the nuclear power programme. There were more than hints of similar Luddite forces at work in the Arab world and, indeed, the revolution against the Shah of Iran in 1978/9 was a reaction of traditional Islam against the Shah's breakneck policy of westernization. Whether there was much that was positive about the Ayatollah Khomeini's Luddism remains to be seen. But throughout the Islamic world, there was a current of mistrust for the West, a defiance of that industrial development and modernization which had once seemed so attractive.

At its most extreme, the ecological movement called for an era of zero-growth, in the economy as much as in population. The alarming political implications of zero-growth were first explored by the British Labour cabinet minister Tony Crosland in 1976, who pointed out that it involved putting not just the economy, but social change too, into a kind of permafrost. Zero-growth presumably meant, he argued, that his constituents remained unemployed, while the affluent continued to drive their Rolls-Royces to the French Riviera. If growth was to be stopped, then even if the population remained static, there would be no more goods to go round. A fairer share for the poor would therefore mean the disposession of the better off. This was a recipe for class war. And if population growth did not suddenly cease, and it showed no signs of doing so outside the rich, Western world, then the poverty of the Third World would become not simply endemic, but institutionalized.

Ironically, Crosland argued his case just as industrial change was sapping at the class basis of the Labour Party that gave him his authority. The Labour vote was falling, the old craft unions of the industrial revolution were giving way to the white-collar and public sector unions. He was already too late, and the social changes that followed this process threatened the old Labour Party from another direction with the birth of the Social Democratic Party owing, perhaps mistakenly, at least a little to the Positive Luddism which had nurtured the Greens in Germany.

But Crosland's instincts and forebodings had been right. If there was a coherence to the politics of Positive Luddism, then it was conservative, in so far as it mistrusted change, and capitalist even though it involved an economy rooted in small businesses, cooperatives and cottage industries, rather than in the factories and the assembly lines. The economic motives for Positive Luddism came from a bewildering variety of directions. The decline of the package tour holiday, that symbol of sixties' affluence, was matched by a growth in more obscure and adventurous holidays – helped along by the ruthless competition in the package tour industry which gave the organizers an average profit margin of 2 per cent, compared to the 15 to 20 per cent of more specialized vacations.

While China has recently become more receptive to visitors, goods and ideas from the West (*below:* tourists at the Temple of Heaven), Islam is turning its back on Western influence. This is especially evident in Iran (*right*) where, since the fall of the Shah, women are again wearing the chador, some by force but many by choice.

And as the fiscal base of the capitalist system became endangered through inflation, so capitalism gave another boost to the conservation movement, the prizing of the past's achievements over those of the present, with the boom in the value of works of art, antiques, old books and antique scientific instruments. The wheel of Britain's industrial revolution came full circle in the 1980s, as the North of England Tourist Board began to promote tours of the industrial archaeology of its region. The dark satanic mills which had been its wealth and its shame had become its new tourist pride. The shrines of the original Luddites, the scenes of their struggles, became the source of pilgrimage for their spiritual heirs as the Positive Luddites came to stare and wonder. And across the world, in post-Mao China, Confucius was rehabilitated, and China too began to enjoy a tourist boom and show off the sites of the old emperors and their mandarins who had resisted so much change for so long. 'The past is a great comfort,' observed Confucius. And the future is never inevitable.

How we make the future

RAYMOND WILLIAMS

There are forces no human power can affect: in the great galaxies, in the solar system, in our own earth. Any of these may at some point influence or decide our future. It is reasonable to think of these forces with awe: more so, often, as we begin to understand them better.

But then, at an opposite extreme, we ourselves are making another kind of future, day by day. Unless we are especially unfortunate, many of us are doing what yesterday or last year we decided or hoped we would do. The scale of this kind of making the future varies enormously between people, according to our real situations and resources. But in some degree, along this large scale, most people have the experience of having made some part of their future, and what they then feel is not awe but a reasonable and healthy self-confidence.

The difficult problems begin in the area between these extremes, where our capacity to make or even influence the future, including our own, is often felt to be insufficient but at the same time is very far from negligible. Either of the other attitudes – sheer awe or simple self-confidence – is then inappropriate. Persuaders of different kinds may offer us either of these attitudes neat: in the first case as fatalism, or as an invitation to leave all such matters to various kinds of higher authority; in the second case as a sort of cheer-leading, in which our ways, our beliefs, our nations or parties can be relied upon to see us through. What both attitudes then exclude is *thinking* about the future: not just watching the programmes or reading the books, which are at best only the beginning of serious interest, but active thinking, which always starts from where we are and ends, genuinely, in what we can do. It is a mark of our own time that this kind of active thinking is now especially difficult, quite apart from the fact that various kinds of fatalism and cheer-leading do all they can to discourage it.

What we can best do, as a first step, is to identify those areas between the vast superhuman forces and the most recognizable everyday life, and try to identify the conditions in which, in these areas, actual decisions about the future will in any case be made, whether we ourselves participate in them or not.

The first thing we will find is that there is a radical and increasing difference between those views of the future which are common in relatively stable social orders and those other and increasingly common views which in effect start from an experience of instability and uncertainty. The distinguishing characteristic of late-twentieth-century society is that more and more of us, in otherwise very different circumstances, are in this latter situation, in which instability and uncertainty seem to have become general norms.

Short-term plans: reproduction

It is of course still necessary to remind ourselves that in many stable social orders, of a relatively simple kind, there can be great uncertainty. Simple herding or food-growing societies, with solidly established social relationships, can be exposed to all the uncertainties of the physical world: anxieties about the next season's rains or about phases of diseases, pests and blights. Within the kinds of knowledge available to them, people in such societies perceive much larger areas of life as beyond their direct control. It is in such conditions that magical or religious substitutes for control most evidently flourish. Yet, in and through these uncertainties, at most stages short of full catastrophe, a sense of the future as an intended reproduction of the present persists very strongly. What is looked for is that the families, the land, the flocks, the crops should be reproduced and be fertile, so that life can be continued in its known forms.

Ways to avoid thinking seriously about the future: *(left)* fundamentalism; *(above)* unthinking, unrealistic flag-waving.

But what we then often forget is that in much more complicated societies, most people's major intentions are the same. Beneath the evident futurism of several kinds of politics, science and technology, there is a strong base of largely reproductive intentions, most obviously in the way in which most people think about their families and their institutions and their communities. Even when an important element of willed improvement has been added to these intentions, what is widely desired is still the effective reproduction of known ways and relationships, if possible in better attendant circumstances. Thus to the question 'where do we want to go, and how do we get there?', the majority answer is still, to the first part, 'into the next generation of this kind of life' and, to the second part, 'by continuing to do what we are doing as well as we can'. It is surprising but significant that this majority view of the future is so often overlooked by what can be called 'professional' thinking about the future. Indeed one kind of futurism sees this common wish and intention as unbearably dull, or even ignoble, yet on a closer look it has to be said that there is usually more human substance in the simple reproductive than in the orthodox futurist perspective.

Indeed this is so in all cases except those in which existing or probable instabilities, of a kind which genuinely threaten the otherwise commanding intention of satisfactory reproduction, have been identified and intelligently examined. The problem now is that on a vast scale, extending from global threats to the continuation of all life to more local threats of environmental damage, loss of livelihood and impoverishment of established communities, these radical instabilities exist. There is an intense problem of the relation between these and the closer reproductive desires. Some of the instabilities come through as actual damage or devastation, as in the current reappearance of mass unemployment throughout the industrial world. Some, like the full dangers of nuclear weapons or of ecological imbalance, may be generally perceived but are dependent for their full weight on many kinds of professional knowledge, based on skills which are very unevenly distributed and indeed, for most people, restricted. In either case, however, there is a widespread belief that what is happening, or what could happen, is for all practical purposes inevitable. It is surprising how common this feeling has been even about something as manageable and avoidable as present kinds of unemployment. There is now a major gap between what is and can be known and done about certain obvious and threatening instabilities, and a more general state of mind which is certain of its own immediate desires and intentions but which pushes away, as too difficult, or as in any case useless, a body of knowledge and thinking which is unquestionably central to all our futures.

Unemployment is a major cause of instability in the industrial world. This is a small section of a queue of 20 000 job-seekers who were applying for 200 jobs offered by the A.O. Smith Corporation in Wisconsin in 1983. Many queued for four days in temperatures of minus 8°C.

Conditions of (in)stability

1. The stable order

We have then to think about the conditions of stability and of instability. We can distinguish two broad kinds of instability. There are the long-standing but also still common effects which follow from the continuation of an apparently stable social order. The most obvious examples are the numerous cases of over-grazing of pastures, or over-felling of forests, which at a certain critical stage can devastate or entirely destroy the land on which a settled and satisfactory way of life has been based. In industrial societies there are comparable cases of industrial pollution and poisoning of the food chain, which are still complacently continued in the name of increased production. Less obviously, certain systems of land ownership and inheritance, or of family structure and size,

In herding and food-growing communities, stability is dependent upon the natural world. Dinka cattle in the Sudan.

Electronic invasion: a tele-communications tower in Senegal.

or of the distribution of knowledge and power, can work through to produce unlooked-for effects which often end by disturbing or breaking up the very order which supposed it was dedicated to its own simple reproduction.

Some forms of this reproduction are imposed on majorities by powerful and privileged minorities, and in these cases what has then to be developed is opposition and the organization of alternatives. But there are other cases, including many examples in contemporary industrial societies, in which, while the source of any particular form may have been a minority, significant majorities support or will even fight for its continuation, long after the dangers it contains have been reasonably identified. It is in these cases that the difficult relationship between the deep desire for stable reproduction and the difficult perception of major dangers and threats to it is at its most acute. Yet history is littered with cases of societies which went on too long in known and valued ways, and ended by destroying even what they had.

2. Invasion

On the other hand, there are many more cases in which a particular way of life, which was in its own terms relatively stable and satisfactory, faced by many difficulties but commonly meeting and overcoming them, has been in one way or another invaded or radically altered by more powerful external forces. There are the innumerable cases of foreign conquest, which reached a systematic stage in the organization of empires. There are the less dramatic but often equally destructive cases of the intrusion of alien economic systems, which break up traditional economies and, treating new lands and new peoples as mere raw material for their own operations, first disturb and often destroy the valued ways of life of other peoples. Between them these two kinds of alien intrusion and invasion have extended a radical instability to the whole contemporary world. Moreover they are now being followed up by comparable intrusions and invasions in the field of culture, communications and information, with the same broad results. The general effects of all these vast and extending changes have been profoundly destabilizing. Many of the changes are now in effect irreversible, in the sense that there can be no return to the whole conditions which existed before they occurred. Yet what is most ironic is that so many of these terrible enterprises, especially in their most systematic phases, have excused or justified themselves in terms of bringing a new and higher order of life. Many of them were directly seen and described as progress, and it is in fact true that some elements of their systems have been specifically beneficial. Yet the basic drives of control and repression, whether savagely or even wisely exercised, have provoked and are provoking counter-movements, seeking independence and autonomy, over a range from newly progressive to crudely reactionary impulses, which now shake the whole world. As we consider the future, within this perspective, it is especially necessary to track the disturbances back to their sources, in invasions and intrusions which are in fact still continuing.

3. Technological determinism

There is then a third kind of disturbance, which can be distinguished both from the unlooked-for effect of an otherwise stable internal order and from the measurable effects, of alien invasion or intrusion. It is often in fact related to both, but its particular importance, now, is that it is especially closely connected with ideas about the future and how we shall make it. Indeed there is one kind of futurism which is virtually limited to this kind of change: the introduction and development of new technologies.

Here, very clearly, it is necessary to understand how change has happened in the past if we are to think with any effect about how we are making or might make the future. In the present phase of rapid technical invention a false way of thinking has become popular and even orthodox. It is identified by its critics as technological determinism. The argument is always complex and often difficult, but it is now perhaps more decisive than any other in general thinking about the future.

For if technological determinism is valid, there is really only one way of describing the future and how we shall reach it. Informed forecasts or more dramatic speculations about the next phases of technology offer to fill the whole space of rational foresight or prediction. From the computerized office to the robot factory to space travel, the basic elements of the future have been set in place, and all other human projections are reduced to fitting in with them, adjusting to them.

There can of course be a merely silly reaction to all or any of these technical developments: pushing them away or denouncing them as unwanted or inhuman changes. But this only hides the real question, and indeed by its very silliness serves merely to increase the complacency of the technological determinists. For what has really to be said is that all technical inventions, of an important kind, come out of a particular social order, with already foreseen social purposes. Their specific development and their actual uses depend, at every stage, on decisions currently made within an existing social order. Moreover, at all early stages, there are genuine choices both between possible alternative technologies and especially between the kinds of use to which in their production stages they will be directed. Further, when certain general kinds of use have been embodied in practical systems, there are still decisive choices to be made about particular kinds of use. The computer network can vastly extend the speed and range of necessary public information, or, from the same basic technology, can be used to support repressive controls by recording and tracking people more intensively and extensively. The robot factory can be used to save human labour and expand free time, or, as now commonly, to reduce labour costs and destroy many kinds of livelihood. Space technology can gain new scientific knowledge or, as is now often projected, take new military systems to levels from which they could control or destroy the world.

The alternatives are in fact fairly obvious, but the special vice of technological determinism is that it describes the future as an internal series of technical changes, each of which carries certain inevitabilities of development and use. We can best correct this from past examples. It was not the invention of the internal combustion engine which caused the near-destruction of public transport systems, in the most developed industrial countries. It was the combination of the invention, at each stage, with calculations of manufacturers' profit, leading to investment in the private car; with contested policies of public investment, leading in most cases to the deliberate rundown of public transport systems; and with several broad changes in the deliberate siting of workplaces and settlements, which in turn favoured one kind of development rather than another. When all these choices had been made, the results could be presented, by propagandists, as technologically inevitable, though the real development, throughout, was a complex of economic, political, social and technical decisions. It is this general lesson that we have to learn when we are presented with the next and then the next technical stage, and are asked to believe that its forms are inevitable and that we have merely to learn how to adjust or change.

4. Deadlock

The central difficulty of the kind of thinking which has absorbed the real lessons of technological development and is capable of applying broader criteria to each new proposed or actual change is that it depends, in depth, on various kinds of specialized knowledge and forms of thought which do not relate easily to the most characteristic contemporary processes of public decision-making. In particular they relate unfavourably to the actual exercise of power, though differentially in different political systems. There can then be mutual abuse between the representatives of the two kinds of process: on the one hand contempt for vote-grabbing, short-term-thinking politicians, or by extension for the electorates or publics which respond to or tolerate them; on the other hand contempt for impractical intellectuals or academics, or for conspiratorial and irresponsible scientists and planners. In the noise of this mutual abuse, many people see nothing better to do than to keep their heads down and get on as best they can with their immediate lives.

In fact we can move beyond this familiar deadlock, but only if we think again, very carefully, about the real conditions of stability and instability. This can be shown in one familiar contemporary example. From their own natural feelings, and from remembered experience and current observation, people do very strongly want to avoid being conquered by an alien power, and real majorities are prepared to do almost anything to resist this. Thus a very powerful position, based in the deep desire for reproduction, is already generally available, and can quite quickly be translated into political terms by this or that group of leaders. Versions of history which in serious terms are always disputable, in the complex and dynamic real relations between peoples and states, are persuasively generalized and disseminated for the purposes of identifying the probable or actually threatening enemy. Once this crucial ground has been won there can be little effective argument about what to do next: the enemy must be armed against, to the limits of current technology and beyond. Objections to this or that new weapons-system can be widely dismissed as merely sentimental or even as disloyal.

But the surpassing confidence of this kind of position, resting on majority support, can continue well beyond the point at which two decisive objections have to be entered. First, it can be shown in detail that the selective histories which brought particular peoples to identification of their enemies are mutually reinforcing: that is to say, they read very much like each other, on different sides of the frontier, and within this each proof that the other is an enemy becomes the hostile propaganda that is cited to reflect and complete the mutual hostility. Each people is convinced that it is peace-loving and that the other is the threatening aggressor. From this situation, the very desires that were enlisted in the original demand for security have been enfolded in the very process that can most readily destroy that security. Moreover, within this now reciprocal hostility, a point can be reached in the development of weapons-systems in which the very means that are deployed to guarantee security have undergone a qualitative change.

People who have been accustomed to thinking of defence in terms of sword and shield, field-gun and trench, bomber and radar-controlled fighter, find their actual states in possession of nuclear weapons which cannot be entered on any traditional scale of relative advantage or competitive attrition but which have transformed the nature of fighting itself, in that even without any use by the designated enemy – and that use is certain, given the interlocking logics of mutual threat and hostility – the weapons cannot be used without damaging or devastating or in the worst case actually destroying not only the territory of the enemy but the common atmosphere and life-forms on which the contending peoples and even their non-participating neighbours depend. At the same time, every demonstration of this common danger, from specialized and often complex inquiry, is capable of being absorbed into the crude initial

"Of course there's no harm in your knowing!"

CARELESS TALK COSTS LIVES

British Second World War propaganda.

positions on which the whole development rests. Politicians can still talk of weapons capable of destroying all life on earth as if, in the rhetoric of an old society, they were some 'sure shield', or even, in a kind of grotesque farce, an 'umbrella'.

The example highlights the general problem of how we are ever, consciously, to make our future. Other examples might be added. There is a particularly instructive case in the current contradiction in our attitudes towards buying and trading. On the one hand there is a majority insistence on buying what we want when we want it from wherever it is most available at the best quality and price. Old reproductive loyalties come at once into play: we have worked hard for our money; we deserve this and our families deserve it. On the other hand, in the immense and intricate complexities of actual world trade and monetary systems, reinforced by profound changes in actual methods of production and comparative costs, these market choices, presented in the attractive terms of individual freedom, can work through to disturb, to damage and increasingly to destroy our own actual livelihood or that of our neighbours. Moreover, when such a case strikes home, and our own livelihood is diminished, it is easy simply to hit out at a closely experienced but still only half-understood threat: often by demanding protection of our own trade, but free trade, for our prosperity, in everything else.

The real argument that has then to begin, in the intricate and specific identification of trading patterns and current production decisions, needs not only specialized knowledge in those who are contributing to the argument but extraordinary patience and attention if the argument is really to be followed through and its complicated alternatives and relative advantages assessed. It is the gap between this necessary level of the argument and either the solid complacencies of stable reproduction or the crude over-reactions to some isolated instability that is now the hardest general problem in thinking about the future, let alone taking part in making it.

Long-term plans

We can then go on to identify four important ways of assessing and trying to influence or control the future, and consider them in relation to this general problem. They can be briefly identified as Plan X; revolution; single-issue campaigns; democratic planning.

1. Plan X

It used to be said that the ruling classes or ruling groups of particular peoples were characteristically conservative. They wanted mainly to preserve the conditions on which their own power and privilege rested. It is not difficult to find many contemporary examples of ruling groups which still think in this way. They can be recognized by their language, which is full of references to the past, to tradition, to heritage, to old values. This is in fact the language of relatively stable societies, in which simple reproduction is at once the possible and the preferred purpose. But it is one thing to think in these ways when there is genuine stability, or a good chance of it. It is quite another to employ this residual rhetoric in conditions of major instability or, even worse, as an accompaniment to policies which are deliberately designed to bring about change. Yet this is often, in the short term, politically successful. It speaks with great force to those many people for whom change means only instability and unwelcome disturbance: people who still mainly want to be left alone to reproduce their own kinds of life in their own ways. But the simple conservatism which the language indicates, and even more that explicit kind of reaction which wants to restore earlier conditions and is prepared to use force to do this, are in effect by definition no ways to influence or control the future. What each represents is a refusal of the future, in favour of an indefinitely prolonged present or of some real or imagined past.

At the same time no actual ruling class or group, in conditions of general instability, can really act in such ways, though they may talk themselves into trying. What has then begun to happen, in our time, is a specific mutation of this kind of conservatism, in which the future is very carefully studied and imagined, in its many possible 'scenarios', with the already determined aim of controlling or containing the now admitted instabilities. We can call this attitude to the future Plan X, because on the one hand it rests on detailed professional inquiry and planning, for a range of possible situations, and yet on the other hand it has no qualitatively identifiable future in view: rather the future is this unknown complex X, within which it is necessary to plan for what are significantly called crisis-management, damage-limitation, containment.

The most obvious example of Plan X is shown in long-term strategic thinking about weapons-systems, which is of a highly sophisticated and professional kind. For public effect there may still be an emphasis on eventual disarmament, or on some established system of security, but in all practical terms what is being looked for is some competitive edge, itself dependent on projecting the X-plans of others, which is not meant to be a ground for either general disarmament or stable security but rather an advantage, however temporary, in what is seen from the beginning as an indefinitely continuing instability.

In the intelligence of many of its detailed studies, ranging from weapons to political tendencies to availability of resources and to crises of hunger and population, this kind of planning in effect ratifies the gap between specialized knowledge and public opinion. No attempt is made to close it, because it is assumed in advance that general publics and electorates will not understand or even want to try to understand the complex calculations being undertaken. Indeed, typically, the gap is left to be covered by political figures talking mostly about the past, where it is known that there is some public connection. At the same time, Plan X is entirely dependent on these same political figures for the command of research and resources, and this is in fact the major difference between Plan X people and other kinds of future planners and researchers. In their command of research and resources, through their ruling political connections, their projections of systems and markets and strategic areas of intervention are very much more likely to be put into place, and then to

The ultimate in crisis-management on the Plan X model: an emergency nuclear shelter in Southwark, London.

become the definition of the real world, the only practicable future: the political limits and the technological inevitabilities within which the rest of us must learn to think and to adjust.

2. Revolution

The principal apparent alternative to Plan X is the idea of revolution. This begins from an analysis of the existing political and economic system which shows itself to be the source of the instabilities and dangers which all are experiencing. It therefore proposes the ending of this system: either by its direct destruction or by a more prolonged process of its transformation into a radically different system. There are many shades of emphasis within this general position, but as a whole it is deeply rooted in the modern world. Moreover, although from any short-term view the prospect of something as large as a revolution can be made to seem improbable, the actual history of the last two centuries, and with a quickening pace in the twentieth century, is full of its actual examples.

But there are then two obvious problems. First, it seems probable, from just this history, that revolutions occur when some previous social order has become not only intolerable but even in its own terms unstable. Once any particular revolution has happened, it is quickly related by those who have benefited from it to the intolerable and unstable social order which it replaced. Many of the most powerful and now relatively stable modern nations in fact celebrate, in just these terms, *their own* revolutions. But of course at the time, in the actual struggles and their consequences, and especially as these are viewed by other peoples, a revolution is not so much seen as a response to intolerable dangers and instabilities but rather as the very source and origin of them. Nor can this, in a limited way, ever really be denied. To get to the point of remaking or trying to remake a whole social order is, of course, a deliberate entry into disturbance, instability and its dangers. This is one reason for the early reaction, inside many such

In 1975 MPLA soldiers fought a revolution for Angola's independence from Portugal.

revolutions, towards what are usually very harsh new systems of control. Then both the revolutions themselves and the systems of control which follow them are seen by many as the very type of instability which, dedicated to simple reproduction, they want most to avoid or ward off. People who even speak of the need for such radical changes can be quickly identified as internal enemies.

Yet revolutions still occur, and the specificities of their occurrence help us to understand the second problem. It was widely believed in the nineteenth and into the twentieth century that the old system itself was producing the revolutionary force which would transform it. Thus, at some definite point in the future to which the idea of revolution became

Flying display over the Arc de Triomphe, Paris. The anniversary of the French Revolution is celebrated on 14 July (Bastille day) with a parade in the capital and a national holiday.

very strongly linked, the force for change would be there and would fulfil its destiny. It is common to say now that this belief has been falsified, but it would be truer to say that it was the identification of this force that now stands most in doubt. It certainly seems to be the case that the force originally identified – the proletariat of the advanced industrial societies – has both changed in itself and in almost all cases has rejected the kind of revolution with which it had been identified. But elsewhere, and especially among the displaced intellectuals and the displaced peasants of formerly colonial societies, or these in combination with relatively early formations of industrial workers, the kind of force necessary to attempt and actually make revolutions has been abundant, and movements of this kind have both decisively changed and are still changing the world.

Something can be learned from these contrasted histories about stability and instability. It is common for people in the advanced industrial societies to see their current and recent history as an apparently endless series of changes and instabilities and dislocations, and so, in many local terms, they have been. But the actual pace and scale of change, for effective majorities, have by comparison with those of uprooted colonial societies been relatively slow and, if eventually large, in practice incremental. Moreover, the changes have been directed, in almost all cases, by their own people rather than by foreigners, and it has in practice been easy to identify with what is presented as a national process, however small a minority has been in real charge and however indifferent it has been to actual majority interests. Thus the point can be reached where people who have been radically changed by others can believe that in fact they have changed themselves, by their own decisions, and that everything else is just some abstraction called progress or technology. Within this illusion, they can then be indifferent to explanations of the system within which they have been changed, or, worse, become the habitual enemies of those who, at home or abroad – even when seeking no more than to control their own lives in their own ways – are seeking to revolutionize the system and to make a different future.

3. Single-issue campaigns

It can be safely predicted that we have not seen the last revolution, but within these problems and current reactions to them it is clear that most thinking about the future in the advanced industrial societies, even among those who still insist on the need for systematic change, has moved away from this track. What has come through as the dominant process is a curious and unfinished combination of two different kinds of future-oriented activity: the institution of what have come to be called single-issue campaigns, and the projection, based on limited practice, of some models of democratic planning.

Greenpeace banners hanging from chimney stacks during International Acid Rain Week, in an attempt to alert the public and governments to the danger of sulphur dioxide emissions into the atmosphere.

It is at first sight not easy to distinguish the single-issue campaign from the more familiar pressure-group, and in practice they often overlap. But there is now a whole range of future-oriented campaigns, especially in the increasingly active ecological movement. The distinction from pressure-groups is usually evident there. The important groups, often better called environmentalist, which mount specific campaigns in defence of particular habitats and species, or more generally against pollution and other forms of environmental damage, are quite properly concerned mainly with the past and the present, against what is seen as a threatening future. These necessary emphases often obscure the broader ecological campaigns, in which there are sustained attempts to raise issues of a medium and long-term kind which are characteristically marginal to or even absent from mainline politics. Decisive issues in the general use of resources in a future about which key decisions are already being made have been powerfully raised, and will go on being raised. There are then two problems: how these issues can be related to the more familiar agenda of public opinion; and how they relate to existing political agencies.

The full ecological case, including the intense and necessary arguments inside it, depends to an extraordinary extent on access to various kinds of specialized knowledge and on skills of assessing evidence. It can be popularized to this or that slogan, and on the other hand it is frequently caricatured by those opposed or indifferent to it, who take pleasure in collecting examples of what they call crankiness. But it is just because it is hard, complex evidence, over a range of very specific but in the end connecting issues, that it is important. It is a set of questions about a whole social order which, though they may be presented as projections, are certain to come through in pressing and sometimes overwhelming forms in an immediately foreseeable future. Yet just because it opposes or questions certain assumptions now dominant – the idea of unlimited industrial expansion, the conversion of all agriculture into agribusiness, the insistence on allocation of resources by market mechanisms alone, the inevitability and desirability of a more centralized metropolitan civilization, the universal extension of culture and communications from certain dominant metropolitan centres – it has great difficulty in engaging with any effective political processes.

One reaction to this has been the theory and practice of small, differently based communities. But these can be projected as marginal alternatives to the dominant trends – as which they most often flourish or are attempted, significantly, in the countries in which the dominant trends are most powerful. Or they can be offered as broader models for a more general reconstruction, as now among socialist ecologists. The difficulty in the latter, more hopeful case, is that they run head-on into the popular assumptions which the existing social order reproduces and demonstrates: the idea of the competitive nation-state, which would be radically weakened by the development of self-managing communities; and the idea of increased production (any production) as the prime cure for poverty. Within a politics dominated by internal competition within competitive nation-states, and by competitive versions of expanded production, a foothold is very difficult to find. This can result in further self-isolation by the movement, turning away from a politics that is seen as hopeless.

4. Democratic planning

The more actively hopeful direction is the attempt by education and publication to alter the political agenda, in the belief that the orthodox political agencies will in any case be forced by events – as in the oil-supply crisis – to face the underlying long-term issues. This in turn can take two forms: the generalized appeal, often made in the early years to leaders of world opinion, which over a range from the Club of Rome to the Brandt Report has had very little success, or the engagement with particular groups and agencies which are already being affected by early stages of the problems.

It is the latter which is now making headway. There is effective cooperation on a range of issues which will be the real politics of the future. These include the evident crisis, in supply and cost, of all forms of energy; the intricate crisis of food production and distribution, in a world in which there are both stored surpluses and famines; the crises of public transport; the beginnings of actual breakdown both in some inner cities and in impoverished rural hinterlands, evidenced in forced flows of emigration and immigration; the new forms of problem in public health, in relation both to stress and to addiction; and the mounting problems of structural changes in employment, with the old expanding wage-labour system beginning to collapse.

In each of these areas real progress is now being made in connecting specialized knowledge to already active public issues. But the next stage of this work is the crucial one. Very few of these problems can be solved, though some can be mitigated, in isolation. It is only by certain general changes, all of them difficult, none quite certain in its outcome, that positive and sustainable resolutions can be found.

This perspective indicates the most hopeful and practical future which can now be envisaged. Its model is what I described, many years ago, as an educated and participating democracy. The emphasis on education is essential. Some of these issues cannot even be focused, and certainly none can be effectively discussed and resolved, without an expanded and reformed public education process. It is almost incredible that what is now happening, in some societies, is an actual cutback on this process, and a narrowing of education to defined but then necessarily limited and probably short-term vocational skills. Highly specialized education will of course survive, though there are now many pressures on its direction of research. But all recent history shows that the knowledge which this generates depends on a much broader public education if it is to be applied successfully to actual political and economic decisions. Moreover, at current levels of social complexity, there can be no effective democratic participation unless public education, on a new scale, is also there. The alternative is either electoral manipulation around short-term habits and perceptions, or, as the issues become more critical, a conscious if partly concealed movement away from democracy, in which power advised by experts, as in Plan X, takes over even in formerly open and plural societies.

Yet education has to be matched by genuine opportunities for participation. This is the emphasis of some, but only some, of those who now advocate democratic planning. It is significant that there is now widespread resistance to planning, and an ideological option for its replacement by free market forces. But the latter is a delusion. The market is not free, for it is already heavily determined by the existing concentration of ownership of capital, which guides both entry and operation. Further, the market is itself heavily planned, by market research, advertising, and differential political policies on taxation and investment. Choice is exercised, by almost all of us, only after all these forces have put a limited set of choices in place.

On the other hand, few of us see much probable improvement in the rival institution of a political monopoly with its own public plan. Even democratic parties now typically conceive planning in this way, and argue

Inner city street disturbances marked the summer of 1981 in Britain. Masked rioters in Toxteth, Liverpool.

that general elections are sufficient to ensure a democratic choice of plan. But this is absurd. There are always too many intricate issues, requiring sustained information, discussion, discrimination and amendment, bundled together in these manifestos and platforms for much specific and intelligent choice to be exercised.

We are now moving towards some alternative models. One early amendment is the proposal that any political party offering some kind of public planning should offer at least two or three alternative plans, with the choices and problematic priorities fully explained and costed. This is better than reducing choice to party alternatives, each with its own settled monopoly of proposals. Moreover, it is as a model for democratic government that such a system has major advantages. The practice of shaping and deciding between alternatives would be a qualitative alteration of democracy, making it active and above all specific. Particular communities and interest-groups would have the opportunity, and indeed be obliged, to move to a constructive stage well beyond the current damaging interaction of power and protest. The complexity of this true democratic process can be readily admitted, and should indeed be emphasized. But as the need for it becomes clear, so, in practice, its supporting technology is becoming available. The new multiple and diverse communications technologies, with their unrivalled facilities for storing and distributing information and their novel opportunities for sustained interaction unlimited by distance and the old difficulties of getting enough people together, offer the practical means for this qualitative transformation. It will be merely stupid if we reduce these extraordinary opportunities to new kinds of distraction and market reproduction.

Of course the technologies will not solve the problems. Only people can begin to do that. But it is now possible to see reasonable ways in which we can begin to understand and then to influence and as far as possible determine our own futures. It is the quality and direction of this process that matter. There are important controversies between different singular visions of the future: big or small communities; nation-states or federations of smaller autonomies; industrial, post-industrial or organic. But it would be astonishing if in all our diverse traditions and circumstances, including many major and unalterable physical and climatic conditions, we all wanted the same or even broadly similar solutions. What matters is the expansion of our actual powers to decide, in the range from issues that affect only our own small groups to those decisive general issues that affect larger numbers or in the end the whole world. We can describe the future as black or golden, lived in this way or that, but what matters much more is to regain the confidence and to find the means and institutions in which more and more of us can take active and informed responsibility for it. The rising demand for such a future, against many still powerful destructive and short-sighted and ignorant forces, is now, in its very activity and diversity, the relevant revolution towards the new millennium.

About the authors

Isaac Asimov was born in the USSR in 1920 and moved to the United States with his parents three years later. He studied at Columbia University, New York, and received his doctorate in chemistry in 1949. His now classic science fiction novels *I, Robot* and *Foundation Trilogy* brought him world-wide acclaim. Altogether, he has written over 250 books on a wide variety of subjects, as well as on many aspects of science. His *Foundation's Edge*, the long-awaited sequel to *Foundation Trilogy*, was published in 1982.

Frank Barnaby is guest Professor of Peace Studies at the Free University of Amsterdam and Director of the World Disarmament Campaign. Formerly a nuclear weapons research physicist, he was Director of the Stockholm International Peace Research Institute from 1971 to 1981. He has written widely on military technology and disarmament, and his books include: *Man and Atom*, *The Nuclear Age*, *Prospects for Peace* and *Future War*.

Christiaan Barnard was born in 1922 in Cape Province, South Africa, and educated at the University of Cape Town. He graduated as a doctor in 1946, later specializing in cardiac surgery. He performed the first successful open-heart surgery, and, in 1967, the first successful heart transplant. He is the author of many specialist and general medical works, and several novels.

Duncan Campbell was born in Glasgow and graduated from Oxford University in 1973 with first class honours in physics. Since 1978 he has been a staff writer for the *New Statesman* and has acquired a reputation for his investigative reports on civil liberties, intelligence and defence. His books include: *Policing the Police* (1979), *Big Brother is Listening* (1980), *War Plan UK* (1983) and *The Unsinkable Aircraft Carrier* (1984).

Robin Clarke is a British writer and consultant who specializes in development and the environment. After working with Unesco, he set up an 'appropriate technology' community called Biotechnic Research and Development. He now works chiefly for the FAO and other UN agencies. His books include: *The Science of War and Peace* and *Technological Self Sufficiency*.

James Coleman was born in 1926 in Indiana, and received his doctorate from Columbia University in 1955. Since 1973, he has been Professor of Sociology at the University of Chicago. His books include: *Union Democracy* (1956), *The Adolescent Society* (1961), *Adolescents and the Schools* (1965), *Resources for Social Change* (1972) and *Power and the Structure of Society* (1973).

Michael Elkins was born in New York City, and worked as a film writer and producer in Hollywood and Europe before settling in Israel in 1948. Since then he has served variously as correspondent for CBS, *Newsweek* and the BBC. He has won international acclaim for his radio broadcasting and is the author of *Forged in Fury*, a book about Jewish resistance in World War II.

Humphrey Evans is a London-based freelance writer. He has worked on the staff of the London magazine *City Limits* and is a regular contributor to the 'Young Observer' section of the London *Observer*.

Betty Friedan was born in Illinois in 1921, and graduated from Smith College in 1942. Her first book, *The Feminine Mystique* (1963) was a major catalyst of the women's movement in the United States. She founded the US National Organization for Women, campaigning for abortion rights and equal opportunities. She is currently Senior Research Associate at Columbia University. Her latest book, *The Second Stage*, was published in 1982.

Ian Graham, a physics graduate of the City University, London, is a full-time writer and journalist specializing in computers, videos and information technology. After working as editor on various electronics magazines, he now runs his own freelance business in Hampshire, UK. He is the author of a dozen or more books on computers and video.

Mick Hamer is a freelance journalist and transport correspondent for the *New Scientist*. He is a regular contributor to many British newspapers and magazines, including the London *Observer*, the *Mail on Sunday* and the *New Statesman*, and a television and radio commentator on transport policy. He also writes a jazz column for the BBC magazine, *The Listener*.

Richard Hawkins studied history at Pembroke College, Oxford, and medicine at St Thomas's Hospital, London. After six years' practice as a surgeon, he began a career in medical journalism. He is currently Editor of the *British Journal of Hospital Medicine*. He was written extensively on medical subjects, ranging from surgical oncology to postgraduate medical education.

Norman Myers is a writer and consultant specializing in genetic resources and eco-development. He is widely travelled in the Third World, and has carried out research and development for, among others, UN agencies and the World Bank. His books include: *Conversion of Tropical Moist Forests* (1980), *A Wealth of Wild Species* (1983) and *The Primary Source* (1984). He lives in England.

Bruce Page was born in 1936 and educated at Melbourne University. His long career as a journalist has included periods with the *Melbourne Herald*, London *Evening Standard*, *Sunday Times* and *Daily Express*. From 1978 to 1982 he was editor of the *New Statesman*. He is co-author of *Philby, an American Melodrama* and *Do you sincerely want to be rich?* and author of *The Yom Kippur War* (1974) and *The British Press* (1978).

Magnus Pyke was born in 1908 and attended McGill University, Montreal, and University College, London. During World War II he worked in the Scientific Advisers Division of the Ministry of Food. More recently, his television appearances as scientific and nutritional expert have made him very popular with the British public. His books include: *Nutrition* (1962), *Food, Science and Technology* (1964), *Food and Society* (1968) and *There and Back* (1978). He lives in London.

Dan Smith is a freelance writer and researcher. He graduated from Cambridge University in 1973, and later worked for the Campaign for Nuclear Disarmament. In 1980, he co-edited with E.P. Thomson the influential *Protest and Survive*. More recently, he co-authored *The War Atlas* (1983) and *The Politics of Militarism*.

Martin Walker was born in 1947 in County Durham and studied at Balliol College, Oxford, and Harvard University. Since 1972 he has been a journalist with *The Guardian*, and is a frequent broadcaster on BBC radio. His books include: *The National Front* (1977), a study of the extreme right in British politics, *Daily Sketches* (1979) and *Powers of the Press* (1982).

Raymond Williams was born in 1921, in Abergavenny, Wales, and educated at Trinity College, Cambridge. During World War II he saw service in the Guards Armoured Division. Since 1961, he has been Professor of Drama and Fellow of Jesus College, Cambridge. A central figure in post-war cultural criticism, his books include: *Culture and Society* (1958), *The Long Revolution* (1961), *The Country and the City* (1973) and *Towards 2000* (1983).

PICTURE CREDITS

Index

Totalitarianism, 37
Trade unions, 118, 122, 259, 264-266
Transplant surgery, 217-220, 223
Transport, 155, 172-185; electronics in, 177-178, 181; pollution from, 182-183; public, 176-182; use of computers in, 174-177
Trolleybuses, 181-182
Typhoid, 55, 230

UNO, *see* United Nations Organization
USA, *see* United States of America
USSR, *see* Union of Soviet Socialist Republics
Unemployment, 196, 248, 270
Union of Soviet Socialist Republics, 49, 64, 106, 109-110, 119-120, 132-133, 141, 152, 163, 170, 234
United Kingdom, 43, 58, 65, 90, 93, 129, 152, 169-170, 173, 176, 198, 208, 217-218, 221, 234, 237, 239
United Nations Organization, 43, 55, 60, 81, 84, 87, 117, 121, 224 236; Universal Declaration on Human Rights of, 117, 122-124
United States of America, 19, 25, 37, 43, 46, 49, 51, 56, 59-61, 63-64, 68, 80, 84, 97, 103-104, 109-112, 114-115, 117, 123-124, 129, 132-133, 135, 141, 145, 147, 162, 167, 169-170, 185, 198, 200-203, 213, 218, 219, 230, 234, 237-239, 246-247, 250, 253, 255, 265
Utopianism, 17, 35

Verne, Jules, 12-13
Vietnam War, the, 19, 38, 105, 110-111

WHO, *see* World Health Organization, the
Warfare, biological, 145; chemical, 145; conventional, 135-140; electronic, 140-141; 'hi-tec', 138; nuclear, 103, 110-114, 131-135; space, 141, 145, 165-167
Water supply, 43, 86; agricultural use of, 87, 89; domestic use of, 87, 89; industrial use of, 87; pollution of, 86-94, 107
Wells, H.G., 12, 18
Wheat, 64-65
Witch doctors, 53-54
Women, 251-257; discrimination against, 118, 124; rights of, 118, 124, 235, 252
Women's movement, the, 251-256
World Bank, the, 108
World Health Organization, the, 43, 50, 53, 57, 230
World War I, 13, 108
World War II, 13, 58, 104, 110, 113, 156-157, 172, 184, 187, 231, 263

Zaire, 66
Zimbabwe, 149